A Cognitive-Behavioural Approach to Clients' Problems

I0123793

Dr Mike Scott

Routledge
Taylor & Francis Group

LONDON AND NEW YORK

First published in 1989
by Routledge

This edition first published in 2015 by Routledge
27 Church Road, Hove BN3 2FA

and by Routledge
711 Third Avenue, New York, NY 10017

Routledge is an imprint of the Taylor & Francis Group, an informa business

Publisher's Note
The publisher has gone to great lengths to ensure the quality of this reprint but
points out that some imperfections in the original copies may be apparent.

Disclaimer
The publisher has made every effort to trace copyright holders and welcomes
correspondence from those they have been unable to contact.

A Library of Congress record exists under ISBN: 0415017408

ISBN: 978-1-138-85769-8 (hbk)
ISBN: 978-1-315-71832-3 (ebk)
ISBN: 978-1-138-85833-6 (pbk)

A COGNITIVE-BEHAVIOURAL APPROACH TO CLIENTS' PROBLEMS

DR MIKE SCOTT

R

TAVISTOCK/ROUTLEDGE
London and New York

First published 1989
by Routledge
11 New Fetter Lane, London EC4P 4EE
29 West 35th Street, New York, NY 10001

© 1989 Dr Mike Scott

Filmset by Mayhew Typesetting, Bristol
Printed in Great Britain by
Billing & Sons Ltd, Worcester

British Library Cataloguing in Publication Data

Scott, Mike, *1948–*
A cognitive-behavioural approach to clients'
problems. — Tavistock library of Social Work
practice.
1. Cognition. Psychosocial aspects.
I. Title II. Series
153.4

Library of Congress Cataloging in Publication Data

Scott, Mike, 1948–
A cognitive-behavioural approach to clients' problems / Mike
Scott.
p.cm. — (Tavistock Library of social work practice)
Bibliography: p.
Includes index.
1. Cognitive therapy. 2. Social case work. I. Title.
II. Series.
RC489.C63S36   1989
616.89'142'08803 — dc19   88-29692 CIP

ISBN 0-415-01740-8 (hbk.)
0-415-01741-6 (pbk.)

CONTENTS

TABLES AND FIGURES

APPENDICES

GENERAL EDITOR'S FOREWORD

Fisher *et al.*, in their study *Mental Health Social Work Observed* (Fisher *et al.*, 1984) concluded, 'With few exceptions, social work practice was not directly concerned with the alleviation of the mental health problem; rather, effort was directed at ameliorating the environmental stresses associated with it'. 'Amelioration' took several forms: the provision of practical services and financial or material help; liaison, co-ordination, or advocacy designed to facilitate the provision of help from other agencies, or to improve communication and understanding with some of the client's social relationships; and the provision of advice or information to the client or to other family members (p.193). Whilst the value of this ameliorative work is noted, the authors reach the important conclusion that such work 'fails to contribute to the resolution of underlying problems or to prevent the recurrence of social difficulties. Thus it tends, in effect, to perpetuate needs, so that social work resources become absorbed in long-term and aimless work to the exclusion of new referrals' (p.193). The authors attribute this failure to a variety of factors, including client expectations, lack of training in therapeutic skills, and lack of confidence in working in a therapeutic manner. Whatever the reasons, the authors were in no doubt that 'there remains a need for a more therapeutically orientated service' (p.194).

Although the primary focus of this study was on social work with the mentally disordered, there is little doubt that this is the situation which would be found in nearly all current social work practice. Yet the need for a more therapeutically orientated service is clear. Its achievement is dependent upon a number of factors, including agency expectation; an informed management; a practice which is based upon a clear definition of the problems to be resolved, the goals to be achieved, the strategy of intervention, and the measurement of the success in meeting stated goals. But, perhaps most of all, it is subject to a clear understanding of appropriate therapeutic techniques and skill in their application. This book promotes one such technique.

The emergence of cognitive behaviour therapy during the past decade provides the promise of a valuable technique available to social workers in their attempts to successfully resolve the wide range of emotional and behavioural disorders and interpersonal difficulties which confront them. This volume describes and critically evaluates the cognitive-behavioural approach and its use in a wide range of client problems. Most important, it demonstrates the technique and skills of application, and provides numerous case examples which clearly demonstrate its use in practice. It should prove of value to all who wish to develop this therapeutic technique.

The Tavistock Library of Social Work Practice series was prompted by the growth and increasing importance of the social services in our society. Until recently there has been a general approbation of social work, reflected in benedictory increase in manpower and resources, which has led to an unprecedented expansion of the personal social services, a proliferation of the statutory duties placed upon them, and major reorganization. The result has been the emergence of a profession faced with the immense responsibility of promoting individual and social betterment, and bearing a primary responsibility to advocate on behalf of individuals and groups who do not always fulfil or respect normal social expectations of behaviour. In spite of the growth in services these tasks are often carried out with inadequate resources, an uncertain knowledge base, and as yet unresolved difficulties associated with the reorganization of the personal social services in 1970. In recent years these difficulties have been compounded by a level of criticism unprecedented since that attracted by the Poor Law. The anti-social work critique has fostered some improbable alliances between groups of social administrators, sociologists, doctors, and the media, united in their belief that social work has failed in its general obligation to 'provide services to the people', and in its particular duty to socialize the delinquent, restrain parents who abuse their children, prevent old people from dying alone, and provide a satisfactory level of community care for the sick, the chronically handicapped, and the mentally disabled.

These developments highlight three major issues that deserve particular attention: first, the need to construct a methodology for analysing social and personal situations and prescribing action; second, the necessity to apply techniques that measure the performance of the individual worker and the profession as a whole in meeting stated objectives; third, and outstanding, the requirement to develop a knowledge base against which the needs of clients are understood and decisions about their care are taken. Overall, the volumes in this series make explicit and clarify these issues; contribute to the search for the distinctive knowledge base of social work; increase our understanding of the aetiology and care of personal, familial, and social problems; describe and explore new techniques and practice skills; aim to raise our commitment towards low status groups which suffer public, political, and professional neglect; and promote the enactment of comprehensive and socially just policies. Above all, these volumes aim to promote an understanding which interprets the needs of individuals, groups, and communities in terms of the synthesis between inner needs and the social realities that impinge upon them, and which aspires to develop informed and skilled practice.

M. Rolf Olsen, 1988

Reference

Fisher, M. *et al.* (1984) *Mental Health Social Work Observed*, London: Allen & Unwin.

INTRODUCTION:
BEHAVIOURISM AND BEYOND

A decade ago, behaviourists were operating almost entirely on three models, classical conditioning, operant conditioning, and social learning theory. Since then, there has been a quiet revolution and behaviour therapy has 'gone cognitive' with cognitive-behavioural (CB) models joining the previous trio. Acceptance of CB models into the theoretical base of behaviour therapy legitimizes a focus on individuals' interpretation of events. No longer does the focus have to be entirely on discrete and visible behaviour, or on changes which are visible on some physiological measuring instrument. The cornerstone of CB models is the assumption that individuals' interpretation of events can have an important influence on their emotional state and behaviour. Though there are divergences amongst CB models there is a consensus that thought processes, emotions, and behaviour are interdependent.

GOING COGNITIVE

Traditional behaviourist formulations, based on classical and operant conditioning, posit people as essentially passive creatures whose behaviour can be altered by modifications to their environment. Behaviour was seen, largely, as a product of rewards and punishments. Bandura (1977) went further and suggested that environmental manipulation may not be the sole determinant of behaviour. He hypothesized that behaviour could also be changed simply by observing the behaviour of others and its consequences. Learning theorists such as Skinner (1938) and Bandura (1977) have elaborated a theoretical base (discussed in the next chapter) on which it has proved possible to build wide-ranging therapeutic interventions for disorders as diverse as child behaviour problems and agoraphobia. Even more importantly there is evidence, from controlled trials, of the efficacy of behavioural treatments in these problem areas (Jansson and Ost 1982; Scott and Stradling 1987). Both Skinner (1963) and Bandura (1978) set the scene for the evolution of cognitive-behavioural models. In 1963 Skinner wrote 'it is particularly important that a science of behaviour face the problem of privacy. . . . An adequate science of behaviour must consider events taking place within the skin of the organism . . . as part of behaviour itself'. Bandura (1978) also paved the way for the development of a cognitive perspective within behaviour therapy with his concept of reciprocal determinism in which cognitions, behaviour, and the environment are seen as interdependent. This model also suggests that interpersonal factors in the environment can influence cognitions and behaviour in a reciprocal fashion, but emotions seem to be curiously underemphasized.

From both a theoretical and a therapeutic point of view the work of Aaron Beck (1976) has done much to bring the once-taboo mentalistic terms and concepts, like thoughts and feelings, firmly to the awareness of the behaviour therapist. As Beck puts it, 'The thesis that the special meaning of an event determines the emotional response forms the core of the cognitive model of emotions and emotional disorders. The meaning is encased in a cognition – a thought or image' (Beck 1976: 52). His model of emotional disorders suggests that those affected characteristically misinterpret their daily experiences in a self-defeating fashion. Adverse experiences are over-selected, over-magnified, and attributed to personal deficiencies. Standards are often set so high they are rarely attained. In the event of an individual achieving a success, this is likely to be minimized or discounted. Difficulties are seen as disasters and the worst is often expected. Within this framework, Beck has developed cognitive therapy (CT) in which the therapist helps individuals identify, evaluate, and modify their dysfunctional thought patterns. Tasks are often set for clients to test the validity of their basic assumptions about themselves, other people, and the future. Whilst Beck has concentrated on the distorted thinking about the self, the life situation, and the future, other cognitive theorists, such as Ellis (1962), have focused on the person's irrational beliefs, whilst Meichenbaum (1977) concentrates on the subjective thinking regarding particular threats experienced by people.

INTRODUCTION

The cognitive developments within behaviour therapy have not been met with universal approval. To some, attempting to modify cognitive processes that are not directly accessible to consciousness is a pointless endeavour. Cognitive therapy is seen by its critics as a dilution of behaviour therapy, jeopardizing the hard-won scientific status of the latter. For example, Silverman and Eardley (1984) take cognitive theorists such as Beck to task for suggesting that in depression-prone people dysfunctional attitudes are not conscious but latent; this seems to them 'an undignified retreat'. From a practitioner's point of view the most important question is whether a given treatment 'works'. Specifically there is a need to know what treatment works with what group of clients under what circumstances. Quite how and why a treatment works is usually a less pressing concern to those at the 'coal-face' as it were. Whatever the theoretical problems with Beck's model it has proved extremely fruitful. A number of controlled trials have demonstrated both the immediate impact of CT and its ability to prevent relapse (Rush *et al.* 1977; Blackburn *et al.* 1981; Simons *et al.* 1984, 1986; Ross and Scott 1985). These studies include both fee-paying US clients and clients attending an inner city general practice in Britain. Both group and individual CT have been shown to be effective.

Overall the cognitive revolution has been a fairly quiet one. No doubt this is, as Salkovskis (1986) points out, because of a continuity between behaviour therapy and cognitive therapy, the latter integrating many of the techniques of the former. As Blackburn (1986) suggests, perhaps it has been more of an evolution than a revolution. In Chapter 5 Beck's model of emotional disorders is described. This is followed by Chapters 6 and 7 describing the treatment of, respectively, depression, anxiety, and agoraphobia using CT.

The effects of maladaptive thought patterns are likely to go beyond the individual possessing them. For example a spouse who is prone to what Beck calls the mind-reading error is likely to discount his or her partner's protestations of affection with a reply such as 'but deep down I just know you don't really care' with a consequent escalation of conflict between them. Similarly a person who has concluded that they are worthless might well decide that in company the best policy is not to speak for fear that others discover their worthlessness. This may well lead others to conclude that the individual is aloof or remote. In turn other people may tend to avoid the person, who sees this as further confirmation of his worthlessness! In Chapter 8 a cognitive behavioural perspective on interpersonal problems is described. This is followed by Chapters 9 and 10 describing the strategies and techniques used in, respectively, marital therapy, social skills, and assertion training.

The notion that thought processes can have a major influence on emotions and behaviour is not unique to cognitive therapy. As early as 1955 George Kelly elaborated a system called 'the psychology of personal constructs'. Kelly's personal construct theory (PCT) is organized around eleven propositions. One of these explains individuals' current behaviour in terms of the way in which they anticipate events. For example slowing down on approaching a red traffic light may be explained in terms of an individual anticipating an horrendous accident if he or she doesn't. Kelly emphasizes the individuality of interpretations. Whereas one person might slow down approaching a red traffic light another might accelerate if they saw it instead primarily as a 'challenge'. A cornerstone of PCT is that an individual's behaviour 'makes sense' to them. Thus clients and client groups, such as drug addicts and anorexics (Chapters 11–13), who are traditionally difficult to engage in treatment may be seen not as 'resistant' or 'unmotivated' but as unwilling to make life less personally meaningful by countenancing change.

Cognitive-behavioural approaches can differ considerably in style. Ellis's (1962) Rational Emotive Therapy (RET) is considerably more direct than the Socratic dialogue of Beck's CT and may be preferred for certain client populations, for example, adolescent drug abusers (see Chapter 12). However it remains to be demonstrated whether any particular cognitive-behavioural treatment modality is better than any other with specific groups. A satisfactory answer to Paul's (1967) important question 'What treatment, by whom, is most effective for this individual with that specific problem under which set of circumstances?' is still some way off.

NEW FRONTIERS IN PRACTICE

Beck's cognitive model is being utilized in the treatment of an ever widening range of client groups including the depressed elderly (Fry 1984) and depressed multiple sclerosis sufferers (Larcombe

4

and Wilson 1984) (see also Chapter 6). The initial findings from both these studies was that CT clients showed clinically and statistically significant improvement compared to clients in a waiting-list control condition. Although promising, these findings are very much in need of replication by further studies. It cannot simply be assumed that because CT has been shown to be an effective treatment with one group of depressives (i.e. those with a diagnosis of primary major depressive disorder, uncomplicated by physical illness and of working age), it will necessarily be as effective for other groups of depressives. It may be, for example, that it will prove more difficult in general to effect cognitive change in the depressed elderly than with their younger counterparts. Nevertheless, given the ubiquity of depression amongst the elderly, an effective treatment is at a premium and CT shows promise. CT employs a variety of cognitive and behavioural techniques and it may be that different elements are the active ingredients for change with different client groups. Research evaluating the individual components of CT has scarcely begun but will hopefully produce more finely tuned packages. The use of CT with multiple sclerosis sufferers raises (in a particularly acute way) a problem that goes to the heart of Beck's cognitive model. The therapeutic utility of the model rests primarily in seeing emotional distress as a product of cognitive distortions, but the negative cognitions of the MS sufferer could, on the face of it, easily be reflections of negative realities, rather than faulty conceptualizations. Exploration of just how far CT can go in alleviating the depression of those with progressive diseases is an important research goal. From the point of view of Beck's model it is interesting that only a minority, approximately a quarter (Braceland and Griffin 1950; Morris 1979), of those with progressive diseases are in fact clinically depressed.

The problem of how far it might be possible to generalize from the existing studies of CT for depression also becomes particularly acute when it is intended to apply treatment to a population of quite different social characteristics to those in the original studies. The sociologists Brown and Harris (1978), from their study of life events in the development of depression in women in Camberwell, London, and the Outer Hebrides, agree with Beck that the individual meaning a person attaches to an event has a crucial bearing on whether that person will go on to develop depression, and that a propensity for depression cannot be inferred from the occurrence of 'negative' events *per se*. However they suggest that the ratio of faulty conceptualizations to realistic negative cognitions will differ from population to population. It might be anticipated that in populations where this ratio is small CT would be less effective. Further studies of CT conducted in inner city areas are necessary to test this hypothesis and have an added importance because the prevalence of emotional distress is at its highest in such places. (The strategies and techniques of CT described in Chapter 6 are those used by the author in a controlled trial in Toxteth, Liverpool.)

Not only has CT been applied to a wide range of client groups but it is increasingly seen as appropriate with disorders other than depression. Recently, the treatment of anxiety has become a particular focus (Beck *et al.* 1985) (see also Chapter 7). Beck suggests that the pathologically anxious client's distress arises from a combination of one or more of the following four errors: 1) overestimating the probability of a feared event; 2) overestimating the severity of the feared event; 3) underestimating coping resources (i.e. what you can do about it); 4) underestimating rescue factors (i.e. what other people can do to help you). CT for anxiety involves identifying the negative thoughts in anxious situations. For example, a client repeatedly experiencing light-headedness, a pounding heart, and panic at a supermarket checkout may be fuelling their panic by thinking 'This means I am going to have a heart attack'! Initially this client might be taught a distraction technique, perhaps focusing on an object and describing it in detail using all the senses when the first signals of panic occur. Later the client would be taught to view the belief that a heart attack was imminent as a hypothesis rather than a fact. The client would then be helped to weigh the evidence for and against the hypothesis. The therapist would encourage the client to continue to confront the feared situation. Finally the client would be encouraged to identify and challenge some basic assumptions, in this case perhaps the notion that unless one's performance in public is flawless one will be thought less of. CT for anxiety has not been evaluated in large-scale controlled trials. Until such trials are conducted it is not possible to say how effective it is as a treatment of anxiety disorders. However Lindsay *et al.* (1987) randomly assigned forty anxious clients to four modes of treatment, CT, anxiety management training, treatment by benzodiazepines and a waiting-list control group. Both psychological treatment groups improved as the trial progressed with the most significant and consistent changes seen in the CT group. However, at follow up there was no difference between the two groups receiving psychological treatments. This suggests that for anxiety CT holds considerable promise but that there is a need for further replications given the small number of clients in each of the groups. Anxiety plays a prominent part in the manifestations of agoraphobia. Behavioural treatment of agoraphobic sufferers has typically been successful with 60–70 per cent of clients (Jansson and Ost 1982). However the remaining 30–40 per cent of clients have not shown gains. It has been suggested (Friedberg 1985) that integration of a cognitive component into the traditional behavioural programme would increase effectiveness. In Chapter 7 a cognitive behavioural approach to both anxiety and agoraphobia is described.

Paralleling the common reasoning errors identified by Beck for depression, Garner and Bemis (1982) have suggested that similar ones operate with sufferers from anorexia. They claim that the most important cognitive distortion is the idea that 'weight, shape or thinness can serve as the sole or predominant reference for inferring personal value or self worth'. Marshal *et al.* (1986) have explored what might constitute a specific CT for anorexia nervosa but have yet to evaluate the techniques in a controlled trial.

Behavioural marital therapy (BMT) has been demonstrated (Jacobsen *et al.* 1984) to be superior to non-specific marital therapy or a waiting-list control treatment. BMT in the studies reviewed by Jacobsen encompassed communication training, problem solving, and contingency contracting. Cognitive components have recently been added to many BMT packages in pursuit of increased effectiveness. Epstein (1982) has adapted Beck's cognitive model for use with distressed couples. He has developed a relationships belief inventory (Eidelson and Epstein 1982) which includes sub-scales assessing five potentially dysfunctional beliefs: disagreement is destructive, mind reading should be expected between spouses who love each other and are sensitive to each other, partners cannot change their relationship once it has an established pattern, one must be a perfect sex partner, and the sexes differ dramatically in their personalities and needs. The questionnaire provides a sample of the sort of idiosyncratic beliefs

7

that might be modified in a cognitive approach to marital therapy using much the same procedures as in CT for depression. The case for including a cognitive component in behavioural marital therapy finally rests on whether it enhances treatment effectiveness.

SERVICE DELIVERY ISSUES

Cognitive-behavioural approaches to clients' problems are essentially psycho-educational. In essence clients are seen as lacking the prerequisite skills to overcome their difficulties and the therapist teaches the required skills. The teaching is time limited, all the programmes described in this volume are usually completed within twelve weeks and some (such as the parent training programme) within six to eight weeks. Compared to many forms of family therapy and psychodynamic interventions CB approaches are very brief. A particular bonus is that many of the CB approaches described in this volume can be applied effectively in groups. At a time of scarce resources in both the National Health Service and local authorities, interventions that achieve their objective with a minimum of therapist time with a maximum number of clients are at a premium.

There is always a danger that procedures are taught in a mechanical or cookbook-like fashion, with the therapist forgetting that cognitive-behavioural approaches are at least as much art as science. If a therapist fails to adapt strategies to the idiosyncracies of the individual or fails to convey the human qualities of empathy, warmth, and positive regard then this is likely to be reflected in a measurably poor outcome which in turn ought to lead to consideration of the possibility that the therapeutic style is awry. There is no evidence to my knowledge that inexperienced CB therapists actually make clients worse than they were originally. Perhaps because CB approaches are highly structured they are relatively easy to learn. Most of the author's students have been able to work quite effectively with this approach by the end of a three-month placement.

Historically, relationships between social workers, clinical psychologists, and members of the medical profession have been fraught with difficulties, good working relationships have been the exception rather than the rule. Part of the problem has been the medical practitioner's difficulty in conceptualizing the role of the non-medical mental health professional. This difficulty has often been exacerbated by the tendency of therapists in these professions to describe their work in a somewhat esoteric fashion. To some extent this may be attributed to the complexity of the theoretical model underpinning the therapist's work. It seems likely however that if therapists cannot convey adequately their way of working to the medical practitioner, then there is much less chance of clients understanding the treatment rationale! Teaching is a role that is familiar to the public and medics alike and is a reasonable representation of the cognitive-behaviour therapist's *modus operandi*. Portrayal of the therapeutic task as teaching may ease working relationships. There is a further reason why cognitive-behaviour therapy might find a resonance with medical practitioners. Medical training falls largely within a scientific paradigm, therefore the emphasis on measurability of results prominent within a CB perspective is also likely to commend itself to medics with a consequent improvement of interdisciplinary relationships. Given that in Britain a general practitioner is the first port of call for many clients, factors which affect their relationship with non-medical mental health professionals are of crucial importance. Health visitors and psychiatrists also play a gatekeeping role with, respectively, parent-child problems and clients attending or admitted to hospital, making relationships with these professionals also of importance. Again it might be expected that communication would be eased for therapists operating on a CB model.

If cognitive behavioural therapy is to be considered a form of teaching, then at least some therapeutic programmes, particularly group programmes, ought justifiably to be made available in educational settings. This would be for many less stigmatizing than attending statutory National Health Service or local authority provisions. The voluntary sector along with the educational sector could enable the public to have direct access to mental health services. Co-operation across professional boundaries and agencies would be needed to ensure that the public had a wide range of mental health facilities available with each agency fully understanding its limits of competence.

Part 1

A COGNITIVE-BEHAVIOURAL APPROACH TO CHILD BEHAVIOUR PROBLEMS

Chapter One

CHILD BEHAVIOUR PROBLEMS: THEORY AND ASSESSMENT

Cognitive-behavioural approaches to child behaviour problems encompass a number of different models and no one model is sufficient to adequately describe the complexity of all possible difficulties. These models in turn generate a wide variety of strategies and techniques for the cognitive-behaviour therapist. From a practical point of view the focus is necessarily on those aspects of the client's functioning that are accessible to intervention. This is not to deny that genetic and constitutional factors will also be interacting with past learning and environmental influences on behaviour. But genetic and constitutional factors are largely outside the sphere of influence of the therapist. Nevertheless it is important to be aware of their role.

CONSTITUTIONAL FACTORS

The origins of temperamental differences amongst children are unclear but some evidence indicates a genetic component (Torgersen and Kringlen 1978). However the heritability of a propensity towards conduct disorder is not entirely clear. Children of biological parents with a history of anti-social behaviour have an increased risk for anti-social behaviour even when the child is separated from the biological parents (Robins 1979). Yet, having an adoptive parent who has anti-social behaviour, in addition to a sociopathic biological parent, further increases the risk of a child's anti-social behaviour (Hutchings and Madnick 1975). A number of studies have shown early child temperament to relate to the later development of behavioural problems. The New York longitudinal study (Rutter 1964) showed an association between temperamental differences and later rates of referral for psychiatric help. Graham (1973) found a similar association between temperamental differences and later disorder. More recently Walkind and De Salis (1982) have developed a scale to measure temperament and found that four month temperament, as reflected on this scale, related to the presence of behavioural problems when the children were aged forty-two months, with 'difficult' children developing higher rates of problems. It has never been suggested that a 'difficult' temperament will in itself cause a behavioural disturbance, but that problems may arise when a child with this characteristic is mishandled or confronted by stress. One analogy (Cameron 1977) has been to see the temperament as a 'fault line' and the family or other stress as the 'strain'. Both are needed to produce the behavioural difficulty or earthquake. In the Walkind and De Salis study, temperament was the fault line and maternal psychiatric disorder was the stress. Thus there were patterns of mutual influence between child and caretaker leading to eventual outcome.

A RECIPROCAL MODEL

It is simplistic to view children as the passive recipients of the influences of parents. The final outcome of the child's socialization and personality growth cannot necessarily be attributed to the manner in which they were treated by their parents. However, as Bell and Harper (1977) have pointed out, scientists in child development research have followed an unidirectional viewpoint on parent-child interactions for over fifty years. A variety of studies have shown a significant association between different styles of parenting and children's behaviour. For example, Wilson (1980) on different forms of parental supervision, Newson (1982) on different disciplinary styles in relation to delinquency, and Cox (1982) in relation to schoolgirl pregnancies. However, these findings were purely correlational and did not indicate which variables had a causal influence. Probably the most frequent conclusion drawn was that aggressive children are so because of the primitive styles of their parents. Bell and Harper suggest that from the data it is just as likely that aggressive children create primitive parents.

The issue of causality in parent-child interactions has been addressed by the studies of Berkley and Cunningham (1979) and Humphries *et al.* (1978). These studies examined the effects of tranquillizing drugs on the mother-child interactions of hyperactive children. If the child's behaviour is the result of parental directiveness, then reducing the child's hyperactivity with tranquillizing medication should result in little change in parental behaviours. But if the parent's directiveness was in fact a response to the child's excessive behaviour, then decreasing the child's excessive behaviour should reduce parental directiveness. In fact when medication reduced the hyperactive behaviour and increased compliance, parents dramatically reduced their level of commands. These studies serve to underscore the notion that the child's behaviour can exert control over parental responses, in addition to the traditional view that parental behaviours influence child responses. Further, the selection of one person in the dyad as having the greater influence in the interaction sequence is not necessarily as arbitrary as it may at first seem.

To redress the imbalance caused by the unidirectional view of parent-child interactions Bell and Harper propose that parents have expectations for a child's behaviour in a given situation. If a child's behaviour is excessive in terms of frequency, duration, intensity, or age-appropriateness for a given situation it is said to exceed that parent's 'upper-limit threshold'. In contrast, when a child's behaviour is deemed by a parent to be inappropriately deficient along the same parameters it is said to exceed the parent's 'lower-limit threshold'. Such expectations can differ across settings, parents, and time. In the case where the child's behaviour exceeds the upper-limit threshold of the parent because it is excessive, high-rate, or aversive, the parent is likely to respond with the 'upper-limit controls', frequently consisting of ignoring the child's behaviour, usually progressing to restrictive commands, negative affect, and physical disciplining of the child. Where the child's behaviour remains within the parental expectations or limits, parental reactions are likely to consist of positive interactions, questioning, occasional praise, and mild physical affection; these are 'equilibrium controls'. Where the child's behaviour falls below the parents' lower-limit threshold, the parents emit 'lower-limit controls'. Such reactions include drawing the child's attention to activities, coaxing, prompting, and encouraging as well as providing provocative commands and physical guidance. These behaviours are intended to increase the frequency of behaviour that is infrequent in the child and would be seen in parents of retarded children. Bell and Harper also hypothesize that parental reactions are probably hierarchically and sequentially organized such that when initial reactions prove unsuccessful, other reactions next in the hierarchy of that set of control behaviours will be emitted. Should no behaviour within the parental repertoire serve to affect a child's behaviour, it is likely that disengagement from and future avoidance of the child will be the result.

MODELS IN CHILD BEHAVIOUR THERAPY

In traditional child therapy the focus has been on changing a child's behaviour via control of the child's environment. In the newer cognitive perspectives the focus is primarily on remedying the cognitive deficits or dysfunctions that have an aetiological role in conduct and emotional disorders. The behavioural parent training programme in Chapter 2 is based on the traditional behavioural models, and the basis for the strategies used may be best appreciated from the more detailed discussion of classical conditioning, operant conditioning, and modelling, which follows. This discussion is itself followed by an elaboration of the cognitive models which offer explanations for behaviours such as inadequate impulse control, anger arousal, and childhood emotional disorders. The cognitive models differ as to whether the target is to supply the child with a new way of talking to him/herself, remedy a deficit in thinking, or to teach a child to modify existing maladaptive thought processes. These models underpin the cognitive approach to parent-child behaviour problems described in Chapter 4.

CLASSICAL CONDITIONING, OPERANT CONDITIONING, AND MODELLING

The classical conditioning model has been at its most useful in explaining the learning of simple reflex-like behaviours. Pavlov (1927) noticed that whenever he placed meat powder in a dog's mouth it began to salivate. The meat powder was called an unconditioned stimulus (UCS) because it automatically produced the salivation response, an unconditioned response (UCR). Repeated pairing of the UCS with a neutral stimulus, for example, a ringing bell, resulted in presentation of the bell alone eliciting a response very similar to the UCR. The response produced by the bell alone (after pairing) was called a conditioned response (CR) and the bell was therefore a conditioned stimulus (CS).

Pavlov and his colleagues found that the strength of the learned association was related to the number of repeated pairings of the CS-UCS and of the intensity of the UCS. They also found that presentation of the CS alone eventually results in the CS losing its ability to cue the CR, a process called extinction. Therapeutically, this suggests that if a neutral stimulus has become a noxious conditioned stimulus, the durability of the CS will depend on the frequency and intensity of the distasteful learning experience. Further the CS can lose its power to evoke the CR and this procedure can be accelerated by strategies such as relaxation training to weaken the connection between stimulus and response. The strategy of 'systematic desensitization' is based on classical conditioning. In systematic desensitization the child is first taught deep muscle relaxation, then a hierarchy of the child's fears is constructed. Whilst in a state of relaxation the child is asked to imagine the least threatening item in the hierarchy, when this image is tolerated without distress, the child again uses the relaxation procedures and progress is made to imagine the next least threatening item and so on ascending the hierarchy. An alternative to systematic desensitization is to use another classical conditioning-based technique, 'flooding'. This entails prolonged exposure, either in imagination or *in vivo*, to the most anxiety arousing stimuli. The extinction model underlying flooding predicts that inappropriate, learned emotional responses can be unlearned by repeatedly presenting the stimuli conditioned to elicit them in the absence of an intrinsically aversive stimulation.

The operant conditioning model developed by Skinner (1953) draws on the earlier experiments of Thorndike (1911). He put a cat in a cage secured by a simple latch. A piece of fish was placed out of reach of the cat outside the cage. To begin with the cat tried to stretch out and reach the fish but to no avail and subsequently gave up. Whilst moving about the cage, the cat accidentally bumped into the door and opened the latch and made directly for the fish, which it ate. The cat was then placed back in the cage, and a new piece of fish laid outside; eventually it inadvertently freed itself and ate the fish. After a number of repeated trials the cat gradually took less time to free itself and consume the fish. Thorndike called this trial-and-error learning 'instrumental learning' to emphasize the active role played by the organism in discovering an appropriate response to the stimulus. The key feature emphasized by Skinner in operant conditioning is that behaviours are altered by their consequences. Clearly parents may organize reward of the behaviour they want in a child, but whether the prescribed reward actually constitutes a reward from the child's point of view can only be determined by whether the desired behaviour increases in frequency or not. It may be that a parent is perhaps inadvertently rewarding inappropriate behaviours, e.g. giving attention to a child's temper tantrum and that behaviour is then set to continue.

MODELLING

Children may learn behaviour patterns not only on the basis of classical and operant paradigms but also by observation of other people. For observational learning to occur, it is not necessary that the child actually perform the response nor that the child receive direct reinforcement or punishment. Learning can occur in the absence of response consequences but whether the response that has been learnt will be exhibited will depend on the consequences to the child. Bandura (1969) sees modelling as explaining most of the learning of children, particularly how behaviour is learnt in the first instance. It also goes some way to explain the finding that children who are abused by their parents are more likely to abuse their own children. Deficits in the interpersonal behavioural repertoire of children, such as an inability to approach, greet, or converse with others, may be attributable to following an inappropriate role model. Modelling has been used to help children overcome fears, phobias, and problems of social withdrawal, and to teach parents child management skills.

COGNITIVE DEFICITS

The works of Luria (1961), Vygotsky (1962), and, more recently, Zivin (1979) have served to highlight that children, in the course of normal development, learn to control their behaviour by self-directed speech. Failure to learn this private self-talk may result in impulsive or angry or aggressive behaviours. Meichenbaum (1977) has developed self-instruction training (SIT) as a strategy for instilling self-talk in children as an effective regulator of behaviour. Theoretically, self instructions are effective through assisting the child to develop an internalization of verbal commands. SIT usually involves teaching a child to adopt a five-stage approach to making a problem manageable; each state is modelled by the therapist then rehearsed by the child. The first stage focuses on encouraging the child to ask 'What exactly is my problem?'; in the second stage the child asks 'What is my plan?', it may be, for example, to list and prioritize homeworks from various teachers before making a start; the third stage involves the child asking whether they have put the plan into action; in the fourth stage the child evaluates what progress has been made; if necessary a coping verbalization can constitute a fifth stage in which the child utilizes a special routine if the plan of action is proving unsuccessful; for example 'I'll go back to the beginning and take it very slowly'. Essentially SIT teaches a child to think before acting. However, to achieve this cognitive goal Meichenbaum uses traditional behavioural strategies such as modelling and therapist reinforcement for each successive approximation the child makes to completing a stage of the SIT routine.

Impulsive children can also be seen as deficient in generating and scanning a range of alternative solutions to problems and further failing to impede inappropriate solutions; as such they are poor problem solvers. Social Problem Solving (SPS) training may be used as an adjunct to behavioural or cognitive interventions, a form of treatment in its own right, or as a way of ensuring maintenance of treatment gains. SPS has been evaluated and shown promise (D'Zurilla and Nezu 1982) with a wide range of client groups and target behaviours. Most of the research on SPS has been based on a model which includes the following five general skills or operations: a) problem orientation, b) problem definition and formulation, c) generation of alternatives, d) decision making, and e) solution implementation and verification.

COGNITIVE DYSFUNCTIONS

Not only can the absence of self-talk cause problems for a child but so too can unrealistic self-talk. The function of Meichenbaum's self-talk is to induce self-talk whereas approaches based on Beck's (1976) or Ellis's (1982) work are focused on modifying maladaptive thought patterns. In work with children Meichenbaum's model has been predominant. Partly, Beck's cognitive therapy for depression, developed with adults in mind, has been little used with children because of doubts that childhood depression could exist. However within the last few years a consensus has emerged that childhood depression is a distinct syndrome with symptoms that parallel those of the adult disorder (Orvaschel *et al.* 1980). Depending on the cognitive sophistication of the child, with suitable children, cognitive therapy for depression may be an appropriate treatment regime. As in the adult version of CT, treatment would initially focus on increasing a child's sense of achievement and pleasure, moving from a behavioural phase to a cognitive phase in which the child's dysfunctional silent assumptions are first made explicit and more realistic assumptions substituted. For example a depressed child may be operating on the silent assumption that 'If I work hard enough, always be there for my mum, then maybe she will say she loves me; if she doesn't say that it means I am not working hard enough'. This could be an example of the logical errors listed by Beck as often leading to depression and personalization; essentially, the child is thinking 'If something goes wrong it must be my fault'. Teaching the child to note such dysfunctional thought processes and produce rational responses to maladaptive thoughts is the cornerstone of a CT approach. The CB models of Beck (1976) suggest that in the development of fears, anxiety, or phobias, children, like adults, may make five possible types of errors in the processing of information and come to make a number of dysfunctional silent assumptions. Personalization is just one of the types of logical errors. The others are arbitrary inference, selective abstraction, magnification/minimization, and overgeneralization. The logical errors are not necessarily mutually exclusive. A child may systematically utilize a particular logical error or combination of errors in forming a self-image. If the child's sense of worth becomes entirely dependent on the achievement of certain goals, then should the attainment of these goals be threatened the child will experience considerable anxiety. A common source of anxiety amongst children arises from what Ellis (1982) calls discomfort anxiety. The basis for discomfort anxiety lies in the belief that it is terrible, awful, and horrible when something goes wrong, or when something difficult or dangerous is confronted. The therapeutic thrust is devoted to helping the child reconceptualize the problematic situation as difficult or irritating, but essentially manageable, so that some discomfort is seen as a normal part of the pursuit of a goal.

AGE OF THE CHILD AS A VARIABLE IN THE SELECTION OF TREATMENT

The age of the child may be a crucial variable in considering an appropriate treatment response. Where for example a parent is almost totally in control of the child's environment with, again for example, a six year old, it may make a great deal of sense to teach the parent child-management skills using the traditional behavioural strategies outlined in the next chapter. However the programme may well be much less viable with a non-compliant older sibling, say a fourteen-year-old, whose life is increasingly led outside the confines of the home. Directly teaching the child anger control strategies, either individually or in a group, may be a much better proposition.

The level of cognitive development of the child will also greatly influence the strategies adopted. It is only when the child is in the formal operational period (normally about 12 years and older) described by Piaget (1926) that the child will be likely to have the reasoning power to cope with CT or RET. Indeed, some emotionally disturbed adults are still in the concrete stage of development (normally lasting from 7 to 11) necessitating a therapeutic focus on intensive analyses of specific situations rather than probing the validity of certain general basic assumptions. Certainly with children under seven, if cognitive strategies are to be used at all they are likely to be of the SIT variety rather than those of a more disputational nature.

ASSESSMENT

Ideally, assessment of child behaviour problems should be as comprehensive as possible, involving direct observation of parent-child interaction, completion of self-report measures indicating the nature and frequency of the perceived behaviour problems, measures of parental emotional distress, and measures of parental social stresses and supports. Assessments of child behaviour problems along these dimensions are not without their difficulties and these are discussed below. It is likely that a busy practitioner will have to make a judicious selection from the available assessment measures and strategies.

Observational methods

Naturalistic observation of parent-child interaction provides a direct sample of the child's behaviour in the actual setting in which it occurs; ideally data from in-home observations should complement that obtained by standardized instruments. However it seems that the presence of an observer, in conjunction with the expectations of the child being observed, can affect the behaviour being observed. Reactive effects have been observed for as long as six sessions (Lobitz and Johnson 1975). Whatever coding system is or is not used, the therapist in the natural setting certainly would be utilizing the ABC of behaviour therapy, where A focuses attention on the antecedents (on what happens before the problematic behaviour occurs), B is the behaviour itself, and C is the consequences of the behaviour.

Although less desirable, observations in contrived or simulated settings represent another alternative to the problems associated with naturalistic observation procedures. There is an advantage, with a simulated observation, that a low-frequency behaviour, or one not occurring in an observational period in the home setting because of the observer's reactivity, can still be observed through the presentation of specific antecedent stimuli. A major issue however is the degree of generalization that is warranted from the behaviours observed in the simulated situation to the behaviours that occur in the natural environment. The Thorley Role-Play Test (1982) elicits three broad types of parent/child interaction, the central features of which are: 1) temper tantrums, 2) a learning difficulty, and 3) the occurrence of a low rate, but desirable, behaviour. Each of these features is contained in separate role-play scenes. Parents' performance of the role plays are rated as to whether they manifest positive social reinforcement, mild social punishment, time out from reinforcement, modelling, or extinction.

Self-report measures of behaviour

There are three standardized scales that have been fairly widely used by therapists working with conduct problem children. The Walker Problem Behaviour Identification Checklist (WPBIC) (Walker 1970) was designed to be used by teachers to assess a child's behaviour in the classroom. Because norms for the WPBIC were not provided for the rating of children by their parents, however, the applicability of this scale in assessing problems that occur in the home is limited.

By contrast the Becker Behaviour Rating Scale (Becker 1960) was developed to be completed by parents and contains an eight-item Conduct Problem Scale that asks parents to rate their children on dimensions such as: strong-willed/weak-willed; dominant/submissive; tough/sensitive. The nature of the scale makes it useful as a measure of parental attitudes though it does not describe the specific problem behaviours exhibited by the child. As such this scale has little 'prescriptive utility', i.e. it does not provide much information that is particularly useful in planning interventions.

The third and possibly the most widely used instrument for the assessment of child conduct disorders is the Peterson-Quay Behaviour Problem Checklist (Peterson and Quay 1975). This scale contains fifty-five items and three primary sub-scales: Conduct Problem, Personality Problem, and Inadequacy/Immaturity. The Conduct Problem Scale is a relatively brief point-rating scale, containing sixteen items. Many of the items describe broad conceptual categories (e.g. boisterousness) rather than more behaviourally specific problems.

The Eyberg Child Behaviour Inventory (ECBI) (Eyberg and Ross 1978) was designed to meet the needs of both therapists and researchers for a comprehensive, behaviourally specific instrument for the assessment of conduct disorders. As such it is an aid to pinpointing targetable behaviours – items such as 'verbal fights with brothers and sisters' being selected over ambiguous terms such as 'aggressive'. Excluded from the scale are behaviours that are clearly applicable to a limited age range, such as thumb-sucking, or unobservable to the parent, such as school-specific behaviours. The ECBI consists of thirty-six typical problem behaviours reported by parents of conduct problem children and two scales: 1) the Problem Scale, to identify which specific behaviours are problems, and 2) the Intensity Scale, to indicate how often these problems occur. The Problem Identification Measure requires the parent to circle 'yes' or 'no' when asked 'Is the behaviour a problem for you?'. The Total Problem Score (between 1 and 36) is calculated by summing the number of problems circled. The frequency ratings range from 1 (never) to 7 (always), and are summed to yield an overall problem behaviour Intensity Score with a potential range of 217 points (36 to 252).

The Self-Control Rating Scale (SCRS) (Kendall and Wilcox 1979) is of particular use in evaluating cognitive-behavioural interventions. The SCRS contains thirty-three items to which the parent can make a response on a seven-point scale. The scale taps self-control, e.g. 'Is the quality of the child's work all about the same or does it vary a lot?'; impulsivity, e.g. 'Does the child butt into games or activities even when he or she hasn't been invited?'; and a combination of the two, e.g. 'Does the child break basic rules?'. Where parents have rated a particular item highly this can be a focus for cognitive-behavioural interventions.

RATIONALE FOR WORKING PRIMARILY WITH THE PARENTS

Children arrive in therapy usually at the behest of parents or teachers who have found the child's behaviour disturbing. The child may well not see his or her behaviour as problematic. If this is the case the child is likely to be an unwilling participant in therapy. In such instances therapeutic efforts are probably better directed at working with the parents. Traditionally parental involvement has been more by way of informing them of the nature of the child's emotional disturbance; but a more important reason is that parents are in a far more powerful position to influence the child's thinking and behaviour than a therapist could ever be. Direct work with the child will almost certainly involve, particularly so initially, much time-consuming off-task endeavours in the interest of establishing rapport and trust. If the therapist is successful in working with the child it is doubtful whether the child could maintain the cognitive and behavioural changes if the parents are reinforcing old behaviours and thoughts. In the next chapter parents are seen as agents of change with regard to the perceived problematic behaviours of their children. The ethical choice is not between parents who modify their child's behaviour and those who do not, but between a parenting style that produces distress and one that does not; whatever the style it constitutes an attempt to control the child's behaviour.

Chapter Two

A BEHAVIOURAL PARENT TRAINING PROGRAMME

THE EXTENT AND SERIOUSNESS OF CHILD BEHAVIOUR PROBLEMS

Behavioural disturbances in childhood have been found to predict anti-social and aggressive behaviour in adolescence. There is a considerable overlap between the concepts of hyperactivity and conduct disturbance used to describe the childhood behavioural disturbances. The usefulness of the two concepts may be assessed by examining the relative contributions of each in the aetiology and outcome of childhood behaviour disturbances. Loney *et al.* (1978), for example, found in a follow-up study of hyperactive children that a child's aggressiveness was a significant predictor of aggressive and delinquent behaviour in adolescence, while the level of activity was a weak predictor only of school achievement. More recently August (1983), in a follow-up of hyperactive boys with and without conduct disorders, investigated the outcome during early adolescence and found that hyperactive behaviours in childhood did not necessarily lead to major behaviour problems in adolescence. Inattention and impulsivity remained stable cognitive styles over time. The anti-social and delinquent behaviours observed in adolescence depended more on the early presence of aggressive under-socialized conduct disturbance.

Cantwell (1977) has estimated that in North America between 5 and 20 per cent of primary school children could be diagnosed as suffering from the hyperkinetic syndrome. Behaviourally defined the syndrome includes motor restlessness, distractibility, impulsiveness, and excitability. In contrast in Britain according to Rutter *et al.* (1975) this diagnosis is made in only 1–2 per cent of children seen by child psychiatrists, and is reserved for children showing these characteristics both at school and at home. The majority of the North American hyperkinetic children would probably be diagnosed as suffering from a conduct disturbance in Britain. The essence of 'conduct problems' according to Peterson (1961) includes: disobedience, irresponsibility, destructiveness, impertinence, negativism, distractibility, fighting, attention-seeking, tantrumming, hyperactivity, irritability, and inattentiveness.

The behavioural parent training programme described in this chapter has non-compliant child behaviour as its primary focus. Before going on to describe specific 'how to' guidelines for implementing the programme, a summary of the research on its effectiveness is provided. A more detailed evaluation is provided in Scott and Stradling (1987).

THE EFFECTIVENESS OF THE BEHAVIOURAL PARENT TRAINING PROGRAMME

The programme was intended for the typical social service clientele of single-parent, low-income or state benefit families and consists of six 90-minute sessions run at weekly intervals during which a variety of behavioural techniques are taught, largely through role play, with a seventh follow-up session a month later.

The programme was evaluated by a range of before-and-after measures on both a treatment group and a waiting-list control group, and maintenance of treatment gains was tested at three and, for some measures, six-month intervals. The programme significantly reduced: the perceived number and intensity of child behaviour problems, parental depression (inward irritability and outward irritability), and the level of perceived child conduct problems (impulsivity and anxiety). It significantly improved parents' child-management skills. Improvement in parental depression and irritability was maintained at three months, and reduction in child behaviour problems was tested for and found at both three and six months.

The programme may be administered in group or individual format depending on the exigencies of the therapist's situation. It should be borne in mind however that the systematic evaluation detailed applies to the group format only. For reasons of cost alone the group format may be preferred. However clinical experience suggests the programme works just as well with individual parents.

In deciding between group or individual methods of service delivery there is something of a trade off between the group cohesion and support on the one hand and the extra attention afforded by the individual format.

RECRUITMENT

The child management group tends to run most smoothly when five to eight parents are recruited initially; this usually means that in fact three to six parents will actually complete the programme. The group leader needs an assistant or co-leader. At the outset the co-leader need not be too familiar with the material as what is important is her/his capacity to relate to group members and willingness to help the group leader with role plays. 'Ordinary' mums have been used as co-leaders and it has been found that their feedback to the group leader about sessions is invaluable. The prime role of the group leader is to teach the child-management skills. The leader and co-leader have to bear in mind that the majority of parents are highly anxious, both when they are being assessed for the group and when the group begins. Almost anything that serves to reduce this anxiety is welcomed, e.g. an informal setting with comfortable chairs and coffee. Perhaps an informal get together before the group begins, where parents hear from another parent who has already successfully gone through the programme, and they have an opportunity to get to know at least each other's names.

Parents referred to the programme by other professionals often have had a conspicuous lack of success in dealing with authority figures about managing their children. It is therefore important to 'sell' the programme to parents by underlining what parents usually achieve by completing it. The tenor of the whole programme is changing children's behaviour by altering the way they are handled, and is thus very much task orientated. This task orientation is most important for parents who come to the group because they are often initially depressed and guilt-ridden; the programme moves them away from depressive ruminations. Their feelings of personal inadequacy can be reduced by saying that what is taught in the group is a development of the techniques that they probably use in some form anyway. (For example, sending children to the bedroom when they are naughty is quite a common practice with parents, but with some children it just doesn't seem to work; for them, it has to be modified in some special ways and this is the technique called 'time out' which we teach.) This begins also to ward off the criticism often voiced by parents in the first session when planned ignoring (ignoring all but the most deviant behaviour) is taught, that 'It's not worth doing that, I do it anyway, it doesn't work!'

ASSESSMENT

The parent training programme has been assessed using a number of self-report measures and a role-play test. For the implementation of the programme the Eyberg Child Behaviour Inventory (1978), shown in Appendix A, is an indispensable aid in the initial assessment of parent-child difficulties. The advantage of the Eyberg Child Behaviour Inventory is that it is very specific. Parents rate how often a particular behaviour occurs on a seven-point scale and whether such behaviour is a problem or not. It is possible for parents to identify thirty-six behaviour problems. If completed with the parents it encourages them to elaborate on the behavioural difficulties and this can be illuminating, as well as strengthening rapport between group leader and clients – but it is obviously more time-consuming than getting clients to complete the Eyberg alone. Parents typically report fifteen to twenty behaviour problems. The biggest single problem is usually non-compliance, where the child simply ignores parental commands, and the programme is constructed with this in mind. It is realistic and encouraging to parents to tell them that, if they stick with the programme, they will probably reduce their number of child behaviour problems by about one half but that some problems will, as with all children, still remain.

There are numerous possible additional assessments that can be made, including home observation and role-play tests. Home observations are often useful if there is time, although there is then the problem that the child may simply act differently because of the therapist's presence. The Thorley Role-Play Test (1982) is a useful guide to how parents actually handle their child. It involves three scenes, one of which is designed to test how much social reinforcement a parent provides; for this a stooge play acts a child doing something that could reasonably be thought worthy of being reinforced, and the parent's response is observed and charted. There are similar scenes with regard to temper tantrums and the child learning new skills. The value of this test obviously depends on the extent to which the parent actually mirrors how he or she acts in similar situations at home.

Parents may have so many other problems, financial, housing etc., that it may be difficult for them to concentrate on the parent training programme. The social stresses on the parent can be gauged by using Corney and Clare's (1985) Social Questionnaire (Appendix B) which looks at satisfactions and difficulties across the social spectrum. Action should be taken to reduce these stresses if possible, as they may impede compliance with the programme.

The parents' emotional state may be assessed using the Irritability, Depression, Anxiety Questionnaire (IDA; Snaith *et al.* 1978) which assesses the parents' inward irritability, outward irritability, depression, and anxiety. In addition the Conners Parent Questionnaire (1978) can be used to gauge whether a child might be considered hyperactive. The Eyberg is of key importance to the programme. The other assessment devices may or may not be used depending on the individual parents and the group leader's energies.

SESSION ONE: CONSISTENCY

The primary aim of this first session is to teach parents consistency, so that the child knows what to expect as a result of certain behaviours.

1. *When . . . then* Often, the pleasant things in the child's life coming from parents are almost entirely independent of his or her behaviour. The child gets something nice because 'Mum's in a good mood' rather than because of his/her behaviour. Not surprisingly the child begins to think it doesn't much matter what his/her behaviour is. This can be explained to the parents first of all by an analogy with a worker in a factory, 'Suppose you started work in a new factory and a workmate told you it doesn't matter whether or not you produce anything, you would still get paid at the end of the week. So that first week you just sat about, did nothing and sure enough on Friday there was the pay packet. Half way through the next week the foreman comes along and bawls you out, saying if you don't do any work this week there will be

no pay packet. This worries you a bit until your workmate comes along and reassures you saying "Ah he's just in one of his moods", and sure enough on Friday there's the pay packet just the same. In the middle of the next week the foreman comes along and bawls you out again. This time you quite enjoy having an argument with him, it breaks up an otherwise dull and boring week, and you know he never carries out his threats. So you reach the stage that your behaviour isn't at all affected by your foreman; if he makes a request "it's just him". Eventually however the firm would disintegrate and the foreman might instead turn on a fellow foreman for not doing his bit. However a new Manager is appointed; he's heard of what's called Grandma's Law, which means he controls behaviour by the consequences – this means that he's always saying "when . . . then", e.g. "When you have made three cars in a week then you will get £120". He sticks to this and the firm avoids bankruptcy.' In the home it is really a question of parents becoming a new manager whenever possible, saying 'When you have done this then you can have that.' Probably most parents have used this strategy at some time or other albeit in an unsystematic manner.

The group should be asked if they can think of any examples of their using 'when . . . then'. It is important to wait for examples to come from the group. These might possibly include 'When you have eaten your dinner then you can have a pudding', or 'When you are dressed and in bed then I will read you a story'. Encourage parents to set themselves some specific homework task using 'when . . . then'. The group leader can get ideas of what this might be in advance by looking at the completed Eyberg, at items such as 'refuses to go to bed on time'. Leaders may in fact have to feed in their own suggestions here.

Parents sometimes object that this is bribing. This may be countered by saying that bribery is something illegal, and that what we are suggesting is that the parent, like the manager, makes the getting of the reward depend on a definite behaviour. We are suggesting only what is necessary to survival. It is very important that the parent spell out to the child exactly what behaviour they want and exactly what the reward will be. There is then less chance of argument – vagueness produces argument. The key to success lies in the parent giving the reward *only* after the behaviour.

A child may be so unused to having to alter their behaviour to what the parent desires that when the parent begins to use 'when . . . then' the child may start throwing temper tantrums and becoming abusive. Parents should be encouraged to stick to their original 'when . . . then' decision and practise planned ignoring.

2. *Planned ignoring* Planned ignoring involves ignoring in a special way all but the worst of a child's behaviour. It can be used for misbehaviour such as whining and temper tantrums but wouldn't be used for more severe behaviour such as the child hitting the parent or his brother or sister. What is special about planned ignoring is that it involves absolutely ignoring the child when he is indulging in minor misbehaviour. For example, when a child has a temper tantrum parents can often think they are completely ignoring it but in fact get drawn into an argument with the child when the child says, for example, 'You're mean to me, I like my dad better' or 'You let John do . . . but not me, it's not fair.' If parents respond to these provocations by getting into an argument they are playing into the child's hands; the child has the attention he or she wants even if it is painful. For the child, what is often important is getting attention, and if not for good things then it might as well be for bad. By drawing the parent into an argument during the temper tantrum, the child learns that tantrums bring attention, and will carry on having them because they work.

The best way of coping with temper tantrums and whining is to follow the steps on Sheet 1 (see page 42). This sheet should be given out to parents and read through. The following scenes should then be play-acted (role played). The group leader and co-leader would role play the first scene, doing it first correctly then repeating it, leaving out one of the elements of planned ignoring and asking for feedback from the parents about what was done wrongly. Thus, to begin with the focus is on the leaders, pressure is taken off the parents and they can enjoy the spectacle of the authority figures making idiots of themselves! Subsequent scenes are role played using one of the leaders and a parent, the most extrovert of the parents being coaxed to join in the role play first. After each scene, group members give feedback on whether all of the elements of planned ignoring were included.

The scenes to be role played are:
1. Stuart on his way to school complains his bag is too heavy

to carry. He starts whining and asks Mum to carry it. Mum insists that it is not too heavy and that he must carry it himself, at which point Stuart begins to stamp and scream.

2. Helen asks for a biscuit and Dad refuses because she has only just had a full meal. At this Helen begins to sulk 'It's not fair . . .' and goes on about how badly she is treated compared to other children.

3. Joanne has been in bed ten minutes when she begins crying that she doesn't like being by herself. Dad goes up to comfort her, comes downstairs again and ten minutes later there is the familiar wailing from Joanne.

4. Anne interrupted Mum's chat with an insurance agent having been told twice not to do so. After the second occasion Anne becomes abusive.

Homework

Towards the end of session one, during the last twenty minutes or so, each parent should be given specific homework tasks that relate both to the material being taught in the session and the problems they originally identified on the Eyberg. It is important that the homework tasks are as *specific* as possible. So that rather than get Mrs A. to practise planned ignoring when her daughter Mary is naughty, it should be to 'practise planned ignoring when Mary has a temper tantrum passing the sweet shop on the way to school'. The more specific the homework task the more likely the parent is to carry it out. If possible, homeworks should be set that incorporate both 'when . . . then' and planned ignoring. Before the session begins the group leader ought (by reference to an individual parent's Eyberg, and the material being taught in the session) to have formulated in rough a homework assignment for each parent. This forms the basis of discussion with parents in the last twenty minutes as they modify the assignment to take account of their particular circumstances. If the group leader has not spent some time planning the homework assignments, the sessions themselves become inordinately lengthy. Typically sessions last 1¼ to 1½ hours once a week.

The programme represents a simple and most cost-effective way of altering a child's behaviour by imparting child-management skills to parents. It should be stressed however that there can be important temperamental or congenital differences between children and that the dominant influence can be that of the child on the parent. Thus the parent must be actively dissuaded from thinking it is necessarily his or her deficiency in child-management skills that causes the behaviour problems. If the parent is initially led to believe that he or she is definitely responsible for the child's problems this may produce depression and impede any change. Rather, parents should be encouraged to practise these approaches as a first aid, as an experiment to see how they solve their problems with the provision that, if they don't work, it may be necessary for more 'major surgery' with, say, a professional working with the parent and child at home.

SESSION TWO: PRAISE AND NEW SKILLS

1. *Review of previous week's homework* The first twenty minutes of this session should be spent reviewing the previous week's homework assignments. As the group members begin assembling it is usually possible to pick up which parents have had some success, so that when the session begins these parents can be asked to recount their experience to the group. This sets a positive tone for the session. For those parents who didn't meet with success it is usually necessary to help them to be specific about what went wrong. Often they say simply, 'It didn't work' and this needs much closer examination. For example, was it that the child's behaviour got worse instead of better? (A common initial consequence of practising planned ignoring, and something parents were told to expect in the first session!) Or has the parent been trying to apply planned ignoring to inappropriate situations (e.g. Joan hitting her little sister, for which techniques taught in later situations are more appropriate)? The focus with parents who have had little or no success should be on problem solving rather than letting their negative feelings dominate the group. Whilst parents with success should be encouraged to talk at length, the underlining of the link between successful practice and what was taught at the previous session should be strengthened by summaries from the leader about what the parent has said.

2. *Praise* The new material for this session primarily relates to praising the child. Often busy parents only notice their child when they are being disruptive and their contact with them is thus fairly

negative. If this continues for any length of time the children begin to look on the parent simply as the 'nagger' and ignore any requests, even reasonable ones, on the grounds that 'it's her again'. The technique is to catch the child being good and praise those behaviours. For example, if there is a big problem with a boy hitting his sister, the parent would make a particular point of praising the child when he is playing non-aggressively with her. In fact the child would be praised any time he does anything other than problem behaviour. Punishment techniques, which are discussed later, only work if there is already a positive relationship between parent and child, and to develop a positive relationship there has to be appropriate praise.

The way of praising the child is as important as the praising; if parents don't praise the child using all the elements on Sheet 2 (see page 42), then the child's behaviour will not change as a result of the praise. Using the elements of praise on Sheet 2, role play the following scenes. As in Session One it is recommended that leader and co-leader do the role play first, then repeat it, making deliberate mistakes and asking for group feedback. Then parents are encouraged to take part in the remaining role plays. The scenes to be role played are:

1. Joanne has come home from school, taken out her lunch box from her bag and put it on the fridge as Mum has been telling her to.
2. Mark and Paul have been happily playing with a jigsaw together for the past five minutes.
3. John is reading a book instead of watching TV.
4. Mary is offering around her chocolate sweets to her brother, sister, and parents.

3. *New Skills* As well as catching the child being good and giving praise, parents can improve their relationship even further by teaching their children new skills. (It should be noted that it is only in the context of a positive relationship that the punishment techniques mentioned later in the programme have an effect.) New skills that parents might teach their children could include: cutting paper with scissors, doing a jigsaw, threading a needle with cotton, catching a ball, riding a bike, etc. The way of teaching a new skill is first of all to praise the child (using the first five steps of Sheet 2)

for at least attempting the new skill, then to give specific instructions, e.g. 'Try looking three paving stones ahead of yourself instead of putting your head down when riding the bike.' Sometimes it might also be necessary to physically aid the child as well, e.g. hold the child's hands whilst threading the needle with cotton. If the parent demonstrates how to perform the activity, i.e. models the behaviour, this is also helpful.

Homework

In preparation for Session Two the group leader should have formed an idea of what appropriate homework tasks for parents might be set at the end of this session. This can be accomplished by looking at the Eyberg and noting those behaviours that, say, sometimes happen and are a problem to the parent. For example, one of Mrs X.'s problems with her child might be that her son 'sometimes' acts defiant 'when he is told to do something'. The group leader can thus make a note that it would be appropriate to suggest to Mrs X. that one of her homework tasks might be to praise her child on the few occasions he doesn't act defiant when told to do something. Often, the homework task the group leader has in mind for a particular parent only becomes practically feasible once the parent's anxieties have been talked through. For example, a parent may be worried that if she just 'planned ignores' a child after he/she is put to bed, what will the neighbours think and will this not mean I am a cruel mother? Homework set should involve not only the praise and new skills material from the session but also the approaches learnt in the previous session. Parents should be encouraged to try to spend say ten to twenty minutes a day just playing with their child and in this context they can often teach new skills.

SESSION THREE: TIME OUT, FINES, AND PENALTIES

As before, this session should begin with a review of homework. The group leader should encourage parents who have had some success to relate their experiences. Then the group leader should focus on parents who didn't have success, and engage them in problem solving rather than let their negative feelings swamp the group. It should be borne in mind, however, that some parents have so many other difficulties in their lives – e.g. severe marital problems, housing problems, a grandparent living with them who spoils the child – that progress for them is going to be slower than for other parents, and they will need a great deal of encouragement to keep going. For them the social dimension of the group may be particularly important. By this stage in the programme parents are likely to be more forthcoming and some allowances can be made for off-task comments between parents, in the interests of increasing group attractiveness, whilst making sure that the material to be taught is properly covered.

1. *Time out* Parents should be given Sheet 3 which describes 'time out' and the group leader then explains the procedure as detailed. Time out from anything pleasant is appropriate for the more serious misbehaviours. The following role plays should be carried out to check that parents do understand the technique. It is often only when a parent is asked to demonstrate a procedure that it emerges that he or she has got the wrong end of the stick! In giving parents feedback on role play, emphasize first of all the elements of the procedure they got right, and give specific suggestions as to how they might alter the elements they left out or got wrong. After the feedback they should be asked to role play the scene again. The scenes to be role played are:

1. John throws food on the floor while seated at the dinner table.
2. Jane is standing on the coffee table, Mum asks her calmly to get off the table, but when she does she kicks it over.
3. Stuart has hit Neil because he would not loan him his felt tip pens.

2. *Fines and Penalties* The second part of this session deals with fines and penalties and is described in Sheet 3. Fines or penalties involve the withdrawal of a specific privilege for a particular misbehaviour, e.g. a television viewing for smoking. The withdrawal procedure should be explained to the child, at a neutral time before the misbehaviour occurs.

Homework

Homework should be set involving material from previous

sessions. In addition situations should be identified in which the parents could use time out and fines or penalties. Parents are sometimes reluctant to practise 'time out' because they predict their child will not go to, or stay in, the quiet area when told to do so. The response to this can be to say to parents:

i) 'You may be right, but give it a try though and see'.

ii) It may be necessary to suggest that the parent physically hold the child there and say that they will not be allowed out until they are quiet. Should the parent not feel physically able to carry out this procedure alone, it can be recommended that initially it is only practised when a partner or friend is at home. Another strategy is to forewarn the child that, should they come out of 'time out' before permission is given, there will be a penalty, e.g. losing the pudding after dinner.

SESSION FOUR: RECAP

The primary aim of this session is consolidation and stock-taking. As usual, the session should begin with a review of the previous week's homework assignments, encouraging those who had met with some success with time out and fines to relate their experiences. The leader should then help the less successful parents problem solve. It is important to stress to parents that time out and fines procedures only work in the context of a good relationship. Praise, playing with their children, and teaching them new skills need to become a normal part of communication with them. The group leader can briefly run through the elements of praise and new skills on Sheet 2. After this the leader can emphasize that 'time out' is only for the more serious misbehaviours, that the minor ones are probably best dealt with by planned ignoring. Again the group leader can briefly run through the elements of planned ignoring on Sheet 1 and reiterate the usefulness of 'when . . . then'.

The material covered so far forms the 'core' of the programme. Parents should be asked to complete another Eyberg in the session so that the impact of the programme so far on the originally identified behaviour problems can be gauged and any still unresolved problems indicated. The group leader should expain that these Eybergs will be used to plan the session.

Some parents may have made little or no progress with their

child's non-compliance. They may have so many other problems – marriage, finance, job, emotional – that it is difficult for them to concentrate sufficiently on implementing what they have been taught. Group leaders should make it clear that they understand the difficult circumstances, and, where possible, should make arrangements to talk privately with the parents about these stresses. At the end of Session Four homework should be set that involves all the previous material taught.

PLANNING FOR SESSION FIVE

The focus of Session Five is on problems that are unresolved. For some parents the number of identified child behaviour problems as indicated on the Eyberg could well already have gone down by as many as a half. The main focus of the programme to this point has been on dealing with child non-compliance, usually the most common problem that parents worry about. The leader can now address other problem areas as well, such as bed-wetting and concentration. It can be explained that one in seven five-year-olds still wet the bed at night, and of ten-year-olds, one in fourteen wet the bed. The simplest approach to try is awarding the child a star for each dry night. If previously the child wet the bed four nights a week, then it would be appropriate to make an agreement that if he or she gained four stars in a week, i.e. achieved four dry nights, then there would be some special reward at the weekend, say 50 per cent increase in pocket money. If the child gained four stars, then the next week he or she would have to gain five stars to qualify for the pre-arranged award. It is important that the parent praise dry nights *not* scold the child for 'slips'. If the child is over six or seven and the star chart is not producing results in, say, two weeks, and the parent doesn't feel able to wait for the child to grow out of the difficulties, then it is appropriate to suggest that the parent go through the school medical services to acquire a bed and pad. This is a special mattress attached to an alarm. As soon as the child begins to wet the bed the alarm goes off and the child has to get out of bed and switch it off. The bell and pad works with 90 per cent of children in about four to six weeks.

Children's concentration may be improved by noting first of all, say, just how long a book they are now capable of reading, and praising them when they read it, then giving a tangible reward, e.g. a cake for reading a slightly longer book, at the same time praising them when they complete it. The procedure is to identify the starting point and to increase concentration in very small steps with a tangible reward and praise after accomplishing each small step.

Charts may be useful aids in changing the behaviour of younger children. For example, if a child has difficulty playing alone, it is possible to make a ladder consisting of four steps, and for, say, each 15 minutes the child is occupied alone he or she can move a star one step up the ladder. When the star gets to the top of the ladder the child is allowed some pre-arranged award, e.g. TV time after normal bedtime. Charts such as this are intended to be phased out within a few weeks, it is therefore extremely important to praise the child as he/she progresses on this chart. For an older child who has not responded to any of the strategies mentioned so far it may be worth trying a points system. An excellent example of such a system is provided by McCauley (1977). Basically points are awarded for various 'good' behaviours and deducted for 'bad' behaviours. The points left over at the end of the day are then exchanged for various rewards which the parent and child have negotiated in advance and which can be 'bought' at a certain 'price'. In constructing a points system for a particular child it is important to identify what would count as rewards – what is rewarding to one child may not be to another. The system should be arranged so that it can be anticipated that the child will have some points to exchange for rewards at the end of the day. Thus the maximum points that can be gained for good behaviour are made greater than the maximum points that can be lost for bad behaviour. The system has to be modified to meet the needs of an individual child. For example if a child refuses to go to 'time out' or stay in 'time out' then he/she could, say, be made to lose fifty points on each occasion. Again the points system is a temporary measure. It will *not* be possible to successfully phase it out unless the parent has also been using the social reinforcement skills described in Session Two.

SESSION FIVE: UNRESOLVED PROBLEMS AND MANAGEMENT OF FUTURE MISBEHAVIOUR

This session begins with the customary revision of homework from the previous session. Then the leader should give each parent feedback on the Eyberg they completed the previous week, and suggest strategies for any unresolved problems. Depending on the volume of unresolved problems, this could take most of the 1½ hours of the session (including the setting of homework).

SESSION SIX: MANAGEMENT OF FUTURE MISBEHAVIOUR

The session should again begin with revision of homework, then Sheet 4, containing a problem-solving strategy, should be referred to. To illustrate the use of this sheet, ask the parents how they would advise another parent who complained of a) having problems with Johnny's getting on with his sister, b) having problems with Sue's laziness. Ensure that parents understand the role of the steps on Sheet 4 in resolving the difficulties in these examples.

The latter half of this session can be made a social occasion. At the end of this final session the group leader should schedule a follow-up session to take place about one month later. This aids in disengaging from the group members, and encourages them to continue practising their skills, thus increasing the likelihood of gains being maintained.

ONE-MONTH FOLLOW-UP SESSION

At this session the group leader reviews with the parents any problems that have arisen since the programme ended, and whether the gains at the end of the programme have been maintained. To do this each parent should complete the Eyberg again. New problems mentioned should be tackled by parents by reference to the problem-solving procedures on Sheet 4. At this stage the parents themselves should be doing the problem solving. The group leader's role is simply to create an awareness that there is a definite problem-solving process.

SHEET 1
PLANNED IGNORING

For behaviours such as temper tantrums and whining:

i)   as soon as the misbehaviour begins walk away from the child more than three feet

ii)   try not to show any expression at all that is visible to the child

iii)   refuse to get in any argument or discussion with the child whilst he or she is in a temper tantrum

iv)   if you think that the child deserves an explanation for whatever is upsetting him or her then it is legitimate to say '*When* you have calmed down *then* we will talk about it, but it will not be discussed whilst you are in a temper tantrum.' It is crucial that the parent say no more than this during the temper tantrum.

When planned ignoring is first begun the child's behaviour usually gets worse instead of better. This is because the child sees that he/she is losing control of the situation and is desperately trying to regain lost ground. Planned ignoring shows results in the end with constant practice, but it does take perseverance.

SHEET 2
PRAISE

Praise involves all of the following steps:

i)   Look at the child

ii)   Move within three feet of him or her

iii)   Smile

iv)   Give a non-verbal sign of approval, e.g. put your hand on his/her shoulder or put your arm around him/her

v)   Put into words your approval of his/her behaviour

vi)   Praise the child within five seconds of seeing the good behaviour. If you delay your praise the child will not easily make the connection between the behaviour and the praise

vii)   Praise the behaviour not the child, e.g. rather than merely saying 'Good boy' explain why you are pleased, e.g.

'That's very good of you to play quietly while Mummy was doing the ironing.'

New Skill
Teaching the child a new skill involves:

i)   Praise – as described in steps i to v above.
ii) Specific instructions telling the child exactly what to do
iii) Physically aiding the child and/or demonstrating how to perform the new skill

Praise for any further development of skill no matter how small is very important.

If time permits, role play scenes teaching new skills, e.g. catching a ball, threading a needle, or doing a jigsaw.

SHEET 3
TIME OUT, FINES, AND PENALTIES

1. 'Time Out' means removing your child from anything interesting or enjoyable for two to five minutes. At the end of this time the child is only allowed to resume normal activities if he or she is being quiet. In preparation for the use of time out, tell your child the serious misbehaviour that you have decided definitely will result in time out, e.g. hitting parents, brother, or sister. For less serious misbehaviours give a warning to the child that time out will follow if the misbehaviour does not cease, e.g. 'Stuart, if you don't stop teasing Helen, you'll have to go to time out.' (As always, a threat such as this must be carried out if the warning is not heeded.)

Time out involves all of the following steps:

1. Give the child a reason why he is going to time out, e.g. 'Christopher you are going to time out because you bit Melanie.'
2. Tell the child to go to the time out area, or physically take him or her there within seconds of serious misbehaviour occurring.
3. Make sure that where you place the child has no distractions – it could be a corner of the living room or hall. Keep an

eye on him, but without making it obvious, to make sure he hasn't wandered off or is playing with something.

4. Avoid at all costs getting drawn into an argument with your child, ignore 'It's not fair', 'You're mean, not like . . .'.

5. For a young child of three or four years old, move at least three feet away from the child, and keep the time out period to no more than three minutes. For a ten-year-old, five minutes is more appropriate. But do *not* use longer than this.

6. *Only* let the child out of time out when he/she is being quiet.

2. Fines and penalties can be used as the price the child has to pay for certain misbehaviours. The particular fine for a particular misbehaviour should be spelt out to the child before it occurs.

Example One

John was always late for school and it was decided that on each day that he does not leave the house by 8.45 a.m. his 10p daily biscuit money would be withdrawn.

Example Two

Jane is always pulling items off the supermarket shelf when she visits it with her Mum. Before entering the supermarket, mother explains to Jane that she is not to touch items on the shelves. She is to hold on to the shopping trolley with one hand, and in the other hand she can carry around a bar of chocolate. The child is allowed to eat the chocolate afterwards if she complied with her mother's request, otherwise it is withdrawn (it is useful to get the child to repeat the instructions to check that she has understood them).

It is important that the withdrawal of privilege follows immediately on the misbehaviour. The withdrawal of privilege should not, however, last so long that it breeds frustration in the parent and the child forgets what he is being punished for (for example, the child is deprived of playing out with his friends for a month for stealing 10p). In short, 'Don't make threats you will not or cannot carry out – that just makes matters worse'.

SHEET 4
COPING IN THE LONG TERM

What to do if new behaviour problems occur.

Ask yourself the following questions:

1. What exactly is it that he/she is doing wrong? If you are being vague, e.g. 'Johnny is just being naughty', it is difficult to think what to do, but if you are being specific, e.g. 'Johnny won't go to bed when I tell him', then possible solutions will occur to you.
2. How often is the misbehaviour actually occurring?
3. Am I slipping back into the old habit of just repeating commands over and over? It is important that if a request is ignored more than once there is always a very definite punishment, e.g. time out.
4. What behaviour would I prefer? Make up an incentive or reward programme that will encourage the child to adopt this alternative behaviour.
5. What punishment technique, e.g. fines, time out, point system, would be suitable for the inappropriate behaviour?
6. Give your strategies to cope with the new behaviour problems at least two weeks before judging their effectiveness. Notice how often the problem behaviour is now occurring. If after two weeks the misbehaviour is still happening as much as previously, review your programme and modify your strategy.
7. If the problem is still unresolved contact your group leader.

Chapter Three

PARENTAL ANGER CONTROL AND COMMUNICATION TRAINING

The behavioural parent training programme described in the previous chapter is essentially a first aid approach to the conduct problems of the younger child. A minority of parents completing the programme fail to perceive reductions in the number and frequency of the targeted behaviour problems. Such perceptions appear to be most closely linked with the parents' outward irritability (Scott and Stradling 1987). It may therefore be appropriate to make anger control training a therapeutic focus for the non-beneficiaries. In this chapter a parental anger control training programme is described. The programme is predicated on the assumption that any parental deficits in child management skills either have been addressed or are being dealt with concurrently. The anger control programme is appropriate for parents who have beaten their children or are in fear of hurting them in an angry rage. It is assumed that other possible causes of anger such as a psychosis or alcoholism have first of all been excluded.

PARENTAL ANGER CONTROL

Parental abuse is a leading cause of child abuse (Kempe 1976). One of the many causes of child abuse is the inability of parents to control angry impulses (Ambrose *et al.* 1980). In the face of provocative child behaviour, parents who lack anger management skills may produce aggressive overreactions.

The programme outlined here is a development and elaboration of one detailed earlier by Nomellini and Katz (1983). Their programme involved six to eight 90-minute sessions in the parent's home. They evaluated their programme with three families.

During and after anger control training, parents showed significant reductions in aversive behaviour, along with decreases in angry urges and overall proneness to provocation. These changes were maintained over follow-ups that ranged from two to six months, during which there was no recurrence of abusive behaviour. The children were not involved in the programme. With such a small study and using a single case design considerable care has to be taken in generalizing from these findings. Nevertheless there seemed to be fairly significant benefits for an investment of on average only 10½ hours of therapist time per family.

It is necessary first of all to obtain a measure of the level of parental anger. This may be done most simply by having the parents complete the Novaco Anger Scale (1976) in which they rate their anger on a five-point scale in the context of eighty situation descriptions. Parents in Nomellini and Katz's study scored over 300 on this scale at the beginning of intervention and reduced to under 200 by completion of the programme. A complementary, if time-consuming, way of assessing level of parental anger is by direct in-home observations of positive and aversive parent and child behaviours coded according to the categories described by Patterson *et al.* (1969). If parents are asked to record the frequency of angry urges on a daily basis during treatment this can also serve as a useful outcome measure.

Anger control training consists of three interrelated components: a) teaching parents about the determinants and physiological cues of anger arousal; b) teaching them to use self-monitoring, self instruction, deep-breathing relaxation, and self-reinforcement to control angry feelings in anger-producing situations, and c) providing them with opportunities to practise these responses under simulated conditions. Such training essentially involves the reduction of aversive behaviours rather than the promotion of positive behaviours. It seems likely that the efficacy of an anger control training programme may be enhanced by the inclusion of strategies to promote positive behaviours. Approaching the problematic interactions from both directions in this way parallels the dual focus in the Behavioural Parent Training Programme detailed in the previous chapter. In the programme to be described anger control training and communication training strategies are integrated.

The programme begins with an assessment interview in which

the most anger-arousing situations are pin-pointed and targeted for intervention. The 'high-risk' situations are often quite idiosyn-cratic and the therapist needs to give the parent ample time to explore what these are. One parent for example was most fearful of harming her child when she was about to go out with him and his baby sister. She would have the four-year-old ready first then change the baby; if he wasn't immediately available for departure in the same state she had left him, she would become very angry. In this interview the rationale for the programme can be explained as finding new ways of thinking about and handling the 'danger-ous situations'.

SESSION ONE

The goal of this first session is to develop a specific routine for one of the high-risk situations, and this is not an easy task. At this stage parents are usually full of 'shoulds' which may amount to the parent saying 'The child ought to be reasonable and see things my way!' The perceived moral rightness of the parent's position can inhibit consideration of alternative ways of handling the situa-tion. A parent may well say 'If I said half the things *he* says to me, to my father he would have hit me with his belt', or 'If John next door spoke to his Dad the way he speaks to me his feet would not touch the ground!' In these examples the parents are appealing to a moral consensus to justify their positions.

To clear the ground for the development of a coping routine for a high-risk situation it is often necessary to refocus discussions on the utility of present coping strategies rather than on their rightness. The question can be posed 'Why continue to use a way of handling the most troublesome situation that doesn't work?' An analogy is often useful here such as 'If you tried fixing your TV only one way and it never worked, what would you say to a friend who asked you why you always do a repair in a way that produces no picture and no sound? Would you tell him "Well, I am doing it the *right way*!".' Any negative emotional consequences the parent has noted as a result of existing strategies can be reiterated to the parent, following as closely as possible the actual language used by the parent. If the parent begins to deny the negative emotional consequences, a statement such as 'So you are saying your way of handling your son doesn't produce any upset for you at all' usually results in the parent being more precise about the negative effects. Ultimately the therapist can suggest that present coping strategies cannot be working that well or the parent would not be sitting in the session! It is counter-productive however for the therapist to adopt an adversarial role about the rival merits of coping strategies. One of the aims of this session is to identify with the goals of the parent, help them make their goals explicit, and underline their laudableness. Typically parents want a relatively hassle-free existence; on occasion however they carry around a basic assumption that 'the whole world ought to be organized to meet my every need'. In instances of the latter it may be necessary to introduce the idea that the price to be paid for intolerance of a small amount of frustration is usually the forced acceptance of an even greater amount of frustration. Some parents have a dich-otomous view of their child, as either a saint or a sinner, and the notion of being just reasonably content with their child is foreign. Ideally the therapist should be seen to endorse the client's goals albeit that on occasion these goals will have been elaborated with the therapist. A therapeutic alliance is a precondition for further interventions. The therapeutic task then becomes the identification of the most efficient means to reach these goals.

The development of a specific routine for coping with a high-risk situation should begin with a discussion of the first signs of anger arousal surrounding the elected situation. The situation focused upon should be seen by the parent as very relevant and preferably one also in which there is some immediate likelihood of success. For example, it would be unwise to choose initially a problematic situation which involved a number of family members, because there are likely to be too many variables which might mitigate against the speedy success necessary for parents to continue to engage in treatment. It is useful to ask parents to do slow motion action replays of the targeted situations – in their own minds or verbally – and note when in these 'videos' they first notice their emotional temperature rise. A thermometer can then be drawn with a 'luke-warm' mark on it and the scene associated with this temperature placed alongside it. To use the example of the parent mentioned earlier with problems of getting her children ready to go out, 'feeling luke-warm' might occur when she first begins dressing her son. 'Feeling hot and bothered' might occur when she looks at the clock and finally the parent may feel at 'boiling point' when she inspects her son again after having changed the baby. The emotional thermometer is an aid to teaching parents to discriminate emotions and to identify the antecedents. Charting a high-risk situation in this way can serve as an exemplar for the parent of how to self-monitor. (A homework assignment at the end of the first session should involve a recording of angry urges, the events that preceded them, and the consequences of any displays of anger.)

The parent is then taught to use the first signs of anger arousal, in this instance dressing her son initially, as a cue for 'going through my routine'. The routine begins with a stock-taking statement such as 'Right, all I have to do is keep my cool'. A mini-routine can then be utilized to help the parent change gear and begin thinking straight, this might involve taking say ten deep breaths and breathing out slowly after each one whilst visualizing what number breath they are up to. This should be followed by a statement that challenges the beliefs underpinning the next marking on the emotional thermometer. In this example the parent might say 'The clock says . . . well what's the hurry to be out? Is the world going to end if I am late? I am not late until I arrive.' It is important that these self-statements use the parent's own words and represent his/her rational response to the dysfunctional attitudes that make for much of the emotional distress. The self-statements should not be imposed by the therapist.

Finally the parent utilizes an antidote to the beliefs that have her at boiling point. In this example the parent might say 'Is my son really getting himself untidy just to annoy me? Does his appearance when we go out seem to bother anyone else? Maybe he just looks an ordinary boy?' The routine is rounded off by the parent asking herself if she is feeling any less outwardly irritable than in the past in the same situation. The parent is asked to evaluate any reduction, however small, in outward irritability as a success and to congratulate herself on the achievement.

It is important to stress to parents that the time scale for the efficacy of any routine devised is uncertain; a routine may need considerable practice or need subsequent modification if important elements of the particular high-risk situation have not been taken into account. This prepares them in advance for any disappointment with a routine practised after the first session. Before practising their 'routine' *in vivo* parents should role play the situation and routine with the therapist. The therapist should shape the parents' behaviours and thought patterns in the role play by providing feedback in the way described in the Parent Training Programme in the previous chapter. It is difficult for parents to test out the efficacy of their new coping routine if the problematic behaviour typically does not occur very often. It is useful then to have the parent spend ten minutes a day imagining him/herself going through the routine. A number of cards should be prepared with the routine on them and placed by the parent in strategic places to serve as reminders.

Particularly at this early stage of the programme, some parents will probably have need of an emergency procedure for those occasions when they are literally beside themselves with anger, and their actions seem to take on a life of their own, happening almost automatically. Parents ought to be advised that when this happens they ought to leave the scene. There are a number of possible options including going into the garden to get some fresh air; relaxation techniques – tensing each muscle group in turn for 15 seconds, after tensing a particular group the parent is asked to relax that muscle and feel the tension flowing away 'like the tides of the sea'; slightly exaggerating the significance of the event therefore introducing humour to put it into perspective, e.g. 'Am I really saying that what X has just done merits the guillotine!' A combination of such strategies should be developed and rehearsed with the parent as the special all-purpose emergency procedure.

SESSION TWO

This session begins with a review of the previous week's homework assignment. If any parent has not attempted to use the previously devised anger control strategy the reasons for this should be explored. Praise should be given for attempting to use the anger control strategy – 'success' at this stage should be regarded as a bonus. Any reductions in irritability noted by the parent should be underlined by the therapist. Where parents have experienced at least limited success with the new strategy they are likely to be further motivated to apply these techniques to other anger arousing situations. Primarily it should be left to the parent to choose another not too dissimilar anger arousing situation which might be targeted for treatment using the coping self-statements. Again however the therapist ought to guide the client to consider initially only those situations that do not contain extraneous factors e.g. the presence of an over-indulgent, unsympathetic grandparent.

The prime aim of this session is to enhance communication between the parent and child, ensuring that communication is assertive rather than aggressive. The assertive parent is essentially balancing his or her needs against the needs of the child, whilst the aggressive parent totally ignores the child's needs. Dubey *et al.* (1983) have suggested the following guidelines which form a useful handout for parents:

1. Use 'I' statements rather than 'you' statements and avoid mind reading. In this way parents own their own emotional responses, e.g. 'I don't like it when you ask for clean items of school uniform when you are getting ready for school', as opposed to 'You know how much I have to do first thing of a morning, you are just trying to be awkward asking for clean clothes then'.
2. Try and summarize first in your own mind what you think your child is saying to you. Before making a reply yourself check out with the child that your summary of what they are saying is accurate.
3. Give the child ample space to explain him/herself without interruption.
4. Signal that you have heard what your child has said by either a non-verbal reply such as nodding or a verbal reply.

Parents should be asked to recall and describe any possible instances of mind reading with their children and how the subsequent interaction evolved. This can serve to enhance the relevance of the communication guidelines to their situation. Asking parents to recall the last time they finished off their child's sentence for them or abruptly changed the direction of the conversation can further sensitize parents to the importance of the guidelines. For homework parents should be asked to practise the communication strategies and in particular monitor what happens when the guidelines are ignored. This is in addition to practising the coping self-statements for at least two anger arousing situations.

SESSIONS THREE AND FOUR

Once again the previous session's homework assignment should be a focus at the beginning of the session. However it is sometimes the case that parents have been so overwhelmed by difficulties since the previous session that they need an opportunity and space at the beginning of the session to ventilate these. Where possible the therapist should build a bridge between what a parent expresses and the material taught in the previous session. For example it may be that a parent has had an angry exchange with a much-resented relative who had happened to visit. The therapist might reflect back to the parent 'I wonder how you would have felt if, when you felt your emotional temperature begin to rise, you had said "I'm getting uptight. Right I must do something different. I'll excuse myself, tell them I just want to get something from the off-licence", then went for a walk and told yourself "Well, their visit isn't going to kill me, after all they only stay an hour".' In this way the anger control strategies are, initially at least, taught very much through the experiences of the parent rather than as an abstract technique of doubtful relevance to the 'real world'.

If parents have had any success at all with the strategies in the first two sessions they should be encouraged to persist. It should be stressed however that few if any parents never lose their temper with their child. The goal is simply to achieve a level of anger displays that is both comfortable for the parent and without danger for the child. Reaching the point where a parent is just reasonably content with their management of anger is very much a two steps forward and one step backwards process. Accordingly parents should be taught to anticipate a mix of bad and good weeks with the latter becoming gradually more predominant.

Further coping self-statements should be devised and negotiated, covering at least a further two problematic situations that occur in the parent's diary of angry urges.

SESSION FIVE

The session should begin with the customary review of homework assignments unless there are any other very pressing problems. Up to this stage in the programme most of the session time will have been spent helping the client clarify the anger-producing cognitions in various situations, and developing rational responses to the dysfunctional cognitions. The rational responses have then been woven into a set of self-statements. This approach is adopted so that the client might obtain the most immediate relief from the dangerous situations. Failure to do this will quite likely mean that the parent will default from the programme. However though parents will hopefully by now be aware of some useful rational responses and alternative behaviours for the situations that have been considered in the sessions, it is problematic whether they would have the coping skills for any newly arising anger evoking situation. Therefore, the focus of this session is on teaching parents a framework they can use themselves to generate a set of coping self-statements. There are five possible phases in the anger control strategy developed by Novaco (1976):

1. *Preparing for anger* Possible self-statements in this category might include 'I can work out a plan to handle this. Easy does it', or 'This could be a difficult situation but I know how to handle it'.
2. *Confronting anger* Examples of self-statements under this heading might be 'I just have to keep calm then I'll be managing the situation', or 'Blowing my top isn't going to help, I'll just concentrate on what is being said'.
3. *Coping with angry feelings* Possible self-statements in this category might include 'I am getting wound up, take it easy, take things slowly one at a time', or 'I am not going to play this anger the way I did before, it didn't work then and it won't now'.
4. *Reflection: conflict unresolved* Examples of self-statements under this heading might be 'Does it really matter that much? Do I have to win every time?' or 'I can carry on screaming it's not fair but all I'll get is a sore throat. Maybe I'll just let the episode float out to sea then I'll have peace of mind'.
5. *Reflection: conflict resolved* Possible self-statements in this category might include 'I kept myself calm and so handled that very well', or 'It shows you can get what you want without shooting from the hip!'

After explaining the five phases clients should be given a handout containing the above material and asked to develop a set of self-statements for an anger-evoking situation they are likely to meet in the following week. Most clients will probably need some help with this exercise. Once the therapist is sure clients have the basic idea they should be asked to use the handout at home in the development of at least two sets of self-statements for differing situations.

SESSIONS SIX AND SEVEN

These last two sessions are simply for consolidation of what has already been taught and for problem-solving obstacles to the implementation of the strategies. The use by parents of both coping self-statements and the communication guidelines should be reviewed. At the end of the last session the Novaco Anger Scale should be readministered and a follow-up appointment arranged some weeks later to help maintenance of treatment gains and lessen any possible feelings of abandonment.

DIRECT WORK WITH CHILDREN

Both the behavioural parent training programme and the parental anger control programme are based on the parent's definition of the situation. When children are referred for professional 'help' it is usually at the behest of parents and/or school. The child may not share the 'official' definition of the problem. The adult's 'area of concern' may not be the child's. Consequently therapist questioning about the 'problem behaviour' may be seen by the child as irrelevant and greeted by a series of 'don't know' answers. The child's behaviours should be seen as 'making sense' to the child and the therapeutic task is to understand how they construe the situation. Accordingly, there is a need to give the child plenty of space to describe the behaviours with prompts such as 'Tell me a bit more about that'. Considerable caution is needed to avoid premature projection of an adult's meaning of a word onto a child's usage of the word. For example one child's description of a friend as 'clever' turned out to be based on his companion's ability to avoid conflict with his teachers by turning up only to those lessons where staff were known to take registers. Adults might apply a quite different label! Checking the child's verbal labels with questions such as 'How would you know if someone was . . .?' can be important.

Working with a child only becomes feasible if the child at least partly 'owns' the problem. Should a child, for example, continue to construe angry outbursts as valued evidence of 'nonconformity', attempts to engage the child in anger control training are likely to come to naught. The child may perceive the training as a threat to autonomy, and cajoling him or her into therapy will probably result in the sabotaging of therapeutic endeavours. Engagement of the child in therapy may depend on the child's reconceptualization of autonomy in terms of actions directed towards the attainment of the maximum number of goals, and goals as he or she defines them.

Direct cognitive work with children may be anticipated where problems lie primarily outside the area of non-compliance. Bernard (1985) describes four stages in the application of a cognitive approach with children: 1) rapport building, 2) assessment, 3) skill acquisition, and 4) practice and application. Each stage needs attention but not necessarily to the simultaneous exclusion of another stage. These stages are used here to provide a framework for intervention with problems of impulsivity, anxiety, and depression.

RAPPORT BUILDING

A necessary precondition for therapeutic intervention with any client group is the establishment of empathy, warmth, genuineness, and unconditional positive regard. But there are few, if any, client groups for whom this is more important than children. Yet because of the power differential between adults and children there is a grave temptation to 'do what is best for the child' in an efficient adult manner, paying scant attention to the child's view. This is most likely to happen when the therapist comes under pressure from parents to 'Do something!' An enduring intervention, however, can only be built on a therapeutic alliance with the child. The emphasis has to be on working with rather than for the child. Appropriate targets are therefore likely to be the child's hassles, hurts, or worries rather than parental wants. In areas of concern such as childhood depression and anxiety there is likely to be more overlap between parent and child goals than if the difficulties surround problems of, say, impulsivity.

It is important to convey to a child that they are not just a problem, and that they are respected as a whole human being. A too-exclusive focus on 'the problem' will almost certainly alienate and exhaust the child. Enquiring and showing genuine interest in the child's favourite TV programmes, hobbies, and interests is not an optional extra. At least of equal importance is a sense of humour and fun. Focusing on these seemingly 'off task' areas is as much a therapeutic task in sessions as the modification of dysfunctional attitudes. The younger the child, the more relatively greater proportions of session time will be devoted to 'off task' areas.

Socializing the child into therapy by carefully explaining what will happen in the sessions, the likelihood of success, and the duration of treatment may prevent premature termination of a programme.

ASSESSMENT

The assessment has been conceptualized by Bernard (1985) as involving a problem identification and a problem analysis phase. In the problem identification phase the therapist determines whether or not a problem exists. The child's behaviour has to be set against the normal behaviour of the child's peer group. Thus a knowledge of age developmental norms is of crucial importance. In the problem analysis phase the specifics of the child's dysfunctional thought patterns and behaviours are teased out. This may involve discussions not only with the child but also with parents and teachers. The problem analysis phase may be complicated by the child's difficulties in self disclosure. In part this may be due to the child's naïveté about the therapist's role and care has to be taken to explain this in a way appropriate to the child's developmental level. Alternatively the child may simply not have the verbal labels to describe what they are experiencing. In such instances the therapist can make general explanatory statements such as: 'Sometimes children feel really wound up like something bad is going to happen, do you feel this way?' to which the child can then respond.

Standardized instruments are of some help in assessing the nature of a child's difficulties but need complementing by a semi-structured interview. For example the Conners Parent Symptom Questionnaire (1978) has an impulsivity-hyperactivity sub-scale comprising ten questions. Each question is answered on a four-point scale in terms of frequency and a mean score of 1.5 is generally accepted as the lower limit for establishing impulsivity-hyperactivity. The PSQ has been found to identify 74 per cent of hyperactive children utilizing this particular sub-scale. However both the nature and duration of the child's overactivity has to be considered in gauging whether impulsivity-hyperactivity is the primary problem rather than, say, non-compliance for which conduct disorder might be a more appropriate classification. For hyperactivity it is necessary that the overactivity is characteristically unplanned and disorganized, lacking a clear goal, and must have lasted for a year. Childhood depression may be assessed using the Beck Depression Inventory described in detail in the next chapter. For use with children the question on libido is omitted because of its reactivity with an adolescent population.

Another useful measure is the Childhood Depression Inventory (CDI; Kovacs and Beck 1977) which consists of twenty-seven 'depressive' items. Each item consists of three statements graded in severity from 0 to 2. The total score is obtained by summing the individual item scores. The higher the score, the more depressed the child is. The following is a CDI item:

(0) I am sad once in a while
(1) I am sad many times
(2) I am sad all the time.

The cut-off scores used to establish a depressed sample on the CDI result in a third of children being identified as 'depressed' which is almost certainly an overestimate of the extent of depression.

The child's view of themselves is likely to be particularly important if childhood depression is the problem. Butler (1985) has suggested the following line of questioning to elaborate on the child's self-evaluation, beginning with 'Who do you think knows or understands you best?' If the child replies 'Mother', the line of questioning continues: 'Let's say I didn't know you at all. If I were to meet your mother and I asked her to describe you, what might she say? What three things do you think your mother might say about you?' An alternative suggested by Jackson and Bannister (1984) is to ask children to write about themselves as if written by someone who knew them well; writing in the third person it becomes 'Susan Smith is . . .'

Impulsivity

There is little evidence to suggest that a purely cognitive approach to a child's impulsivity will produce enduring change or change that generalizes across settings. However there are a number of strategies that might act as a useful supplement to a child management programme. The key problem with impulsive behaviour is that the child literally doesn't stop to think. As one parent, delightfully, remarked about her ten-year-old son, 'He needs to plug in and switch on his brain before he opens his mouth or does anything'! To this end Campe and Bash (1981) have developed a problem-solving strategy in which the children are taught to ask themselves the following questions: 'What is my problem? What is my plan? Am I using my plan? How did I do?'

A therapist may introduce a wide variety of games to illustrate problem solving. The selection of the game should be governed by the interests and developmental level of the child. For example the younger child may be introduced to O's and X's or draughts, or chinese chequers. To begin with the therapist should model aloud the problem-solving process at appropriate junctures in the game, verbalizing a number of alternatives as he or she evolves a plan. Often the younger child will volunteer solutions for the therapist! A child should be praised for signs that they have used the problem-solving strategy. As it becomes apparent that the child is beginning to grasp the strategy, the therapist's verbalizations should become more hushed. To aid generalization a further game should be introduced. The older child may be intoduced to a game such as Stratego, in which the object is to capture the enemy's flag. Initially the child can be the therapist's coach as he/she plays a colleague. Discussions between the therapist and 'coach' have to follow the problem-solving format. When conversant with the format the child and therapist can play the game. The latter then simply makes occasional comments as the game progresses. Finally the child might be encouraged to play the game at home with the parent. At subsequent sessions the therapist can ask how the child-parent game went, giving light-hearted feedback. Computer games can be a useful alternative or addition. They cover a wide range, including a Fisher-Price Dance Creation, a St Bernard Dog who has to avoid walruses rising out of pools, and the abominable snowman! When sufficient rapport has been established with the child, he or she can be encouraged to use the same problem-solving format in interpersonal situations on the basis that it 'works for games though you can't still win all the time, so it might be worth trying with people'.

Difficulties encountered are seen simply as challenges to develop new plans. Applying the cognitive problem-solving procedures to interpersonal situations is likely to be particularly fraught when children initially perceive changes to be outside their control, e.g. a teacher overly insistent on classroom quiet. In these circumstances the 'tortoise' response may be appropriate. The tortoise pulls in its head and limbs when faced with an antagonist. The child is taught to do likewise, physically withdrawing from a provocative situation, while using the formula: 'I had better think it out again'. This gives them time to generate and consider new alternatives, such as discussing the matter with his/her parents. The focus in treating impulsivity is on helping a child supply task-appropriate verbal self-instructions. Moving to childhood depression and anxiety Waters (1982) suggests the therapeutic task is rather to help the child a) modify distortions of reality (i.e. 'Nobody likes me, they're all against me') and b) modify the child's self-defeating evaluation of situations (i.e. 'This situation shouldn't exist. It's awful!')

Depression

Somewhat different approaches could be used for the younger child and the older child/adolescent. These are discussed in turn.

a) *The younger child*
Care has to be taken to check that the younger child has a wide enough emotional vocabulary. This can be done by drawing simple pictures of a face and asking the child what emotion each one represents. To help the child appreciate that emotions are on a continuum, a particular emotion in its extreme form is represented on paper. The child is then asked to draw and label the complete opposite of this emotion. Subsequently the child represents an emotion on paper that is midway between the extremes. Then expressions are drawn and labels are attached for points intermediate between the midway and the extremes. Effectively the child has developed a five-point scale for a particular emotion. Scales of particular interest would be sad (for depression), worried (for anxiety), and possibly anger and jealousy, as they often occur concurrent with the first two in children. An alternative to actually drawing the emotions is for the therapist to model them and seek labels from the child. As the child recounts experiences of, say, the past week, the therapist can help to fine-tune the description of

events by reference to the scale developed, with prompts such as 'Do you mean you felt as bad as that?' (pointing to a face and label) 'or as bad as that?' (pointing to another face and label). This exercise also helps the child break one of the most common thought processes hypothesized by Beck (1976) to be implicated in depression – dichotomous reasoning, i.e. thinking in black and white. The child may typically think 'My classmates love or hate me'. This may then be compounded by further logical errors such as 'Since I only go around with one or two friends most of the class hates me' – an example of arbitrary inference.

To help children become aware of their self-talk, therapist prompts suggested by Bernard (1985) include:

'What were you thinking when . . . happened?'

'What sorts of things were you saying to yourself when . . .?'

'Tell me the first things which come into your mind when you think about . . . .'

'Picture yourself back in class. What did you think when . . .?'

The next stage is to illustrate the connection between self-talk and feelings. One way of doing this is to ask the child what feelings they would have if they thought a pet cat was outside the room and then to ask what difference it would make to the feelings if they seriously thought a lion was outside. In this way a child can be helped to grasp that what they think influences what they feel. The distinction between 'thoughts' and 'feelings' is not always immediately apparent to children, and may need to be underlined by explaining that different people may react differently to the same situation. For example, the therapist might illustrate the point by saying: 'One child may be happy that the next lesson is a swimming lesson whilst his friend may be frightened. The different sort of things they are saying to themselves about the swimming are their thoughts. They feel different so they're thinking different.'

The final stage of therapy with the depressed younger child is teaching coping self-statements. For example P.W. was aged ten and in foster care, attending a local primary school. He had become depressed and withdrawn following the taunts of local classmates about having no father and 'your mother doesn't want you either'. Unfortunately, about this time his mother's visits had decreased in frequency because of a progressive disease. P.W. was taught to say to himself 'If I am beginning to feel sad I have got to blow my referee's whistle really loud and write in my notebook ''No one can do much when they are injured, Mum tries as hard as she can, maybe she will have some better times.'' I do enjoy it when I go to the match with my foster father. I'll just think about the last match for a bit and if the other kids do go on at me I'll just send them off.' To construct such a set of coping self-statements it is clearly necessary first of all to enter the child's particular world. The efficacy of such self-statements would be reviewed at each session and modified if necessary. The coping self-statement is essentially constructed from a realistic answer to the child's automatic thought 'My mum doesn't care about me' and a challenge to the perceived 'awfulness' of life, a modifying of cognitive distortions and evaluations.

b) *The older child and adolescent*
The older child is more able to develop their own realistic answer to dysfunctional thoughts. There seems to be no reason why treatment of adolescent depression should not closely mirror treatment of adult depression (the subject of Chapter 6). However only one outcome study of a cognitive-behavioural approach to adolescent depression has yet been published (Reynolds and Coats 1986). The results of this trial indicated the superiority of a group cognitive-behavioural programme to a waiting-list control condition, and that gains made were maintained at a five-week follow up. However clients in the other active treatment condition, relaxation training, did just as well at the end of treatment and at follow up.

Waters (1982) suggests that children can be helped to challenge their dysfunctional automatic thoughts by posing the following series of questions:

1. Is this belief based on fact, opinion, inference, or assumption? Where is the evidence that this is really so?
2. Is it really awful? Is it true I couldn't stand it? Is it the worst that it could be?
3. Is this belief getting me what I want?
4. Why shouldn't it be so? Do I always have to get what I want?
5. Where is the evidence that this makes me worthless? How can this make me worthless or less than human?

Anxiety

The transient nature of much childhood anxiety and fear calls into question the wisdom of therapeutic intervention. Further, childhood anxiety disorders have not been found to create a heightened risk for adult disorders. Nevertheless both parent and child will continue to expect as speedy a relief from the anxiety problem as possible and there is some evidence that cognitive-behavioural approaches can act as a catalyst.

Graziano and Mooney (1980) conducted a controlled trial in which they demonstrated the superiority of a cognitive-behavioural programme (CBP) over a no-treatment condition in the alleviation of fear of the dark. The CBP programme contained seventeen children with serious fears of going to bed alone in the dark. These children were taught to relax their muscles in bed, self-reinforce their efforts with praise and tokens, imagine a pleasant scene, and recite brave self-statements. These children were compared on several parent-recorded measures of fear behaviour to an untreated control group of sixteen children with similar fears. Significant differences were found after treatment and were maintained at a three-year follow up. Because the programme contained both cognitive and behavioural components it is not clear which were the active ingredients for change or whether cognitive strategies potentiate the effects of behavioural interventions.

Cognitive interventions with childhood anxiety problems tend to be grafted on to behavioural approaches. In order to gauge the efficacy of the composite package the effectiveness of behavioural interventions alone should be recalled. Behavioural interventions such as systematic desensitization have been used successfully with a wide range of specific fears such as school phobia, dog phobia, bee phobia, treating tics, stuttering, fear of ambulances and hospitals, fear of loud noises, and test anxiety (Hartzenbuehler and Schroeder 1978). Systematic desensitization involves pairing an anxiety evoking stimulus with an anxiety inhibiting response, usually relaxation training. Such training has as its core the progressive tensing and relaxation of the different muscle groups. An often viable alternative to systematic desensitization is participant modelling (Graziano *et al.* 1979). First, the child watches a model go through a graded approach sequence. Then, with verbal assistance and reinforcement, the model leads the child through the same response. The last step involves having the child perform the responses without the assistance of the model.

Nelson (1981) used a cognitive-behavioural approach in the treatment of a child's dental phobia. Treatment focused on teaching the child self-statements to cope with three specific aspects of the dental visits: 1) preparing for dental visits (e.g. 'Worrying won't help anything'); 2) confronting a stress or pain (e.g. 'Remember what the dentist said and it will be over a lot quicker'); and 3) coping with stress or pain at critical moments (e.g. 'Just cool it and relax'). After successful completion of the cognitive strategies the child reinforced herself with statements such as 'I did it'. The self-statements were taught to the child using the procedures of Meichenbaum and Turk (1976). Initially, the therapist modelled the appropriate coping statements (cognitive modelling). Then the child verbalized the same coping statements under the therapist's guidance (external guidance), after which the child verbalized the statements by herself (overt self guidance). Finally, the child role played the scenes while verbalizing the statements to herself (covert self guidance). Besides rehearsing the self-statements, the child was instructed to breathe deeply and slowly when she became aware of her typical rapid breathing and was taught a distraction technique of counting to twenty while visualizing the numbers when she felt overwhelmed by fear or pain. This example illustrates all the main features of a cognitive-behavioural approach to fear. Cognitive-behavioural approaches to childhood anxieties clearly hold a great deal of promise but in view of the paucity of outcome research no definitive statement can be made.

Part 2

A COGNITIVE-BEHAVIOURAL APPROACH TO EMOTIONAL DISORDERS

Chapter Five

EMOTIONAL DISORDERS: THEORY AND ASSESSMENT

Depression and anxiety are the most common of the emotional disorders found in the general population. The emotional disorders pose a major health problem with between 20 and 25 per cent of patients consulting their general practitioner suffering from a psychiatric disturbance. Between 5 and 10 per cent of patients actually fulfil diagnostic criteria for depression. The characteristic course and outcome of depression and anxiety is far from clear, since different studies use different follow-up periods and types of groups (Blacker and Clare 1987). However a study by J.M. Murphy *et al.* (1986) deserves special mention as she and her colleagues have performed the longest follow-up study, seventeen years, of depressed and anxious patients. It was found that 56 per cent of the 'cases' had a poor prognosis in terms of later psychiatric morbidity of variable duration. However nearly 80 per cent of those with initial complete syndromes of both depression and anxiety had an unfavourable outcome, thus making any effective addition to the armoury of treatment strategies at a premium. The cognitive-behavioural strategies described in Part Two of this work have been found to constitute a most useful supplement to existing treatments for depression, anxiety, and agoraphobia.

CLASSIFYING EMOTIONAL DISORDERS

Emotional disorders have distressed and puzzled people down the centuries. Shakespeare's Antonio expressed his bewilderment thus:

> In sooth I know not why I am so sad;
> It wearies me; you say it wearies you;

But how I caught it, found it, or came by it,
What stuff 'tis made of, whereof it is born,
I am to learn;
And such a want-wit sadness makes of me,
That I have much ado to know myself.
(*The Merchant of Venice*, Act 1, Scene 1, 1-7)

The public view would probably be that Antonio was suffering from 'depression'. However modern diagnostic systems such as the Present State Examination (Wing *et al.* 1974), the International Classification of Diseases (ICD-9; World Health Organisation 1978) and the Diagnostic and Statistical Manual 3 (American Psychiatric Association 1980) would all require evidence of symptoms over and above sadness to permit a diagnosis. There is a considerable overlap between the three diagnostic systems, so that a patient diagnosed as a 'case' under one system would probably be so diagnosed under another system. But this is by no means certain as each system emphasizes some symptoms at the expense of others.

THE CRITERIA FOR DEPRESSION

In establishing whether a client is suffering from depression Snaith (1987) has proposed a merger of some of the symptoms held to be important in the PSE with others of importance in DSM 3, constituting what he sees to be the core of depressive disorder. He leaves out somatic symptoms, such as weight loss and insomnia which might occur in a wide variety of bodily illnesses. His list is as follows:

- depressed mood – sadness, misery, low spirits
- loss of pleasure response – a definite diminution in the
  person's interests, either some interests have been dropped, or
  the intensity of the interest has decreased. The diminution
  must be measured in the context of the range and depth of the
  person's usual activities.
- slowing down or agitation
- feelings of worthlessness, self reproach and inappropriate guilt
- hopelessness – the person's view of the future is bleak and
  without comfort
- diminished ability to think or concentrate

Table 1 Extract from Beck Depression Inventory

On this questionnaire are groups of statements. Please read each group of statements carefully. Then pick out the one statement in each group which best describes the way you have been feeling the PAST WEEK, INCLUDING TODAY! Circle the number beside the statement you picked. If several statements in the group seem to apply equally well, circle each one.

1. 0 I do not feel sad
    1 I feel sad
    2 I am sad all the time and I can't snap out of it
    3 I am so sad or unhappy that I can't stand it
2. 0 I am not particularly discouraged about the future
    1 I feel discouraged about the future
    2 I feel I have nothing to look forward to
    3 I feel that the future is hopeless and that things cannot improve

4. 0 I get as much satisfaction out of things as I used to
    1 I don't enjoy things the way I used to
    2 I don't get real satisfaction out of things any more
    3 I am dissatisfied or bored with everything
5. 0 I don't feel particularly guilty
    1 I feel guilty a good part of the time
    2 I feel quite guilty most of the time
    3 I feel guilty most of the time

Clients who experience most of these symptoms are probably depressed, as opposed to 'demoralized', 'grieving', 'frustrated' or 'disillusioned' (Snaith 1987). Snaith sees the loss of the pleasure response (anhedonia) as the most central and reliable symptom. This symptom can be teased out fairly reliably using a few key questions such as: Can one look forward to a usually enjoyed event such as a weekend outing or a visit from a friend? Does one still pursue old hobbies or pastimes with real pleasure? Can one still heartily enjoy a good joke?

Rating scales and self-report measures can be used to gauge the severity of the disorder but they do not constitute a diagnosis. For example, many clients suffering from schizophrenia would score fairly highly on say, the Beck Depression Inventory BDI (1961), but depression would not be their primary disorder and a diagnosis of primary major depressive disorder would not be made. Nevertheless measures such as the BDI are a reminder of the sort of symptoms considered important in depression. An extract from the BDI is shown in Table 1.

The full scale consists of 21 items making a maximum total score of 63. Clients scoring 14–20 are termed 'mildly depressed', 21–26 'moderately depressed', and over 26 'severely depressed'. Most cognitive therapy outcome studies have in fact used a BDI score of greater than 20 (i.e. moderately or severely depressed) as a criterion for selecting depressed subjects.

THE CRITERIA FOR ANXIETY

The Diagnostic and Statistical Manual of Mental Disorders (DSM 3, American Psychiatric Association 1980) distinguishes eight anxiety disorders: generalized anxiety disorder, panic disorder, agoraphobia, post-traumatic stress disorder, atypical anxiety disorder, phobic disorder, social phobia, and simple phobia. The treatment focus in Chapter 7 is on the most common anxiety disorders (the first three in the list) and the defining characteristics of these three disorders in DSM 3 are:

Generalized Anxiety Disorder The essential feature is generalized, persistent anxiety of at least one month's duration without the specific symptoms that characterize phobic disorders, panic disorder, or obsessive compulsive disorder. The diagnosis is not made if the disturbance is due to another physical or mental disorder, such as hyperthyroidism or major depression.

Although the specific manifestations of the anxiety vary from individual to individual, generally there are signs of tension, hyperactivity, apprehensive expectation and vigilance and scanning. Mild depressive symptoms are common.

Panic Disorder The essential features are recurrent panic attacks that occur at times unpredictably, though certain situations (e.g. driving a car) may become associated with a panic attack. The panic attacks are manifested by the sudden onset of intense apprehension, fear, or terror, often associated with feelings of impending doom. The most common symptoms experienced during an attack are palpitations, chest pain or discomfort, choking or smothering sensations, dizziness, vertigo, or unsteady feelings, feelings of unreality (depersonalization), hot and cold flushes, sweating, faintness, trembling or shaking, and fear of dying, going crazy or doing something uncontrolled during the attack. Attacks usually last minutes, more rarely hours.

The individual often develops degrees of nervousness and apprehension between attacks.

Agoraphobia The essential feature is a marked fear of being alone, or being in public places from which escape might be difficult or help not available in case of sudden incapacitation. Normal activities are increasingly constricted as the fears or avoidance behaviour dominate the individual's life. The most common situations involve being in crowds such as on a busy street or in crowded shops, or being in tunnels, on bridges, in lifts, or on public transport. Often these individuals insist that a family member or friend accompany them when they leave home.

DISTINGUISHING BETWEEN DEPRESSION AND ANXIETY

In practice depression and anxiety often coexist. Nevertheless, it is useful to have an assessment device that helps identify the severity of each separately. This can be particularly important because anxiety management techniques often fail unless an accompanying depression is first treated. Snaith and Zigmond (1983) have developed the Hospital Anxiety and Depression (HAD) Scale which consists of depression and anxiety sub-scales. Each sub-scale has a normal, borderline, and pathological region. This instrument takes clients only a few minutes to complete and can be used easily in the community both as an aid to assessment and as an evaluation of progress. (The name of the instrument arises simply because it was originally developed and validated on a hospital sample.)

COGNITIVE MODELS OF DEPRESSION AND ANXIETY

Cognitive models of depression and anxiety differ from traditional behavioural formulations, in that behaviour is not seen simply as a function of the environment. Rather individuals are seen as responding to their perceptions of the environment and are active participants in the creation of their realities! On this model the environment is not a fixed, stable, and external reality, nor is the individual seen as a blank sheet on which the environment writes itself.

Beck *et al.* (1985) liken an individual's construction of a situation to taking a series of photographs, first scanning the environment and then determining which aspect to focus on. The photograph necessarily leaves aspects of the external world out of account. Specific settings (lens, focus, speed) have an enormous influence on the final picture. For example, depending on the type of lens (wide-angle or telephoto), breadth is sacrificed for detail or vice versa. The analogy suggests that specific characteristics of the receiving apparatus (the camera or the cognitive organization) have a decisive influence on what one sees. Moreover the photographer plays a crucial role in selecting particular strategies. In this way the individual is constantly processing information from the 'external world'. Particular processes are more evident in depression and others in anxiety. The information-processing procedures in depression and the anxiety disorders are now discussed in turn.

DEPRESSION

To adequately account for the complexity of cognitive processes in depression Beck (1987) suggests six separable but overlapping models. Each of these models is briefly considered:

The cross-sectional model

This model asserts that negative cognitive content is an integral part of depressive symptomatology. Depressed clients show high levels of self-criticism, negative expectations, and a negative view of past experience. In general depressives have been found to downgrade their personal attributes, exaggerate the insolubility of problems, and forecast negative outcomes. Beck asserts that depressives are not simply mirroring their negative experiences but are presenting a biased sample of these experiences. In part this occurs because of a selective focusing on the negative aspects and excluding the positive aspects of experience. Thus while the depressed person may accurately perceive the negative details of an event, dwelling on them distorts the overall meaning of a situation. If the information processing is biased in some way, there is going to be a corresponding modification in the individual's emotional state and behaviour. Beck does not claim that 'cognitions cause depression', he sees such statements as akin to saying 'delusions cause psychosis'. He sees deviant cognitive processes as intrinsic to the depressive disorder not a cause or consequence. Beck concedes that adverse reality may start a downward spiral in mood but argues that exaggerated negative meanings attached to ongoing experiences are responsible for the build up and maintenance of a full-blown depression.

The structural model

This model helps account for an individual's continuity of thought processes from one depressive episode to another. It also helps explain the similarities in the thought processes of many depressives. It is postulated that early on in life the individual develops basic rules for living (schemata). These schemas have a conditional nature, e.g. 'If people don't like me, I am nothing'. The core schemata are shorn of their conditional nature and take on an absolute form, e.g. 'I am nothing'. Such core schemata would be apparent only at the deeper levels of depression. Depressogenic schemata are activated in depression.

The schemata are thought to be relatively dormant when the individual is not depressed. During depression the negatively toned schemata emerge from the predepressive personality of the client. Beck distinguishes two personality types: the sociotropic and the autotropic. The former places a high premium on interpersonal relations and tends to judge his own worth in terms of the amount of acceptance and affection he receives. The autotropic personality, by contrast, values independence, freedom of action, privacy and self-determination most highly. The nature of a depressed client's reaction to a situation will be influenced by whether it impinges on their particular personality type.

The stressor-vulnerability model

The vulnerability hypothesis postulates that certain dysfunctional silent assumptions become operative only when external factors impinge on the individual's specific vulnerability – like a key fitting into a lock. Beck (1987) gives the example of a person who believed that 'I need to be loved in order to be happy'. This particular predisposing schema is of no significance until the person makes a judgement that he or she is not loved by a particular key person. If this judgement is made the belief that 'Therefore, I cannot be happy' will probably follow in its wake, thereby ushering in depression. Opening the door to depression depends on the coexistence of a predisposing schema and a related stressor. Implicit in this model is the view that chronic stress *per se* does not precipitate clinical depression. This is not to deny the evidence that suggests chronic stress may increase social maladjustment (see for example Breslau and Davis 1986).

The reciprocal-interaction model

The reciprocal interaction model acknowledges the role interpersonal context plays in the maintenance of depression. There is evidence that depressed individuals prematurely disclose negative information about themselves and that non-depressed persons seek to reduce their interactions with them. This can provide the depressed person with further 'evidence' of their 'inadequacy'. In seeking solace the depressed individual may be unwittingly maintaining his or her depression. This vicious circle is obviously not inevitable. Some spouses may react kindly to their partner's expression of depression, or may scold them into partaking in activities that offer at least an outside chance of producing a sense of pleasure or achievement.

The psychobiological model

A comprehensive description of depression has to take account of the psychological, social, and biological aspects of the disorder. The interdependence of the three factors makes an exclusive focus on any one of them arbitrary. Regrettably, but understandably, professionals tend to concentrate on the discipline in which they are trained. This will at best produce a partial description of the phenomenon. Beck (1987) comments that

Negative interpretations of reality may be related less to the direct impact of the negative environment *per se* than to the effect of drugs, toxins or hormones that make the individual sensitive or hypersensitive to the adverse environmental circumstances. Thus, the individual who responds with depression to a generally negative situation (for example, unemployment) may be the one person whose cognitive organization has become destabilized or sensitized by organic factors.

The evolutionary model

At first glance depression seems to run counter to the received wisdom about an instinct for self-preservation. Rather than preserve his/her life the depressive seems more concerned with self-castigation, perhaps even committing suicide. Yet the ubiquity of depression suggests that it must after all have some evolutionary significance. Beck (1987) suggests that the characteristics of depression are suggestive of an underlying mechanism to conserve energy. Historically such conservation of energy may have been an important safeguard against wasting energy in a frenetic search for food or fighting adversaries with little likelihood of success. Some energy had to be reserved for the continuance of the species. An analogy may be drawn between an economic and psychological depression. In both cases there is the expectation of a prolonged reduction in income (material or psychic). Increased productivity would result in only a further depletion of resources. The only solution is to shut down the system until conditions obviously improve.

ANXIETY

Whilst depressed clients take their interpretations and predictions as facts, anxious clients see them as possibilities. Anxious clients keep hope alive, conceding that good times may come and that they may cope better. The negative appraisals of anxious clients are selective and specific; by contrast depressed clients' appraisals are pervasive and global. The anxious person is more tentative about personal defects or mistakes and does not see them as indicating his or her worthlessness, whereas the depressed person does. Thus an anxious student might castigate him or herself for not preparing adequately for an exam or misunderstanding a question; but the depressed student would blame him or herself for global deficits, such as being a stupid or lazy person.

Anxiety disorders may be analogized to a hypersensitive alarm system. Anxious clients fail to distinguish between possible or remote dangers and probable dangers. There is a selective attention to possible dangers. This makes for a pervasive sense of vulnerability which is heightened by distorted thinking. Clients may underestimate possible rescue factors amongst their personal resources (minimization) or be inclined to focus primarily on weaknesses (selective abstraction). Each flaw may be seen as a gaping hole (magnification); or each slip as heralding a catastrophe (catastrophizing). Anxious clients also tend to assume the most negative interpretation when confronted with ambiguous situations. In contrast to depressed clients however, anxious clients do not show a bias in memory in favouring negative material. The information-processing pathology in anxiety lies rather in the facilitation of the acquisition of threat-related information.

The particular form that the anxiety disorder takes – generalized anxiety disorder, panic disorder, or agoraphobia – depends on the anxiety stimuli under focus. With panic disorder the symptoms of light-headedness, dizziness, or palpitations are taken as evidence of impending catastrophe and this leads to a further exacerbation of the symptoms. It is possible for clients to have agoraphobia with or without panic attacks. The agoraphobic client is hypersensitive to specific spatial configurations: too narrow spaces and too expansive spaces. This sensitivity is paralleled in personal relations – the fear of being too close and the fear of being too far away from a caretaker. Any blockage of access to home or the caretaker can itself induce fear and an overpowering wish to return home. It is suggested by Beck *et al*. (1985) that the agoraphobia-prone individual has latent fears of situations that might have constituted potential dangers during early childhood but that are not dangerous for adults, such as crowded shops or open spaces.

Beck sees anxiety disorders as arising from a composite of many interacting factors – genetic, developmental, environmental, and psychological. Whilst genetic factors have been implicated in the aetiology of panic disorders their role in generalized anxiety disorder is much less clear. He identifies three possible immediate precipitants of anxiety disorders: a) increased demands (for example, increased workload), b) increased amount of threat in life situation (for example, the possibility of being one of the candidates for redundancy), c) stressful events that undermine confidence (for example, being one of those selected for redundancy and having difficulty negotiating the maze of DHSS regulations in order to secure the correct benefit). Beck suggests however that these precipitating factors are only potent in so far as they impinge on an individual's specific vulnerabilities. For example the man who had long carried the tacit assumption that the male ought to be the breadwinner in the house, and who saw state benefit as 'charity' and acceptance of it as a sign of personal weakness, would be much more vulnerable when the possibility of redundancy arose.

Chapter Six

COGNITIVE THERAPY FOR DEPRESSION

Cognitive therapy for depression represents a systematic therapeutic development of the ancient notion that 'People are disturbed not so much by events as by the views which they take of them' (Epictetus, 1st century AD). In this chapter the practice of cognitive therapy for depression is described. A necessary first step is of course to check initially that the client is depressed according to the self-report measures and diagnostic systems described in the previous chapter. For those new to cognitive therapy it is particularly useful to add the Dysfunctional Attitude Scale (DAS, Weissman and Beck 1978) – see Appendix C – to the standard assessment measures. The DAS contains forty items answered on a seven-point scale from 'totally agree' to 'totally disagree'. The items provide a wide (but by no means exhaustive) sample of the depressogenic silent assumptions often found amongst depressed clients such as 'If I do not do as well as other people it means I am an inferior human being' and 'I am nothing if a person I love doesn't love me'. Much of the emotional distress of clients in particular situations is reducible to one of these forty silent assumptions. A therapist aware of a client's response to these items prior to therapy can be on the look-out for their manifestation in the distressing situations the client relays or records. The completed DAS can provide the novice therapist with a shortlist of salient depressogenic assumptions that will probably need modification if the client is to overcome depression and perhaps even more importantly avoid relapse. It has to be borne in mind however that there can be many more dysfunctional silent assumptions than those contained in the DAS.

Therapy usually involves fifteen to twenty individual sessions over a twelve-week period. In the first few weeks sessions are often arranged twice weekly. The rationale for this is that the therapist can thereby more easily prompt the client to overcome the inertia characteristic of depression. Anything that involves an effort in terms of behaviour and thinking tends to be avoided by the depressed person. From a practical point of view therapists can find it difficult to provide twice-weekly appointments, and in the Ross and Scott (1985) trial of cognitive therapy the clients who were given individual cognitive therapy were seen on a weekly basis and this still proved effective. Indicating to clients at the outset what the likelihood of 'success' of the treatment will be is important in motivating the client. On the basis of studies of cognitive therapy it seems reasonable to claim that four out of five patients completing CT will recover from depression by the end of the sessions – and for the most part treatment gains will be maintained. To help ensure treatment gains are maintained, clients should be told they will be offered at least three or four booster sessions in the year following completion of treatment. Initially it is advisable to contract with clients for four or five sessions and then perform a stock-taking exercise. There is evidence to suggest that how clients are faring after four or five sessions of cognitive therapy is predictive of the short and long-term outcome of therapy (Fennell and Teasdale 1987). So that if a client had worsened or remained unchanged by the end of that period, alternative treatment might be indicated, perhaps antidepressant medication if they are not already taking it. For those who had shown a slight change the full cognitive therapy programme may be indicated, and for those who seem to have 'recovered' by the fourth or fifth session, bi-weekly appointments may be appropriate provided there are no subsequent signs of deterioration.

At the outset of therapy it is important to provide clients with some coherent written rationale for therapy. A variety of materials may be used. The author developed the *There's Hope!* leaflet for clients in the controlled trial (see Appendix D). This leaflet provides three case histories of clients who had gone through cognitive therapy describing in their own words what their problems were and how they learned to overcome the depression. This enables clients, often for the first time, to appreciate that their feelings and characteristic ways of thinking have been shared by other people and that recovery is possible. The leaflet also contains a potted summary of how to overcome depression, and the main foci in therapy. Most clients are unaware of what therapy might involve and this is particularly so with the lower socio-economic status clients. The initial presentation of an understandable and coherent rationale for treatment can help prevent premature termination of cognitive therapy. Beck and Greenberg (1976) have also produced a very useful client information leaflet *Coping with Depression*. It has been found that clients' initial response to this leaflet is predictive of long-term outcome of cognitive therapy. A client's reaction to this leaflet seems to indicate whether or not they buy into the cognitive therapy formulation of their problems.

A minimum requirement prior to commencing therapy is to have the client complete the Beck Depression Inventory (BDI) (Beck *et al.* 1961) and the DAS (Weissman and Beck 1978). These instruments can be used also as measures of ongoing change in the client. Typically clients express their depressive feelings in conjunction with particular social concerns. It is useful to quantify these concerns using, say, Corney and Clare's (1985) Social Questionnaire (see Appendix B). Sample items from this instrument are, for the unemployed 'How satisfied are you with this situation?' and for the married 'How satisfied in general are you with your relationship?' Clients indicate their feelings on a four-point scale from 'severely dissatisfied' to 'satisfied', or 'no difficulties' to 'severe difficulties' in a wide range of social domains. The Social Questionnaire can help in the construction of agenda items that would be tackled in therapy. In explaining the rationale for therapy, the therapist can draw on material that is salient to the client from the Social Questionnaire. For example J.D. had indicated that he was severely dissatisfied with his job as a computer programmer. In addition, he had indicated perfectionistic attitudes on the DAS. By way of explaining the rationale for cognitive therapy the therapist asked if there were colleagues doing a similar job who didn't get as wound up as he did. J.D. then described one or two colleagues who reacted differently. The therapist then went on to explain that 'In cognitive therapy we do slow-motion action replays of what passes through people's minds when they get upset. In work colleagues may be thinking "I'll do my best to get through the work management has set, but it's their own problem if they set too much", whereas perhaps you are thinking "I have got to get it all done, if I don't it's my fault, I am a failure". The different mental cassette tapes produce different feelings but eventually there is some choice as to which cassette we choose to play.' In this way the important issue of the relevance of therapy is addressed as well as indicating, by analogy, the direction of therapy. Care should be taken however to paint a realistic scenario, and that it is not just a matter of thinking straight and all will be sweetness and light! It is often difficult, particularly initially, for clients to detect what they are thinking when they become depressed, and it may be some time before rational responses to any identified negative thoughts produce a major change at a feeling level. Under pressure the characteristic distorted form of thinking may resurrect itself even after a period of calm and realistic thinking. Clients should be advised that progress in therapy is most likely to be two steps forward and one backwards. But that the backward steps are learning opportunities which can further serve to strengthen the inoculation against further depressive episodes.

THE EARLY SESSIONS OF COGNITIVE THERAPY

The emphasis in the early sessions of CT is more behavioural than cognitive. Cognitions that may be central to the person's depression, often those to do with the client's view of themselves, are not normally challenged at this stage, but should be noted by the therapist for later intervention. Instead the emphasis is on helping the client to participate in activities and behaviours that offer at least the potential for a sense of achievement or pleasure. Often the client has withdrawn from the activities that once gave pleasure or achievement. The therapeutic task is to encourage the client to conduct an experiment in which some previously pleasurable activities are attempted. It should be stressed to clients that it is more by way of a bonus if they get achievement or pleasure from the activity, the prime concern is to get the client moving. A useful analogy for the client is that once you overcome the inertia of a heavy object, movement thereafter becomes relatively easy. To further motivate inactive clients, their inevitably depressed state can be contrasted with the possibilities for mood alteration should they play a favourite piece of music for example, or take a shower, go to a football match, etc. In the active state there is at least the possibility of achievement and pleasure; in the inactive state there is the certainty of depression. Care should be taken however not to ask too much of clients at this stage, as it has to be borne in mind that anything involving decisions or concentration constitutes a major effort. The therapist is seeking simply to underline for the client that, to some extent at least, mood alteration is possible via the activities chosen. This can give clients for the first time some sense of control over their depression. The therapist has to be prepared, however, for the possibility that clients find no initial mood alteration as a result of these activities. In which case the emphasis should be on praising them for making the attempt. It is useful at this point to acknowledge to clients that they are attempting the various activities weighed down by a very real 'lead weight', and even the contemplation of movement is itself a major step forward.

It was mentioned in the last chapter that one of the features of depression is an increased access to and recall of negative memories. This can play havoc with a client's report of the efficacy of a homework assignment that involved some increased activities. In retrospect the client may deny that a particular activity made any difference at all and the therapeutic lesson may be lost. To guard against this possibility it is useful to have the client complete a diary of the week, noting the sense of achievement/mastery and the sense of pleasure experienced each hour of the day, and in two or three words what he or she was doing at the time. Achievement/mastery scores and sense of pleasure should be rated on a ten-point scale from 0 to 10, where 0 is no pleasure or achievement and 10 is the most achievement or pleasure. Pleasure and achievement should be independently rated. Most clients find it more practical to complete the diary at lunch-time looking back on the previous few hours, then tea-time, looking back on the afternoon, and again before they go to bed, looking back on the evening. A completed diary enables the therapist to see the precise influence the activities have on mood, and provides probably more realistic data than the client's recall in the session some days later. Within the session the client's attention may be drawn to the actual impact of the activities.

The diary also helps provide information on a client's low spots in the week. For example it is fairly typical for depressed clients to feel particularly low first thing in the morning, as they lie musing on 'another day!'. Such a client may be advised to experiment with re-arranging the morning routine, perhaps rising as soon as the alarm rings and having a shower. Ideally clients' diaries should reflect a balance of activities producing primarily a sense of pleasure and those producing primarily a sense of achievement. Initially there is usually little of either and the client sees his (but more usually her) week as the discharge of a set of moral obligations. Breaking down some of these obligations into manageable proportions should become a therapeutic focus. For example, at her third session of cognitive therapy J.A. complained that she hadn't done anything in the week since the previous session. It emerged that the day after the last session had been her ironing day, her mood when she rose that morning had been better than average. She set up the ironing board, then went and had a cup of coffee. This was followed by a read of the morning paper which in turn was followed by a telephone call to her friend and a listen to the local radio station. By this time it was mid-morning and she felt guilty she had wasted the 'morning' when there was a day's ironing to do. As the morning wore on her guilt deepened and she sought to assuage it by eating chocolate biscuits which made her feel more guilty as she was trying to lose weight. The therapist suggested that she wasn't managing the ironing because the cost of doing it – a day's total boredom – greatly outweighed any gains. This realization dawned on her at tea-time when she would flop exhausted into the chair, and feel guilty she didn't have any energy to cook the tea and would have to send the children to the local chip shop. J.A. decided to iron for 1½ hours three mornings each week, finishing as a favourite radio programme came on. She would reward herself with a coffee and a single chocolate biscuit then. To help get her started on the ironing she would set up the ironing board and assemble the items for ironing the night before. She was also allowed to drink a cup of coffee as she began but not before ironing.

Clients who are 'depressed about being depressed' are a particular challenge in the earlier sessions. They may default from treatment because they believe that depression is their fault and that if they showed more willpower they would already be over their problems. Often such individuals have prided themselves on their willpower prior to depression. They have a sense of exasperation with their inability to 'pull themselves together' which may be exacerbated by the well-meaning but ill-judged advice of friends and relatives. Such clients often express a wish to be suffering from something more tangible like a broken leg because they wouldn't see it as blameworthy and the path out of the difficulties would be clearer. At her fourth session of cognitive therapy J.G. complained: 'No one else is off sick like me. I say to myself I shouldn't be like this, I should pull myself together, everybody says so . . . I should be making quicker progress. I have been feeling guilty about not wanting to do anything, not even wanting to bother picking my friend up.' The therapeutic strategy adopted in response was to indicate that 1) between 1 in 5 and 1 in 10 of her colleagues at work would be needing professional help for depression at some time, so that she was not perhaps as unusual as she imagined, and 2) a rationale for depression was explained that helped to counter blame. Depression was described as the mind going on strike for better pay and conditions, frustrated that opportunities for achievement and pleasure are lacking. The mind has to use all its energy to sort out how it can regain the pleasure from life, this means that little energy is left over for other people, tasks, or interests. It is as if the mind has hung a 'temporarily out of order – closed for repairs' notice on the outside. The key to begin with is not to get annoyed with yourself that previous enthusiasm, interest, and concern is lacking. Eventually these will return if the client treats herself as her own best friend, attempting tasks in a graded way and checking that how she views situations is accurate (for example, 'No one else is off sick like me'). It was necessary to reiterate much the same ideas at the fifth session so that by the sixth session we were dealing with just one problem, her depression and not two – depression plus depression about depression. In the early phase of cognitive therapy it may be necessary to challenge other cognitive distortions that may make for the client defaulting. They may be expressed as much non-verbally by, say, a client's reluctance to provide information as by comments such as 'I am a private person' which may be reducible to the silent assumption that 'It is a sign of weakness to seek help'.

A particular concern in the early sessions is with the possibility of suicidal intent. Approximately 15 per cent of seriously depressed persons commit suicide. The possibility of suicide may be indicated by the client's response to the relevant question on the

Beck Depression Inventory. Equally of concern, however, is the client who refuses to answer any questions on self-harm or the possibility of self-harm. The seriousness of suicidal intent may be gauged by the degree of detailed planning of the act. For some clients suicide may simply be an idea that has often passed through their mind, in statements such as 'I would be better off dead and wouldn't mind if I didn't wake up in the morning', where no positive actions are contemplated. In such cases the risk is considerably less than for the client who has thought 'If I were to do it, I would probably go down to the docks, at night, when it is dark and nobody is about, and throw myself into a dock'. The suicidal risk is heightened further if the client is impulsive. Obviously a previous history of suicide attempts increases the risk even further.

Hopelessness as measured by Beck's Hopelessness Scale is a better predictor of suicide than the level of the client's depression, thus emphasizing the link between a wholly negative view of the future and suicide. The therapeutic task is therefore to help the client examine the accuracy of a wholly negative conceptualization of the future. Clients may be operating on the assumption that 'Because now is really bad the future must be really bad'. One approach to this is to ask clients how they can be so absolutely sure the future will be a continuance of the present distress. If the pattern of the client's life has been of both 'good' and 'bad' times then it becomes easier to concede the possibility of some joy and move the client away from notions of self-harm.

Having the client elaborate the 'ups' and 'downs' of life can set the scene for a more accurate appraisal of the future. The client will probably still see the future as negative, and perhaps without hitherto important sources of satisfaction (a relationship, a promotion etc.), but not without at least the possibility of some redeeming features.

With a suicidal client it is useful to build bridges between sessions. This may be achieved in a number of ways, agreeing to put a key concern of the client's on the agenda for the next session; offering to find out about or contact someone about a major client concern between sessions.

Table 2 Thought Record

Example . . . .

Date	Situation	Feeling(s)	Automatic thought(s)	Realistic answer(s)	Outcome
	What were you doing or thinking about when you started to feel bad?	What symptom(s) did you notice (e.g. anger, apathy)? How bad did you feel? (On a scale from 0–100 with zero as 'terrible' and 100 as 'fine')	What was going through your mind immediately before you started to feel bad?	How can you answer the negative thoughts realistically and constructively? Is there anything you can do to test out the thoughts or handle the situation differently in future?	How do you feel now that you have tried to answer the thoughts? (On a scale from 0–100 with zero as 'terrible' and 100 as 'fine')
Sept. 27th	Finishing a meal with friends	Anger – 0	Friends' laughter sounded hollow – they are just being superficial. I can't stand people being superficial.	There's a time for being superficial. I am just labelling them as superficial people when all they are doing in fact is being superficial on this occasion. Who says I can't stand people being superficial? What dreadful consequences, if any, would happen.	Quite a lot better 75

88

THE LATER SESSIONS OF COGNITIVE THERAPY

The later sessions of cognitive therapy have more of a cognitive emphasis. The prime skill taught is that of detecting dysfunctional automatic thoughts and the generation of realistic answers to such thoughts. In teaching this skill use is made of a Dysfunctional Thought Record (Appendix E). An example of the use of the Thought Record is shown in Table 2.

Moving across the Record from left to right, the client is asked to consider the situation in which they felt upset, what the emotional response was, their automatic thoughts – what they were saying to themselves to account for their distress, or if not conscious that they were saying anything in particular – what it sounds 'as if' they were most probably saying to themselves to account for their distress. Next comes a column to indicate realistic answers and finally a column indicating outcome. Emotions are rated on the Record for their intensity, as are automatic thoughts and realistic answers for their believability. The Thought Record serves as a useful reminder to the therapist of the skill to be taught to the client. Initially the client is asked to attempt to complete the first four columns. It should be stressed that 'attempt' is the operative word, and that they may well have considerable difficulty identifying the automatic thoughts. Clients often complain that they just suddenly felt low for no accountable reason and cannot find the automatic thoughts. Because they cannot complete the fourth column they may not record the slip in mood at all. Occasions such as this are as important to attempt to record as those in which there is a 'tangible' source of distress. The therapist can explain that his/her role is to help the client discover the silent assumptions that surround upsetting situations. In instances where the client is unaware of the automatic thoughts in a given situation, the therapist can suggest a range of possibilities. The DAS completed by the client at the beginning of therapy can be a useful aid here for the generation of hypothesized automatic thoughts. The therapist should however resist forcing these hypotheses on the client. It is for the client to decide how well if at all the suggested automatic thoughts fit the situation.

Clients sometimes fail to record automatic thoughts because, when written down, the notions seem to them so patently odd that they fear other people, including the therapist, would think them 'stupid' for thinking such thoughts. Consequently clients should be advised not to disown their thoughts and that all dysfunctional automatic thoughts represent opportunities to think straighter and feel better in the future. It is not uncommon for a client's depression to lift after the first few sessions of cognitive therapy, largely as a consequence of becoming more active, and for the client then to express dissatisfaction with later sessions and with the Thought Records because 'they make me depressed'. This can happen because some of the more major items that were put on the agenda at the initial assessment become due for examination. For example P.O. presented a number of problems at initial assessment, including an inability to allow himself time to relax, and a marriage that lacked any personal intimacy. The first of these was relatively easily tackled at the start of therapy, by having P.O., a very methodical person, timetable in periods of relaxation, the way he did most other things in his life. However, in the later sessions when marriage difficulties were addressed, he became more depressed. He was found to be recalling that all previous personal and professional attempts to 'mend' the marriage had failed and begun to doubt the point in his recent activity given the state of his marriage. P.O. was encouraged to see 'non-improvement' in the marriage as a hypothesis and not a fact, and to consider that there are multiple sources of achievement and pleasure of which marriage is but one.

The non-completion of the Thought Records by a client should not be seen necessarily as a therapeutic failure. Some clients are unused to writing, and even after detailed explanation can find it difficult to separate situations, emotions, automatic thoughts, and realistic answers. Particular difficulty may attach to rating the degree of emotional belief. The author found that in a trial of cognitive therapy in Toxteth, Liverpool, only 50 per cent of clients completed four or more thought records. What is probably of key importance with regard to outcome is whether the client actively challenges the negative view of him/herself; this process begins in therapy and has to continue between sessions with or without the aid of Thought Records. Other main foci in cognitive therapy are the client's negative view of the world and of the future.

G.E. Murphy (1985) has helped conceptualize the way in which the cognitive therapist intervenes and what follows is an adaptation of his work. Any dysfunctional automatic thought of a client's may, in principle, be sent for analyses to any one of three columns/laboratories of Table 3. The procedures in each 'laboratory' differ somewhat, and the focal concerns of three are: 1) how realistic is the silent assumption? 2) by what authority is the silent assumption held? and 3) does the silent assumption help achieve a desired goal? The choice of starting point depends on the context of the client's distress. For example R.B. began the eighth session of CT in a very distraught state: 'I'm just useless. I'm O.K. until he comes home, if the kids are acting up he says it's my fault for not being a good mother, my own mother always said I was useless.' The silent assumption here was 'I am useless because my husband and mother say so'. The most obvious starting point is column 2, sub-test 2, which questions the 'expertness' of the authority figures. R.B. was asked whether her husband's constantly raised voice meant that everything he said was true. Then the credibility of her mother's view of her was questioned by remarking that it seemed strange that she had an identical view of R.B.'s only sister. The view of R.B.'s friends was that she was a good mother and this was then contrasted with the views of her mother and husband (column 1, sub-test 2). Gradually R.B. became less certain that she was 'useless'. Effective therapy involves judicious movement between and within the columns. The therapist then conceptually shifted to column 3 and asked whether believing she was 'useless' had interfered with her recently rekindled interest in crocheting. In spite of her distress, R.B. had in fact achieved her weekly target of crocheting. Accordingly the therapist shifted to column 1 and asked how valid it was now to believe she was useless when she had done more crocheting in the past week than in the past year. The emphasis throughout is on asking concrete rather than abstract or, worse still, rhetorical questions. A thorough analysis of an automatic thought will probably consist of a series of sub-tests in different laboratories rather than exhausting all the procedures of a particular laboratory. It is not likely that all 27 (3 × 3 × 3) possible combinations of sub-tests will need to be used to analyse a particular dysfunctional thought.

The case of M.G. further illustrates the use of Table 3. M.G. was very depressed. One of his main concerns was that he had been passed over for promotion. He had had an almost meteoric rise from the shop floor to senior management level. His energies for the previous ten years had been devoted almost entirely to the

Table 3 Questioning Dysfunctional Thoughts in Depression

	1	2	3
		columns/laboratory numbers	
Focal concerns	How realistic is the silent assumption?	By what authority is the silent assumption held?	Does the silent assumption help achieve a desired goal?
Sub-tests	1. is it valid? 2. is it consistent?	1. by a consensus? 2. by an expert view?	1. how close is the achievement of the goal? 2. is a change of means necessary to achieve the goal?
	3. is it useful?	3. by own view?	3. is another goal more appropriate?

next move up the promotion ladder. This had been something of a strain on his wife and children necessitating a number of house moves. Cognitive interventions with M.G. began in laboratory 3 with sub-test 1 in an attempt to clarify what M.G.'s goal was and then to gauge how close to it he was. It transpired that M.G. had no definite goal, but carried an assumption that he must always be upwardly mobile. The focus then shifted to analyses of the assumption 'that upward mobility and happiness were inextricably linked' i.e. to laboratory 1 sub-test 1. M.G. presented data indicating that over the past year or two his happiest times had in fact been outside work, for example playing five-a-side football. This helped call into question the equation between climbing up the company hierarchy and happiness. He concluded that his striving was largely a product of higher management's view that 'There was a pot of gold waiting, if you just put a little more into the job' and that this was not now his own view (a shift from column 2 sub-test 1 to column 2 sub-test 3). The upshot was that M.G. set a goal, of a balance of achievement and pleasure, both within work and outside. Work ceased to be 'the' place in which he 'had' to achieve, rather than one of a number of possible sources. Put simply he stopped putting all his eggs in one basket.

To help clients become aware of how they may be upsetting themselves, Burns (1980) gives them a list of the ten most common self-defeating thought patterns:

1. *All-or nothing thinking* You see everything in black and white like the student with Grade A's who gets one B and then thinks he is a total failure. It 'will set you up for discrediting yourself endlessly. Whatever you do will never measure up'.

2. *Over-generalization* You expect uniform bad luck because of one bad experience. 'A shy young man asked a girl for a date. When she declined, he said to himself, "I'm never going to get a date. I'll be lonely and miserable all my life".'

3. *Mental filter* You seize a negative fragment of a situation and dwell on it. It's like wearing a special lens that filters out everything positive. Burns writes, 'You soon conclude that everything is negative.'

4. *Automatic discounting* One instance of this is the way we often brush aside a compliment: 'He's just being nice'. That's a destructive distortion, Burns writes. Usually a depressive hypothesis is dominating your thinking, some version of 'I'm second rate'.

5. *Jumping to conclusions* Two examples are what Burns calls 'mind reading' and the 'fortune-teller error'. In the first, you assume that others look down on you without checking the validity of your assumption. In the second, you look into the future and see only disaster.

6. *Magnification and minimization* Burns calls this the 'binocular trick' because you are either blowing things up or shrinking them out of proportion. You look at your imperfections through binoculars and magnify them. But when you think about your strengths you look through the other end of the binoculars and shrink everything.

7. *Emotional reasoning* 'I feel guilty; therefore I must have done something bad' is a prime example. Your emotion seems to be evidence for the thought. It rarely occurs to a depressed person to challenge this pattern of distorted reasoning.

8. *Should statements* 'I should to this' or 'I must do that' are examples of the kind of thinking that makes you feel guilty rather than motivates you to do something.

9. *Labelling and mislabelling* If the shares you invested in go down, Burns warns you might think 'I'm a failure' instead of 'I made a mistake'. Such self-labelling is irrational. Your self cannot be equated with any one thing you do.

10. *Personalization* You think: 'Whatever happens, whatever

others do, it's my fault'. Says Burns: 'You suffer from a paralysing sense of bogus guilt'. What another person does is ultimately his or her responsibility – not yours.

This list can help make clients aware of the particular logical errors to which they are prone, thus providing a short-cut to their re-appraisal of a situation. For example R.C. had arranged to meet a friend for lunch, she was looking forward to seeing her as they hadn't met for some time, but she became depressed because she had to eat and this would destroy her diet. On her dysfunctional thought record she wrote 'Whoops, there I go again! *Mental filter*, why don't I think about the pleasant chat rather than the food? Anyway, it's not an *all or nothing* situation, dieting vs seeing my friend. I could always explain to her my problems or maybe a meal for a special occasion doesn't break dieting'.

As a final note, the author has found it quite useful to check by, say, the eighth session what progress has been made on the Dysfunctional Attitude Scale with regard to the items that were rated a 6 or 7. Such items may repay further special attention.

It seems likely that some dysfunctional attitudes are more central to the individual's depression than others. A client's view of themselves probably occupies a key position in this regard. Clarification of the self-evaluation criteria the client uses is often crucial. For example, K.M. concluded that she was worthless because her previous marriage had 'failed' and she was having difficulties in her current marriage. Therapeutic intervention in such instances can focus on the arbitrariness of the criteria. K.M. was asked whether she would consider her friend who was divorced as 'worthless' (applying sub-test 2 column 1), she replied instantly 'Oh no', and the therapeutic rejoinder was 'Does there have to be one law for you and another for other people?' As a result K.M.'s tendency to self-blame decreased markedly.

Probably most clients referred for depression have a mixed diagnosis, depression plus anxiety. Strategies for dealing with anxiety are described in the next chapter. However, about half of depressed women have serious marital problems. It is unclear whether depression causes the marital problems or whether marital problems cause the depression. Interestingly, Beach and O'Leary (1986) found that depressed women who received behavioural marital therapy fared better than depressed women who received cognitive behaviour therapy. Women in both treatments showed reductions in depression, but women who received behavioural marital therapy showed both reduction in depression and increases in marital satisfaction. As Beach and O'Leary stated

> Behavioural marital therapy may allow a clinician to cast a wider net than individual cognitive therapy when trying to treat a co-occurring marital discord and depression. Behavioural marital therapy may prove to help relieve depression while simultaneously providing an improved interpersonal climate which can facilitate personal growth and change. Conversely, cognitive therapy may have less effect on improving the interpersonal environment.

Behavioural marital therapy (BMT) is described in Part Three. Cognitive therapy does however have a wider applicability than BMT in that it does not require both parties to be willing to engage in therapy.

Cognitive therapy's ability to modify the client's psychological environment can be enhanced by emphasis on teaching problem-solving skills. In the latter stages of cognitive therapy clients should be encouraged to complete the proforma in Appendix F in which they focus on distasteful aspects of their environment. For example, W.H. was concerned about his finances. The first stage of the problem-solving process is to define specifically the problem to be tackled. This often means breaking down a major problem into a potentially more manageable unit. W.H. defined his problem as an inability to pay the landlord rent at the end of the month. The next stage is to generate as many possible alternative solutions as possible, putting down even those ideas that at first glance seem most impractical. The client is encouraged to ask others if they can come up with any other ideas. W.H. developed the following list:

1. Don't pay the landlord.
2. Take a part-time job as a barman.
3. Seek a reduction in rent because repairs hadn't been done.
4. Seek other accommodation.

The next stage is to weigh up the advantages and disadvantages of each option. W.H. dismissed the idea of not paying the landlord because of fears of eviction, but did acknowledge that this option would help him if the eviction process proved lengthy. Likewise, he thought it unlikely he could seek other privately rented accommodation because of the need for a down payment, however there was an outside chance of a flat with a housing association. He finally decided to ask in the pubs he frequented whether there was an evening or two's work a week. This would cut into his social life but he wouldn't be drinking, thereby saving and getting paid. He also decided to call at the local law centre to see if they would send a letter about rent reduction and repairs. W.H. gave himself a week to make these enquiries and planned to then review the situation. He quickly found work in a pub but the law centre were unhappy about his tying together a permanent reduction of rent and non-repair of the property. At this stage W.H. reconsidered option 1 and decided not to pay the landlord, but only until the repairs were done. The problem-solving procedure emphasizes chipping away at problems, and ensures the client is task-orientated rather than focusing on perceived inadequacies.

Treating clients in groups for depression has the obvious advantage of saving therapist time, but too little research on group cognitive therapy has been conducted to allow any definitive conclusion to be drawn as to its efficacy. Ross and Scott (1985) found it necessary to provide each group cognitive therapy client with a supplement of three individual sessions at the start of group therapy. Clients are generally more resistant to the notion of group cognitive therapy, although those that complete such a course tend to see it as having been an advantage over individual therapy. Typical advantages mentioned by group CT clients are: i) that they saw they were not unique in their thoughts and feelings, ii) seeing how others upset themselves enabled them to be more objective about their own upsets. The proportion of clients dropping out of treatment seems likely to be greater in group cognitive therapy. Partly this may arise because some clients simply do not fit in to a group either because of age, or intelligence, or because they particularly lack social skills. Though practically all depressed persons show deficit in the exhibition of social skills, in only a minority will the deficit of social skills have a primary importance in the development of the depression. In group cognitive therapy the pressures on the therapist to 'think on your feet' are considerable, and ease and familiarity with individual cognitive therapy is a recommended first stage before contemplating group work.

Chapter Seven

COGNITIVE THERAPY FOR ANXIETY AND AGORAPHOBIA

Anxiety is a part of everyday life. Not to have some anxiety when crossing a busy road, for example, is likely to prove, literally, fatal. Therapeutically, the task is to teach clients anxiety management skills, rather than how to eradicate anxiety. The therapeutic focus is on overcoming a debilitating sense of anxiety rather than anxiety *per se*. If anxiety itself is seen by clients as a danger, then the client becomes anxious about being anxious.

The initial diagnosis of the client's anxiety problem (see Chapter 5) should be followed by the presentation of a coherent rationale for the treatment programme. (The article, 'Coping with anxiety' in Beck *et al.* (1985) is an excellent guide to therapy for clients.) The rationale presented should indicate the 'normality' of anxiety and convey its essence – a 'catastrophic' misinterpretation of forthcoming events. The anxious client is hypervigilant with regard to the possibility of danger and sees perceived threats as beyond his resources. In generalized anxiety disorder (GAD), threat may be seen in a wide variety of situations, whereas in panic disorder the key misperception is usually of bodily sensations. In this chapter therapeutic strategies for GAD, panic disorder, and agoraphobia are presented in turn.

GENERALIZED ANXIETY DISORDER (GAD)

There are a wide range of anxiety management strategies pertinent to the treatment of GAD. Choice of strategies should flow from the particular way in which a client's difficulties are conceptualized. Butler (1987) has provided a useful framework within which the information from the client can be located. The factors which initiate anxiety are derived from two sources, perceived stress (e.g. a wife may be distressed over her husband's move onto shiftwork) and vulnerabilities (e.g. a life-long belief that everything must always run smoothly). It is useful to think of stress and vulnerability operating at Level 1 leading to anxiety at Level 2. There are four aspects or symptoms of anxiety: 1) physiological (e.g. tension pain), 2) behavioural (e.g. poor concentration, procrastination), 3) cognitive (e.g. 'Something dreadful is going to happen'), and 4) emotional (e.g. rushing about, inability to sit down). The anxiety symptoms at Level 2 lead to reactions at Level 3. There are four aspects of reactions: 1) avoidance (e.g. avoiding open conflict), 2) hypervigilance (e.g. noticing that a guest had little to say), 3) interpretation (e.g. assuming that because a guest had spoken little he or she must be dissatisfied), and 4) demoralization (e.g. 'I am pathetic to be like this'). There is a reciprocal interaction between Levels 2 and 3 to maintain the anxiety state. For example, G.S. was fearful about a forthcoming meal to which she had invited people (a Level 2 general fear). At the meal she became very anxious that one of her guests hadn't spoken much and she concluded that he must be dissatisfied (a result of hypervigilance and interpretation at Level 3). This led her to be even more fearful about inviting people to her home (a Level 2 cognition). Not surprisingly she stopped inviting people (a Level 3 avoidance reaction). A vicious circle is created at Levels 2 and 3.

Figure 1 Model of Generalized Anxiety

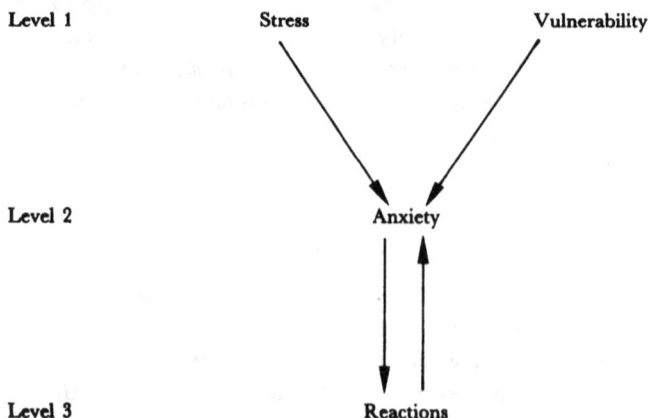

Level 1   Stress   Vulnerability

Level 2   Anxiety

Level 3   Reactions

Butler's framework helps locate targets for intervention, and obviously the targets will vary from client to client. For example, not all clients will be demoralized nor will they necessarily show avoidance reactions. The framework helps ensure that the therapist will range over those strategies pertinent to the targeted difficulties of the client. Strategies relevant to the different aspects of the framework are now described, beginning at Level 3.

1. *Demoralization*

Clients who are both anxious and demoralized present a strong therapeutic challenge and are probably those least likely to do well in therapy. (Though this framework, and these impressions, do require empirical verification.) The client may be so preoccupied with blaming him/herself for the condition that little thought goes into what to do about it. At initial assessment L.C. expressed her self-blame: 'I am a waste of space, I shouldn't be like this. I have just got to pull myself together. I am just wasting your time, you must have much more needy people to see than me'. Unless the issue of demoralization is tackled in the early sessions of therapy the client will be likely to default. The demoralized client typically sees the anxiety problem as a manifestation of a deficit in willpower. The therapeutic task is to portray anxiety largely as a product of missed opportunities and to learn anxiety management strategies. L.C.'s self-blame was tackled by asking her whether, if she went to an ice skating rink and kept slipping over, she would blame herself. L.C. thought she would not 'because everybody takes time to learn things'. It was agreed that with the help of a suitable instructor the learning time could be much shortened. The therapist then asked if she should blame herself if no instructor was available and it was taking a long time to learn. L.C. agreed that such blame would be inappropriate. Finally it was suggested that maybe L.C.'s problems were largely attributable to the absence of a suitable instructor and instruction course. L.C. conceded that her father had been a shy, withdrawn man and 'no help at all'. In this way the client can be moved away from Task Interfering Cognition (TIC) to do with self-blame to Task Oriented Cognitions (TOC) e.g. 'I'll make a start on the meal, by first getting together all the ingredients'. Clients can remind themselves of the mnemonic TIC/TOC when catching themselves engaged in self-evaluation or self-blame.

2. *Hypervigilance and interpretation*

Three basic questions can be used by the therapist to restructure a client's thinking at Levels 2 and 3. According to Beck *et al.* (1985) these are: 1) 'What's the evidence?' 2) 'What's another way of looking at the situation?' and 3) 'So what if it happens?'

1) What's the evidence? L.C. felt that in work most people looked down on her and so she felt she had to perform exceptionally well. When pressed for the evidence on which this assumption was based she said that she had only one or two close friends in the office. The therapist then asked 'What does it mean to you if you only have one or two close friends?' and she answered that 'The others must dislike me'. At this juncture the therapist could have lectured the client on the absurdity of such black-and-white dichotomous thinking, but it is an important feature of cognitive therapy that clients are led to analyse their own interpretations of reality. Accordingly the therapist asked L.C. to list eight people she knew, then to indicate those she was really close to, those she was enemies with and those she could take or leave. It emerged that L.C. was very close to two people, at odds with two others and neutral about the remaining four. The therapist then asked what the evidence was that most people in her office were not neutral about her. She then began to entertain the possibility that others could be neutral about her. A few sessions later L.C. volunteered that she had never actually been admonished in work but this was 'only because I have my standards and work really hard'. Her prediction was of catastrophe if she didn't keep to such high standards, yet when she left work of an evening she was totally drained. Instead of rushing to process as many invoices as possible in her working day, L.C. was set the homework task of pacing herself to just meet her daily quota and to thereby test out her prediction that slave-driving herself was the only solution permitted by her bosses. At the next session she reported that there had been no criticism of her. This case illustrates the importance of tackling problems from both a cognitive and a behavioural perspective.

2) What's another way of looking at it? Most anxious clients have difficulty in creating alternative non-threatening interpretations of situations. Initially the therapist may have to prime the

pump for alternative interpretations. S.C. was a temporary worker in an office and felt sure her boss was soon going to dispense with her services because he had been bad-tempered and irritable when he arrived at work each morning. The therapist suggested that perhaps her boss was no longer guaranteed a lift to work and was having to make do with the vicissitudes of public transport. This was dismissed by S.C. on the grounds that it was more likely he was having trouble with his wife again.

3) So what if it happens? The specifics of a client's imagined catastrophes are rarely spelt out. In order to relieve their distress clients typically prematurely terminate a detailed examination of their worst fears coming true. Clients should be encouraged to stay with their fear rather than brush it aside. Staying with the fear offers the opportunities to discover rescue factors, those aspects of the situation which may make it less than absolutely awful. For example B.S. was afraid that his new landlord might want to renovate the block of flats in which he lived. This would necessitate his temporary rehousing. To B.S. this meant 'once again life is pushing me from pillar to post, you can be sure when life is running smoothly it is actually about to fall apart'. He had failed to notice that temporary rehousing could be at his recently divorced son's, allowing him the choice of a much-wanted renewed acquaintanceship. B.S. had also failed to distinguish between what is possible and what is probable. The therapist explained that 'We sit together in the therapy room because we consider the odds on the ceiling falling in are remote, at most a possibility, if we thought it was a probability we would rush out of the room. Whether you label something a possibility or a probability makes a big difference to what you do and feel'. B.S. agreed that it was possible rather than probable that the landlord would want to renovate the property.

Between sessions clients are encouraged to complete the Daily Record of Dysfunctional Thoughts described in the previous chapter. Material from the Thought Record becomes the subject for in-session discussion between therapist and client. After successive completion of the Records various themes can usually be detected. Beck (1985) has identified three main themes to do with (a) acceptance, (b) competence, and (c) control. The themes

101

may relate to the fundamental dysfunctional schema. Each of these themes is examined in turn.

(a) Acceptance

Clients for whom acceptance is an over-riding concern are excessively dependent on others for a sense of self worth. The prospect of incurring the disapproval of others may fill the client with terror. Consequently the client may go to extraordinary lengths to win approval. S.A., for example, continued to put up with her husband's public derision of her because 'If I just try harder he will love me'. Her core belief was 'I am nobody if the person I love doesn't love me'. This epitomizes the precedence the socially anxious person gives other approval over self approval. It is as if such clients are pursuing a goal of getting everyone's approval. The therapeutic task is to make this explicit to the client and encourage an examination of the appropriateness of the goal. The fundamental logical error is to see other people as a homogenous mass with very tightly defined expectations. M.J.'s Thought Record showed that she was very upset following a blazing row with her boyfriend. She had met him an hour late to go to a party and he was annoyed he had had to wait so long. But she protested that she had only been trying to look her best. In fact she was late because she had been through four different sets of clothes before returning to and settling on the first set. As a homework assignment M.J. was asked to initiate a discussion with her boyfriend of whether he actually had any strong preferences in the four sets of clothing and whether it would particularly bother him if she wore a non-favourite set. To her surprise it transpired that her boyfriend was largely indifferent to what she wore. Her mother however had a considerable aversion to the punk-style clothes. This was used to illustrate to the client the impossibility of pleasing everyone and it was suggested that primarily she should please herself.

Often the source of the client's low self-evaluation has its origins in childhood experiences. R.G. had great difficulty communicating with his bosses and had become distraught about discussing with them a much-needed matter. On the surface this was difficult to understand as R.G. was very able and articulate. The therapist asked R.G. to try and remember the earliest time in his life that he had experienced feelings such as these. Eventually R.G. said that it was when he was about seven or eight and had gone to ask his father for help over his homework. His father became very angry and said not to bother him and he ran away crying to his room. The therapist had the client visualize the scene in detail for some minutes. Then R.G. was asked to look at the situation again as an adult and to try and explain what was happening. R.G. guessed that his father was probably uptight after one of his many rows with his mother and that the incident had little to do with him. In fact some time after that incident his parents separated for about five years. For homework he was asked to practise visualizing himself interacting with his bosses with his new-found understanding. By the next session he was comfortable with the imagery and role played with the therapist a likely interaction. Therapist and client swapped roles in the session until R.G. became comfortable about approaching his bosses and appreciated that there was little evidence they would regard him as 'just a nuisance'. For homework he was to approach his bosses over some minor matters. This went quite satisfactorily and he was encouraged by the experience to raise more serious matters. The essence of the strategy was to help R.G. attend to the data of his experience rather than respond to a childhood belief which was no longer tenable.

(b) Competence

Clients may routinely evaluate their competence across a wide range of social situations where competence as such is not an issue. The client who, at a social gathering, spends so much time wondering precisely what to say that he misses the cues in a conversation, or makes a remark at a tangent to the general flow. Or a lover who is so concerned about a competent performance that he or she completely freezes. In both instances the initial anxieties are compounded by failure experiences. The client's self-efficacy is reduced and a vicious circle begins.

A useful therapeutic strategy is to encourage the client to adopt a coping goal rather than a competent or masterful goal. N.S. was anxious about going on the works Christmas Night Out. He was asked to pick out those in his group that he thought were masterful in such a situation, then those who coped and finally those who seemed decidedly uncomfortable. N.S. acknowledged that he felt most at ease with the 'copers' and agreed that perhaps most people actually did. This helped him relinquish his competence goal and gave him permission to be stuck for conversation, to relish forgetting the end of a joke etc.

The client's excessive emphasis on competence may be focused on one specific area such as work, and this may lead to workaholism. The fundamental dysfunctional assumption here is 'I am what I achieve'. One possible strategy is for the therapist to support the workaholic's goal of being more productive in work, but to question whether ceaseless activity and long hours were the same. With H.H., a departmental head teacher, the therapist began by asking him why he made himself available to colleagues at lunch time and he replied that his department would fall apart if he didn't. In the subsequent week H.H. tested out his prediction and reported that making himself unavailable had only caused minor hassles. H.H. clearly received a great sense of achievement and pleasure from his work but the therapist questioned whether it could be the only source. He decided to take up jogging as a step to a more balanced lifestyle and the effects of believing 'I am what I achieve' on his interpersonal relationships were put on a session agenda. At work, relationships with some colleagues were fraught because they 'wouldn't put themselves out'. He decided that this was in fact a half-truth, and he was angry that 'they wouldn't slave-drive themselves' like him. At home he disparaged his less-educated wife's views and lack of ambition, and this was causing major conflicts. For homework H.H. was asked to construct a pie-chart of the determinants of his 'success'. To his surprise the lion's share of the chart was taken up by factors over which he had no control or responsibility, namely genetics, upbringing, and luck. Subsequently his relationships all around improved.

(c) Control

The fears of clients concerned with control centre on the possibility of being dominated by others or by events outside their control. J.D. always double-checked the work of a subordinate, even though the latter was very competent and no major mistakes had ever been found. To his wife's considerable annoyance, on arrival home from work he would check his financial position rather than play with their young baby. J.D. planned everything meticulously, and long lists of household tasks were written down in advance.

If, for example, something happened that was unforeseen such as a telephone call, this would make him highly anxious. Contingencies simply were not allowed for. It was almost as if he were saying to himself 'I can't cope with the unexpected, I'll protect myself from it by planning for every eventuality'. Not surprisingly he became totally exhausted. The therapeutic strategy is to teach clients to ride with contingencies rather than fight them. The paradox is that clients gain more control over life by settling for less than total control.

3. *Avoidance*

Clients may seek to reduce their anxiety by avoidance reactions, perhaps fleeing from a crowded shop, or refusing to eat in public places. Such reactions do, in the short term at least, reduce anxiety and thereby negatively reinforce and maintain the avoidance behaviour. In the long term however the client leads an increasingly constricted life. Graded exposure to the feared situations constitutes the major behavioural treatment approach and may be complemented by appropriate client self-talk.

The treatment approach outlined later for the agoraphobic sufferer parallels that used for treating social anxieties. To take the example of the client highly anxious about eating in public. First of all the client's goal is identified; this may be, say, having a meal in a restaurant with his wife. Then the present level of client functioning is assessed, perhaps having a coffee with friends at work. A series of intermediate steps is then marked out with the help of the client. The therapeutic task is to climb the hierarchy of items generated. The size of steps in the hierarchy may be too large, too small, or just right. It should be explained to clients that the size of steps is necessarily provisional and will probably need to be adjusted in the light of practice. Clients are placed in a 'no lose' position. If they successfully manage a step they are praised and encouraged to praise themselves, and if the step proves too difficult the therapist assumes prime responsibility for not gauging accurately the size of step that would be manageable. Progression is made up the hierarchy only when previous stages have been successfully accomplished.

4. *Physiological*

Tension and aching joints are common accompaniments of

anxiety, and relaxation exercises can help relieve the tension. Essentially they involve the systematic tensing and relaxing of each muscle group in turn. A script for recording a relaxation tape is provided in Appendix G. Few clients are inclined to record this exercise themselves and most request a therapist's recording. Clients have used the recording in various ways, some to help them get off to sleep, others to clear their mind when they are getting tense and wound up, thus enabling them to think straight. Used early in therapy it provides a simple way of the client getting a 'success' experience and ensuring adequate engagement of the client. A minority of clients have a fear of loss of control, in which case the tape is contra-indicated. Some clients find a favourite piece of music an adequate substitute for the tape.

5. *Behavioural and emotional*

The behavioural and emotional aspects of anxiety may range from extreme procrastination to attempting too many tasks simultaneously. Procrastination may be treated behaviourally by having the client break down the chosen task into small elements and ticking off each step as it is accomplished. In this way the noting of accomplishments serves as a springboard to tackle the next element. D.C. was a student and had great difficulty getting his essays in on time. He would read extensively about the set topic for an essay but had great difficulty putting pen to paper. D.C. decided to break the task down, starting with the assembly of the written materials and paper the evening before he was to begin writing, so that when he came to start writing there was already a tick on his sheet. The next tick was gained simply by writing the essay title, the step after by writing an essay plan which was itself to be rewarded with a cup of coffee. D.C. found that once he had accomplished his plan he had gathered sufficient momentum to complete the essay writing. Cognitively, it seemed that D.C. was reading far more widely than most students because he 'mustn't leave anything out'. When the therapist asked what it would mean to him to have missed out a point in his essay he replied that his teachers would think less of him. For homework D.C. was asked to examine the notion that he needed his teachers' approval all the time. By the next session D.C. had reframed his belief to 'I would like my teachers' approval most of the time but I can get by without it'. His core concern had been that without their approval he counted for little, and he procrastinated to avoid the possibility of a negative evaluation. The paradox was that the procrastination was a greater guarantee of incurring his teachers' wrath than a less than perfect essay.

Anxiety may be accompanied by feverish activity. Clients may begin on one task, in mid-stream they think of another task that needs tackling and move to that, only to leave that typically incomplete when they are distracted by the 'need' to perform yet another task. In this way clients may set themselves up for endless frustration. A useful strategy is to have a client say 'wasp' when he or she catches him/herself 'buzzing' in this way. The letters of the word WASP stand for W-Wait, A-Absorb, and SP-Slowly Proceed. 'Wait' refers to the act of pulling a psychological brake which the client can visualize when saying 'wasp'. The next step is for the client to absorb what he or she is actually doing. This may involve self-talk of the form 'Who says all this has to be done today? Is it the end of the world if it is not finished today? I will just do what I can of this task before going on to another. Moving on today to another task is a bonus, not essential'. Then for a few minutes the client slowly proceeds to make the point that tasks rarely have the urgency with which he or she imbues them. An alternative imagery is for a client to visualize a set of traffic lights when they feel themselves going too fast. At the sight of the red light the client screams 'stop' to him/herself. When the lights change to amber they reconsider the urgency of the tasks at hand and prioritize them. Finally when the lights change to green the client moves off to tackle the priority task in a realistic time interval.

PANIC DISORDER

Panic disorders may be seen within a cognitive-behavioural perspective as having their origin in a catastrophic misinterpretation of bodily sensation. A client may notice say, a missed heartbeat and interpret it as a sign of an impending heart attack, which in turn fuels further panic. This theory may account for panics which arise after an event, such as an argument with a spouse, and those which arise seemingly out of the blue, such as at a particular point in the menstrual cycle. Hyperventilation (breathing quickly and deeply) can produce similar symptoms to panic attacks, light-headedness, dizziness, palpitations, etc., and may often play a role in panic disorder. Having such a client hyperventilate to induce panic feelings in the session is a useful first step in helping them to reconceptualize the panics as being controllable. Increasing a client's understanding of the aetiology of the panic serves as a precursor for teaching slow breathing. Clark, Salkovskis, and Chalkley (1985) have reported that, in their study of panic patients, this method substantially reduced the frequency of panic attacks within two weeks.

Where hyperventilation seems not to play a key role in the development of panic a self-instruction/distraction routine can be employed. First, the client is asked to notice the first symptoms of panic, perhaps a tightening of the stomach, and instead of this acting as a stimulus for further panic it is relabelled as a cue to go through a set routine. The first step in the routine is to focus on an object or image and describe it in detail using all the senses. A client may choose to focus on say a favourite rose, recalling its fragrance and texture, and watching it blowing gently back and forth in the breeze – the more vivid the imagery the better. At the end of approximately two minutes description the clients goes on to tell him or herself that 'I am a little less wound up than I was at the beginning, I am gaining control, I am heading in the right direction'. It is important that clients appreciate that they are not aiming to totally eradicate their panic but simply trying to take the edge off it. At the end of the routine clients congratulate themselves, and if possible give themselves a tangible reward. Clients vary considerably in their use of imagery and some find it easier to focus on an object they can actually see and describe it in detail.

Panic attacks may occur by themselves, or in conjunction with agoraphobia, or generalized anxiety disorder. The self-instruction/distraction strategy is useful when panic attacks constitute the single disorder or figure in the other two anxiety disorders.

AGORAPHOBIA

The most widely used treatment for agoraphobia is graded exposure. This has proved just as effective treating clients in groups as individually. Typically clients are seen initially for an individual assessment. It is important to check that the client is afraid of going out alone and not simply too fed up or depressed to go out. End of programme goals are identified for each area of difficulty, for example the ultimate goal with regard to transport might be 'travelling to town by bus unaccompanied', whilst the goal for shopping might be 'to spend an hour at peak shopping time in a local shopping complex'. A hierarchy of steps is created with respect to each goal. Movement up the steps is planned and practised first within the therapy session.

The usual format for a group session, involving 4–6 clients, is to first review between session practice then to identify with each group member what the next step up their hierarchy would be. This is then followed by in-session practice of the next step. Group members require assistance from therapy staff to complete the in-session work. For example, a member of the therapy staff may have to travel downstairs on a bus whilst the client travels upstairs, or perhaps a client will need to be met after having crossed a busy junction. It is crucial that between sessions clients do not attempt more than they had practised in a session. The homework assignments have to be clearly specified in the light of the in-session practice. Usually clients are asked to practise on two or three occasions in the following week what they had practised in the session. It is important to discuss with the client whether a friend or family member could aid the client between sessions in the way the therapy staff helped with within-session practice.

The quasi-therapist in the community is a vital link in aiding generalization. On what they feel is a good day clients are tempted to try more than specified, this can result in feelings of being back at square one if they fail and a consequent lessening of motivation. Clients may be insulated from the worst effects of failure experiences by the therapist making it clear that the size of the steps in the hierarchy are something of a guess, and if they experience failure at any point it is probably because the therapist has miscalculated the size of the next step. In addition clients are told that, rather like driving lessons, progress is typically two steps forward and one backward.

Thus although graded exposure is obviously a behavioural technique in its application, it involves the integration of elements akin to the cognitive-behavioural strategies used in relapse prevention training with addictions (Marlatt and Gordon 1985). Effective group treatment of agoraphobia requires the same groupwork skills as detailed earlier in Chapter 3. It seems unlikely then that simple graded exposure to feared situations would be efficacious. The scene is set for the integration of a more explicit cognitive component to perhaps enhance treatment effectiveness. Friedberg (1985) has proposed a Cognitive Reaction Inventory which assesses the frequency with which the agoraphobic experiences eight types of thoughts: 1) angry thoughts (e.g. 'I should be able to control these feelings'), 2) anxious thoughts (e.g. 'What if I faint/lose control?'), 3) coping thoughts (e.g. 'These feelings will pass'), 4) depressing thoughts (e.g. 'I'll never get over this problem'), 5) distracting thoughts (e.g. 'I'll think about something else'), 6) escape thoughts (e.g. 'I have to get away'), 7) frustration thoughts (e.g. 'I can't stand these feelings'), 8) relaxation thoughts (e.g. 'I'll just let go of my tension, breathe easily'). The inventory is designed to reveal self-defeating thought patterns that may then become the focus of cognitive change interventions.

Part 3

A COGNITIVE-BEHAVIOURAL APPROACH TO INTERPERSONAL PROBLEMS

Chapter Eight

INTERPERSONAL PROBLEMS: THEORY AND ASSESSMENT

The approach taken to emotional disorders in Part Two of this volume has been to concentrate on intrapsychic processes, specifically dysfunctional automatic thoughts. It is noteworthy, however, that in Beck's most recent (1987) description of the development and maintenance of depression, the role of interpersonal factors is acknowledged. Coyne (1985) has noted that when confronted with a depressed individual people tend to be initially comforting and reassuring, subsequently however they tend to avoid the depressed person. This serves to reinforce the depressed client's view of his or her worthlessness or unlovability and of the hostility of the world. A therapeutic response is to help clients redefine the situation in terms of 'others' feeling frustrated that they lack the skills to 'cheer up' the client and in desperation resorting to avoidance. Depressed clients have also been found to exhibit interpersonal skill deficits; specifically they prematurely disclose negative information about themselves. Accordingly the therapist may need to underline for the client the necessity of a positive and mutually rewarding relationship as the context for disclosure of negative aspects. Kubler and Stotland (1964: 260) have argued,

> emotional disturbance, even the most severe, cannot be understood unless the field in which it develops and exists is examined. The manifestations of the difficulty in the disturbed individual have meaning depending on aspects of the field. The significant aspects of the field are usually interpersonal.

The appropriateness of a cognitive-behavioural interpersonal framework to the treatment of marital discord may be readily appreciated, but it may be much less obvious that a similar framework can underpine social skills training, and have relevance to client groups as diverse as the schizophrenic sufferer and his family, and the shy or lonely individual. This chapter first elaborates the theoretical base of, and assessment procedures for, cognitive-behavioural marital therapy, and presents a conceptualization of social skills training.

A COGNITIVE-BEHAVIOURAL MODEL OF MARITAL DISCORD

A comprehensive cognitive-behavioural description of marital distress encompasses five somewhat overlapping models: social exchange theory, the principle of reciprocity, communication deficits, problem-solving deficits, cognitive deficits. Each of the models are now described:

Social exchange theory

Social exchange theory suggests that the partners in a dyad each seek to maximize their satisfaction and minimize their dissatisfactions. Difficulties arise when one partner's satisfactions can only be bought by greatly increasing the dissatisfactions of the other partner – the latter may see the transaction as too costly. This model of marital interaction assumes that individuals enter and stay in intimate relationships only so long as that relationship is adequately satisfying with respect to both rewards and costs (Thibaut and Kelly 1959). The maintenance of a relationship may depend on partner-given satisfactions that incur little cost and are greatly appreciated by the receiver. Thus partners with similar interests may well find the maintenance of a relationship easier because they each get something out of the giving. The maintenance of a relationship will also depend on the range of alternatives available. The cost/benefit ratio of the present relationship is contrasted with the cost/benefit ratio of other possible relationships and with the ratio for being alone. The positive and negative aspects of a relationship are independent. Partners each have a list of what pleases and what displeases them in the relationship. Action by one partner to eradicate a 'displease' (e.g. by coming straight home from work and not going to the pub first) will simply reduce dissatisfaction and will not of itself increase satisfaction.

Satisfaction for one partner may be dependent on 'pleases' such as a cuddle when the spouse comes home from work.

The principle of reciprocity

The principle of reciprocity assumes that, over a long period of time, members of a dyad reward and punish each other at equal rates. Typically partners presenting for marital therapy each see themselves as the passive recipient of the other's misdeeds. This principle challenges that view, underlining the interactive nature of the difficulties. Put simply coercive responses beget coercive responses and rewarding behaviour begets rewarding behaviour. Acceptance of the principle by clients removes a roadblock to the initiation of rewarding behaviour because such actions will bring their own reward. The principle can be used to capitalize on the self-interest of the client.

The response of distressed couples to negative interaction is more immediate than that of non-distressed couples. It is as if the latter have built up good faith deposits which act as a brake on an immediate and negative response.

Communication deficits

Studies of marital communication have provided consistent evidence of a link between problems in communication and marital distress (e.g. Weiss 1978). Weiss found that the negative interactions of distressed couples were specific to that relationship and different to the communication pattern with other people. Typically, these studies have involved self-report measures of marital communication and global measures of marital satisfaction. For example, Jacobson *et al.* (1980) asked distressed and non-distressed couples to complete a behavioural checklist and global marital satisfaction ratings on a daily basis. His results indicated that daily satisfaction ratings for distressed couples were best predicted by the general category 'negative communication and interaction'. Whilst for non-distressed couples daily satisfaction was best predicted by 'positive communication and interaction'.

More specifically, Gottman (1979) found that non-distressed couples pause to acknowledge that they have understood their partner's difficulties whereas distressed couples enter immediately into repetitive cross-complaining loops. The distressed dyad enters into two monologues; in contrast the non-distressed couple engage in a dialogue. However in terms of their reported message intent, distressed and non-distressed couples were found not to differ but the two groups had very different perceptions of their partner's intent. For the distressed group there is a greater mismatch between messages intended for transmission and the reception of those messages than for the non-distressed group.

Problem-solving deficits

Communication deficits are most manifest when there is a conflict of interests between partners. Such deficits inhibit effective problem solving. Specifically, partners fail to indicate the behaviour of concern in a concrete way, do not generate and evaluate a wide range of possible solutions, and finally fail to experiment with a provisional solution.

Cognitive deficits

It was noted earlier that the research on communication deficits and marital distress has relied heavily on self-report measures of communication. Although scores on various communication questionnaires discriminate effectively between distressed and non-distressed couples, there have been low correlations between reports of communication obtained separately from husband and wife, and low correlations between spouse reports and observer ratings (Epstein *et al.* 1987). This suggests that these instruments have, at least in part, assessed perception of marital communication rather than 'actual' communication behaviour. To borrow Beck's metaphor, a spouse's view of the marriage and the communication process will also depend on the particular camera, filters, lenses, and settings used to focus on it. The main thrust of much behavioural marital therapy to date has been to emphasize the prime importance of communication training but, as Epstein *et al.* have commented (1987), 'to the extent that spouses' self-reports of communication problems reflect cognitive biases rather than accurate perceptions of communication skills deficits, it would be important to consider cognitive interventions as well as communication training.'

Chapter 6 of this volume elaborated upon the distortions in information processing that may lead to emotional disorders. The same logical errors can lead to marital distress. For example, the thought 'He always interrupts me' is likely to be an instance of 'overgeneralization' rather than an accurate description of a spouse's invariant behaviour. In the absence of concrete evidence, the thought 'He thinks I have nothing worthwhile to say' is an 'arbitrary inference' (i.e. jumping to conclusions) and 'I either satisfy my partner or I don't' is likely to be an example of 'dichotomous reasoning' (i.e. all-or-nothing thinking). Spouses' automatic thoughts about their interactions with their partners often include inferences about the possible causes of pleasant and unpleasant events that occur between them. Distressed spouses are more likely to attribute their partners' unpleasant behaviours to negative intent and global, stable traits (e.g. 'He criticized me in front of the children because he is a nasty person and wanted to embarrass me'). On the other hand a distressed spouse will tend to interpret a partner's positive behaviour as attributable to specific, unstable, unintentional causes (e.g. 'She was nice to me only because she had a good day at work today'). The global, stable causal attributions implicated in marital distress are quite similar to those associated with depression and Epstein (1985) has suggested that this may account for the demonstrated link between these two problems.

ASSESSMENT OF MARITAL DISCORD

An assessment of the degree and nature of marital discord is a necessary prelude to treatment intervention. Without some base-line measure of marital satisfaction it is impossible to gauge the efficacy of interventions. The assessment should not however be a once and for all event but an ongoing aspect of treatment, thereby leading to a tailoring of the treatment modality to the particular needs of the couple. Self-report measures of marital satisfaction are the most commonly used assessment devices though they may be complemented by the more time-consuming observational coding systems. Samples of these instruments are described below and the first three of them, the Dyadic Adjustment Scale, the Relationships Belief Inventory (RBI), and the Areas of Change Questionnaire, are reproduced respectively in Appendices H, J, and I.

A behavioural interview can be used to supplement data gathered from the inventories.

1. *Dyadic Adjustment Scale* This provides a global measure of marital distress. It contains thirty-two items which can be grouped into four aspects of adjustment – dyadic satisfaction, dyadic cohesion, dyadic consensus, and affectional expression. Each item of this scale has been found to discriminate between happily married and divorced samples (see Appendix H).

2. *Relationship Belief Inventory (RBI)* This is a forty-item self-report inventory which focuses on extreme expectations that an individual might hold about marital relationships. The scale covers six areas: a) disagreement is destructive, b) mind reading is expected, c) partners cannot change, d) sexual perfectionism, e) sex role rigidity, f) a partner is essential. The instrument can serve to identify cognitive blocks to communication and the performance of new behaviours. It should be noted however that the RBI was not intended to provide an exhaustive assessment of all important dysfunctional relationship beliefs (see Appendix J).

3. *Areas of Change Questionnaire (A–C)* This asks how much change the respondent would like of his or her spouse in thirty-four specific areas of marital behaviour. The spouse is also asked separately whether an increase, decrease, or no change in the areas would be pleasing to their partner. In this way gaps between what one partner wants and what the other partner 'thinks' they want can be explored. In addition spouses indicate those items that are of major importance to them. This instrument readily highlights those behaviours that might form part of a behaviour exchange contract. The A–C has discriminated between distressed and non-distressed couples and is responsive to changes occurring as a result of behavioural marital therapy (see Appendix I).

4. *Marital Interaction Coding System (MICS)* This has been applied primarily to ten-minute video-taped samples of spouses striving to come to a resolution of their difficulties on each of two predetermined problem areas. Topics for these discussions are chosen (often with the help of the therapist) so that both a major and minor conflict area are represented. The therapist leaves the room

to simulate a more natural setting whilst the problem-solving is under way. The MICS can be used to score audio tapes as well.

5. *The assessment interview* The couple's presence in therapy provides the therapist with a ready-made laboratory in which to view their interactions. It also provides the opportunity to obtain further clarification of major problems indicated on the self-report measures. Clearly assessment is not confined simply to intake interviews but is an integral part of each session. The data provided by having spouses 'under the therapist's microscope' has a direct bearing on treatment strategies adopted and perhaps also on the efficacy of previous treatment recommendations.

COGNITIVE APPROACH TO SOCIAL SKILLS TRAINING

Traditional social skills training has encompassed a combination of instruction, feedback, modelling, behaviour rehearsal, and reinforcement. Each of these components is examined in turn.

1. *Instruction* Instructions involve telling the client what to do, how to do it, and when to do it. For example, a client might be instructed to make eye contact with colleagues on arrival at work and say 'Hi'.

2. *Feedback* The function of feedback is to provide the client with a measure of how well they performed and very specifically how improvement might be made. Feedback has to be positive, thereby encouraging further practice, as well as corrective. For example, in a simulated role play of the client's arrival at work, the therapist might comment 'It was great that you made the eye contact and said "Hi" to colleagues but maybe this time make sure you bring in a smile at the same time'.

3. *Modelling* Simple instruction and feedback is usually insufficient to teach a new skill and the therapist may need to model the new skill. This is particularly the case when a combination of skills is taught. For example, maintaining eye contact, greeting colleagues in an audible tone, and smiling.

4. *Behaviour rehearsal* Therapist modelling of a new behaviour is

followed by a client's rehearsal of the behaviour. This in turn leads to feedback and a subsequent behaviour rehearsal. If the client's performance is still deficient the therapist may have to model the behaviour again.

5. *Reinforcement* The final component of social skills training is reinforcement in the form of social praise or tangible reinforcers. Reinforcement is in practice an integral part of providing feedback, each successive approximation to the targeted response is praised, i.e. the client's behaviour is shaped. Often the slightest movement towards the new behaviour has to be reinforced.

Consideration of the components of social skill training in this sequential manner should not be taken as implying that they are so ordered in practice, rather they are intertwined. The premise on which such training is based is that the client's anxiety in social situations is a product of a deficit in the repertoire of social skills. Such deficits give rise to negative social consequences which in turn lead to anticipatory anxiety. However, it should be noted that the original Argyle and Kendon (1967) social skill model was a process, not a component model. It involved the constant monitoring of performance and making decisions about appropriate response in the light of this feedback.

Interest in cognitive factors in social skills training has increased as the limitations of the traditional model described above have become evident. Stravynski and Shahar (1983) have reviewed outcome studies of social skills training, including only those that met minimal methodological requirements, and concluded it is superior to no-treatment, group discussion, short-term psychotherapy, or the provision of written materials. However these studies provided scant evidence of a transfer of learning to real-life situations, leading Trower *et al.* (1982) to comment that the failure to generalize may be a product of inattention to cognitive aspects. The concentration on observable motor behaviours in traditional social skills training (e.g. eye contact) may represent a circumscribed view of social interaction difficulties. A study by Newton *et al.* (1983) suggests that social performance, social anxiety, and self-esteem are all important and potentially independent dimensions in social interaction difficulties.

The self-presentation approach to social interaction difficulties goes beyond the above behavioural dimensions. Schlenker and Leary (1982) focus on the gap between the perceived need to impress an audience and an expectation of a performance that will fail to impress as resulting in social anxiety. It is as if the individual is striving to 'match to a standard'. From the point of view of this model, skill programmes based on the behavioural model would be likely to have a therapeutic impact by improving the expectation of a better performance and so closing the gap. Clearly however, in addition the self-presentation model has distinct cognitive aspects. Specifically, there are expectations about the 'norms' surrounding a situation and beliefs involved about a capacity to perform; these cognitions may be to a greater or lesser extent based in reality. Accordingly the more recent social skills training has often contained strong cognitive dimensions. For example, van Dam-Baggen and Kraaimaat (1986) have developed a three-part programme involving 1) training in basic social skills, both verbal and non-verbal, 2) training in specific social responses such as making and refusing requests, and 3) training in self-management skills – setting realistic standards, setting concrete and realistic goals and sub-goals.

ASSESSMENT OF SOCIAL SKILLS DEFICITS

Social skills deficits according to Trower *et al.* (1978) may be usefully assessed by examining the clients' functioning in the following three main areas:

1. *Past and current relationships* It is important to distinguish clients with a long-standing deficiency in social skills from those who are showing a temporary deficit of skills because of an episode of depression. For the depressed client it is usually simply too much effort to exhibit socially skilled behaviour but the skills are not outside his repertoire. This is not to say that there may not also be a minority of depressed clients whose primary deficits in support-eliciting skills may have led to their depression. This latter sub-category of depressed clients would also seem appropriate for a social skills programme.

The therapist should enquire about the client's ability to mix with others at different stages of the life cycle – childhood, adolescence, post adolescence, etc. Difficulties across two or more stages of the life cycle would be suggestive of social skills deficits.

2. *Social situations* Clients' social difficulties are often very specific to situations. Identification of the problematic situations is a necessary prelude to a more fine-grained analysis of the difficulties. Trower *et al.*'s Social Situation Questionnaire (1978) asks the client the degree of difficulty experienced in various social situations and how frequently these situations are encountered. The SSQ is reproduced in Appendix K. (Trower (1986) has also provided a useful summary of other social skills assessment devices.) The therapist can then take in turn each situation which is rated 2, 3, or 4 (moderate or great difficulty or avoidance) and discuss it with the client. It should be noted that on the SSQ clients rate their perception of difficulty, they may or may not manifest these difficulties as far as an observer is concerned. The therapist should probe what the client's goals are in the situations in which difficulties are experienced. For example, a client reporting severe difficulties entering a room full of people may have as a goal acceptance by all those present. A video of such a client's perfor-mance may not reveal any obvious deficits but nevertheless they report an unacceptably high level of social anxiety. By contrast another client may also have severe difficulties entering a room full of people, but a video of their performance might reveal that they stood in a corner, looking at the floor, refusing to make eye contact with anyone. The first client would require a cognitive intervention, the second a behavioural one. Of course, in specific situations clients are often exhibiting both cognitive and behavioural deficits. The nature of the client's thought processes in difficult situations can be made explicit using the ABCD format. A represents a particular occasion of social difficulty, C represents the emotions experienced, B represents the automatic thoughts or self-talk about A. The Bs – automatic thoughts – are sometimes not formed consciously and the client may be best taught to access them by posing the question 'What does it sound "as if" I am saying to myself'. The 'identified' Bs are a convenient hypothesis, a starting point which gives the client a handle on the situation, and permitting the generation of more rational responses, D, during therapy.

Social interaction has been likened by Argyle (1986) to the play-ing of games – certain situations having certain roles. The automatic thoughts of clients in their difficult situations are often at odds with the rules of the situation. Thus the client attending a works social gathering with the automatic thought that 'It must be purposeful' is likely to be given short shrift by colleagues if attempts are made to negotiate new working arrangements.

3. *Performance* It has already been stressed that the SSQ assesses the client's subjective experiences of social situations. Ideally this should be complemented with observation of the client in his naturalistic setting. But this is no simple matter: there are problems of influencing the client's behaviour because of the presence of an observer; difficulties in deciding what should be measured and what weighting to give to the various aspects of interaction; and not least such observations are extremely time-consuming for the therapists. To help circumvent these problems use is often made of standardized role plays. A key issue in the use of such role plays is the extent to which the skills and anxieties clients manifest in them reflect the 'real' life situations.

Trower *et al.* (1978) have developed a Social Interaction Test, which requires clients to converse with two strangers for twelve minutes. Clients are assessed in twenty-eight micro-domains which include the appropriateness of volume of voice, non-verbal 'grammar', feedback, and the degree of violation of situation rules. In addition clients are rated on thirteen axes, and each axis has a seven-point scale. The axes include happy–sad, rewarding–unrewarding, controlling–uncontrolling. The test is specific to meeting strangers and this may not be a client's main difficulty. Replication role-play tests in which the client attempts to replicate a previously encountered situation may potentially be of greater utility. But so far little research (Kern 1982) has been conducted on the construction and evaluation of such role-play tests.

Chapter Nine

IN MARITAL THERAPY

The cognitive-behavioural treatment programme for marital discord described in this chapter has three interacting components: 1) behavioural exchange, 2) cognitive restructuring, and 3) communication and problem-solving training. Historically programmes ostensibly constructed on the first component have nevertheless had a cognitive goal of a perceived increase in marital satisfaction. Without such an increase any programme would likely be judged worthless. Traditionally the cognitive goal would however have been realized by primarily behavioural means. By contrast in this programme behavioural, cognitive, and communication training strategies are given an equal weighting. This approach reflects current findings from outcome studies of marital therapy and research into the nature of marital communication reviewed in chapters 1 and 8. It seems likely that best results will accrue from tailoring the programme to an individual couple's needs, so that for some couples a greater emphasis might be given to the behavioural elements and a lesser focus on the cognitive aspects, whilst with other couples the reverse may be the case. The initial responsiveness of the couple to the particular component may serve as an indicator for differential emphasis.

The first step in conducting the programme is to conduct a behavioural interview with the couple which examines the antecedents of the behaviours complained about, the actual behaviours, and the consequences of those behaviours. In this connection the focus is obviously on the dysfunctional aspects of the relationship and how they are being maintained. However, spending some time in the assessment interview underlining where there is agreement in the relationship can serve to remind couples that the relationship is not totally devoid of redeeming qualities – often a necessary counterbalance when the couple's energies have been heavily focused on the problem areas. Hope is a necessary ingredient for the active engagement of a couple in therapy. One way of fanning the flames of hope is to have the couple recall in detail a good period in their relationship, perhaps when they were courting, then to suggest that the therapeutic task is one of regaining lost ground rather than having to learn totally new skills from scratch. Most of the therapist's attention in the session will however be on the negative aspects of the couple's interaction. Specifically, the therapist has the opportunity to note dysfunctional patterns of communication between the partners. Do they, for example, infer malevolent intent on their spouses's behalf? In what ways is their verbal and non-verbal communication different to their interaction with the therapist? The observational data and the couple's description of their difficulties should be complemented with their completion of the Dyadic Adjustment Scale (Appendix H), Relationships Belief Inventory (Appendix J), and the Area of Change Questionnaire (Appendix I).

Assessment interviews would normally take between one and three sessions and would include the presentation of a coherent rationale and an outline of the treatment programme. In presenting the rationale for the programme (and the behavioural component in particular) appeal can be made to each partner's self-interest, in that the first phase of the programme is largely concerned with helping each partner to get more out of his/her spouse by altering first his/her behaviour. The second phase of the programme can be explained by contrasting extreme interpretations of a spouse's behaviour, along the following lines 'One person may think that anything his spouse does that he does not like *must* be because of things outside her control, and everything she does that pleases him was *deliberately* done just for him. Another person may think in exactly the opposite way about his spouse. How people think about their spouse's behaviour affects their marital satisfaction. In the programme, before you get low over your spouse, we teach you to pause and check out the accuracy of your thinking'. The need for the final phase of the programme, communication training, tends to require little justification to clients as it seems to have become part of the popular wisdom to attribute marital problems largely to unspecified 'communication difficulties'. If further explanation is required it can be pointed out that just one of the aspects of communication training is teaching couples to keep to one problem at a time, and avoiding bringing in other quite different problems. Typically the programme involves 12–16 hour-long weekly therapy sessions, with monthly booster sessions for three months and a six month follow-up. Thereafter the therapist makes him/herself available in a consultant role.

It is sometimes the case that one partner has felt 'dragooned' into attending the assessment session and is in fact poorly motivated for a programme whose focus is on improving the relationship. Such a partner may not wish to verbalize their disquiet, perhaps for fear of hurting their spouse, but it may be apparent from their completion of the DAS. A partner who had indicated that they thought of divorce or separation most of the time (item 16) and whose feelings about the future of the relationship were on a continuum from 'It would be nice if my relationship succeeded and I can't do much more than I am doing now to help it succeed' to 'My relationship can never succeed and there is no more that I can do to keep the relationship going' (item 32) would suggest that the couple are better candidates for the motivational interviewing strategies described in Chapter 12, in which clients can be helped to make decisions about their future, than for marital therapy.

The programme is now outlined in terms of its three major components.

BEHAVIOURAL EXCHANGE

The focus in the first few sessions is on desirable relationship behaviours that are relatively easy to bring about, that is, without too much couple conflict. This can serve as a necessary reminder to the couple that their partner can be a source of reward. To address the major areas of conflict at this early stage would be likely to result in the all too familiar failure experiences. As discussed in the previous chapter, increasing marital satisfaction necessitates a dual focus, the reduction of negative behaviours and an increase of positive behaviours. Simply removing the negative behaviours does not increase positive couple interaction. The concern in the first phase of the programme is with increasing positive behaviours rather than with the reduction of negative behaviours. This orientation is reversed in later phases of the programme. (There are of course exceptions to the non-conflictual focus in the early phase, for example where one spouse is physically abusing the other partner or being unfaithful.) The behavioural exchanges have the aim of maximizing the rewards to the recipient and minimizing the costs to the giver.

The Area of Change Questionnaire (A–C) (Weiss and Margolin 1977) can help pinpoint those items which might be appropriate for a behavioural exchange. It should be noted that the items on this instrument are couched in highly specific terms leaving little room for debate (or more likely argument!) about whether they occurred subsequently or not. The specificity of the items can serve as a model for appropriate behaviour exchanges. Fuzzy items such as 'I want my husband to get on better with my mother' are clearly ruled out of court. Where a partner has indicated on the A–C that they would like much more of a particular behaviour but that it nevertheless does not constitute a major difficulty, the therapist can open up a discussion of the feasibility of the behaviour in the coming week. This procedure is then repeated using the other partner's A–C. In this way, under therapist direction, partners can be helped to exchange positive behaviours. Having partners exchange A–Cs is an aid to more accurately gauging what would please the spouse and sets the stage for better selection of reinforcing behaviour.

Bob and Jane exchanged A–Cs and found that they both wanted each other to go out more. Both partners were unemployed and living constantly under each other's feet and this created a great deal of stress. The therapist suggested that given Bob's interest in football perhaps he would like to go to a match whilst Jane might welcome an opportunity to visit a friends one evening without the children accompanying her. Verbally they both agreed to this suggestion but non-verbally they had turned to look at each other apprehensively. Accordingly the therapist enquired whether there were perhaps some practical problems or fears that might get in the way of performing these two tasks. After a long pause Bob said without looking at his wife 'If I go to the match she will just give me "flack" for wasting money'. Jane replied indignantly 'I wouldn't, not once in a while anyway. I don't know what chaos I would come home to if you mind the kids whilst I go and see my friend'. Bob bowed his head, sighed deeply and muttered 'There she goes again', at which Jane sat angrily upright and began a volley with 'Listen you . . .'. The therapist abruptly interrupted the cross-complaining by summarizing the positives in the session so far. Permission had been given to meet Bob's needs by going to a football match but a specific game had yet to be specified; the next task in the session was to spell out how Jane's needs might be best met by an evening out. Finally it was agreed that Bob would go to a football match on the following Saturday afternoon and Jane would have an evening out the night before. However to dispel Jane's fears of 'What I would come home to' it was necessary to specify the details of Bob's babysitting. Specifically he would wash the dishes whilst the baby was in the play pen and have both children ready and changed for bed by the time Jane came in at about 10.30 p.m. At the next session the homework tasks were reviewed and both partners reported a great deal of satisfaction with how they had worked out and they had had a fairly pleasant weekend as a result. In the above example the behaviour exchanges negotiated for Bob and Jane were made on a good faith basis; if Bob didn't or couldn't go to the match Jane still had the right to go out to her friends and vice versa. The behaviours were not tied together. An example of a good faith contract is shown in Figure 2.

Figure 2   Example Good Faith Contract

Behaviour Change Goal: Not to interrupt my wife when she is explaining something to visitors.
Reward: Buy myself a new greenhouse on Saturday.
Penalty: Shop for the week's groceries myself.
Record keeping: Put a cross on the homework chart each time I interrupted.

Signed . . . .

In general in the early phases of marital therapy good faith contracts are to be recommended. It is of course possible to tie together the two behaviours in a quid pro quo contract, but if one party fails to comply the whole contract dissolves. Given the importance of success experiences in the early stages of therapy quid pro quo contracts are especially risky. However the long-term goal of marital therapy is to make each partner a source of reward for the other, e.g. 'If you come straight home from work then I'll go for a drink with you for the last hour'.

Theoretically behavioural exchanges constitute a fairly simple procedure, but in practice considerable therapist involvement is necessary to troubleshoot difficulties and ensure adequate specificity of tasks. Returning to Bob and Jane at the next session a behavioural exchange was negotiated in which Bob agreed to mend the front garden fence and Jane agreed to go with him the following Saturday evening to a club, she would also arrange for her friend to do the baby-sitting that evening. Their progress with these tasks was reviewed at the following session. They both looked particularly glum as they sat down at the beginning of the session. Jane's first comment was 'It's just not working, we had an awful week', to which the therapist replied that 'Therapy for most people is two steps forward and one backward but they mostly get there in the end. Maybe we need to do some detective work to see exactly what went wrong because things had gone really well for you last time I saw you both.' With this reply the therapist was accepting that they had encountered particular difficulties in the past week without taking on board Jane's overgeneralization about the therapy and thereby generating hope. It emerged that Jane had kept her part of the agreement and gone out with Bob on the Saturday evening but she hadn't enjoyed it 'Because I was fuming inside that Bob still hadn't done the fence and feeling that it's always me that has to do the giving!' Bob had noticed her scowls and lack of interest in the proceedings and called her a 'pain' and she left the club by herself abruptly and prematurely. Until the session he was unaware of the origins of the downward spiral in Jane's mood. He protested that he had intended to repair the fence on the Saturday but the rain was on and off all day and so he had decided to leave it to the Sunday. By the time Sunday came he felt Jane had sabotaged her part of the agreement and so he was not going to do his part. To which Jane replied that he was just a lazy ****. Once again the therapist interrupted the cross-complaining, this time to focus on the conflict as an exemplar of the cognitive distortions that can bedevil a relationship, thereby paving the way for the second phase of therapy. With most couples general principles are better explained with reference to a highly relevant example. In this case the therapist commented 'Seems to me you're both doing a lot of mind reading. How could you have been sure, Bob, that Jane was deliberately trying to destroy the evening out and not simply unhappy about something? And how can you, Jane, be sure that Bob didn't intend from the outset to repair the fence? Maybe if you could climb inside each other's minds you could know, but short of that it is not too easy to see how you can know.' Jane replied that 'Maybe we both messed it up' and Bob agreed. The therapist then went on to say that 'Lots of couples sabotage their relationship by mind reading and assuming that if the partner does not do something that would please them it is because of some long-standing, almost innate characteristic of the partner, and if on the odd occasion a spouse does something liked by the partner it *must* be by chance, a fluke. What we go onto in the second phase of therapy is putting this naturally occurring way of looking at each other under the microscope and seeing how useful it is and how true it is.'

The session described above does illustrate a difficulty with behavioural exchanges in that although the therapist may not have made one partner's task conditional on prior completion of the other partner's tasks (a quid pro quo), nevertheless even with a good faith arrangement there is inevitably some contamination of tasks. The differences then between quid pro quo arrangements and good faith ones are sometimes more apparent than real.

Behavioural exchanges focusing on the more major difficulties may be negotiated from roughly session nine onwards. As such they form a final part of the communication and problem-solving phase of the programme. There is no evidence that one form of contract applied across the board is superior to the other form. It is rather a question of choosing that form of contract that best meets the needs of a particular couple at a particular time.

COGNITIVE RESTRUCTURING

The therapy sessions themselves provide an ideal opportunity for noting and correcting cognitive distortions. Returning to Bob and Jane the therapist had attempted, fairly successfully, to reframe their understanding of why it was that the homework contract involving 'fence mending' and 'a night out together' had not worked. However when the therapist attempted to reinstate the assignment Jane muttered 'I am not sure I want it mended now, he would only be doing it out of obligation'. To which the therapist replied 'Can you be absolutely sure of that?' Here again the therapist was having to challenge Jane's propensity to mind read. The next session began with the customary review of the homework assignments. Bob began 'I fixed the fence, but she just moaned anyway, it's no wonder I don't bother doing anything.' At which Jane became indignant, 'All I said was that the two planks are not level. If you tell him anything he just takes a huff and sulks for days!' The therapist was aware that Bob had scored highly on the 'Disagreement is Destructive' sub-scale of the Relationship Belief Inventory (Epstein and Eidelson 1981) and accordingly asked Bob what it meant to him if someone disagreed with or criticized him. The bottom line was that he assumed it meant they didn't like him. The behavioural consequences were that he avoided doing anything that would make him the focus of attention. The therapist then focused discussion on the utility of this approach, contrasting the short-term gain of avoiding criticism with the long-term disadvantage of being branded by others and notably his wife as 'lazy, good for nothing'. Bob agreed that 'there isn't much mileage in the way I handle criticism'. From considerations of utility the therapist shifted to the issue of validity. (It should be noted that in the cognitive restructuring component of marital therapy, the conceptual framework used for guiding therapists' choice of interventions is the one elaborated in Chapter 6 on cognitive therapy for depression.) Bob was asked by the therapist whether, if he criticized the way in which someone did something, it meant that he thought less of them as a person. He replied 'Not usually'. The therapist suggested he had two sets of rules, one for himself and one for other people. Bob conceded 'Maybe some people are more like me when they criticize'. A self-instruction routine involving imagery was developed to help Bob cope with criticism. When he felt himself bridling under criticism he was to first tell himself to 'keep calm', then challenge the 'awfulness' of the situation by asking himself 'Am I actually in front of a firing squad about to be machine gunned, or am I getting a clip round the ear which may be deserved or undeserved?' To encourage him to become task focused he was to say, 'I'll stay where I am and sort out what I might be able to do differently'. Finally he was to congratulate himself for not running away from the criticism.

So far the cognitive restructuring has been discussed in terms of trouble-shooting the cognitive blocks to behavioural exchange contracts. Though this is an important function it is not its sole function. Couples are in therapy precisely because they are acting as a stimulus for each other's emotional distress. Having each spouse track, between sessions, those situations in which they experience distress is a necessary precursor to explication and possible modification of the thought processes and behaviours involved. This may be accomplished by having the spouses complete a diary using the format in Figure 3.

Figure 3 Example from 'How I Felt' Diary

1. When you
. . . . came home from work and started working again immediately after tea

2. I felt
. . . . lonely, left out, sad

3. Because I was thinking
. . . . your work is more important to you than me. I don't count. I am just a slave. You're a workaholic.

4. Is there a more realistic and possibly less distressing way of thinking and or behaving in this situation? If so please specify . . . . we've both got a lot on just at the moment. It's not always like this. I could discuss setting aside some special times, maybe to go to the theatre or for a meal on Friday nights.

The format of the diary implicitly takes issue with the often expressed complaint of distressed spouses to each other 'You made me feel . . . ' by suggesting that feelings may, to an important extent, be under the control of the thought processes the individual chooses to utilize. Spouses are advised to complete the diary as soon after an 'upset' as possible. This serves two functions, first of all ensuring that the cognitions recorded in the third section are 'hot', and not as subject to after-the-event rationalizations; second, the format causes the spouse to stop and think before interacting with their partner. The de-escalation of a conflict depends on one spouse at some point in the interaction avoiding making a response beyond the threshold of tolerance of their partner. Completion of the diary helps to make this a possibility. It is useful also to ask a couple to complete the diary on at least two occasions between sessions when their partner pleases them. This can help to counter the mental filter through which partners often view each other's behaviour by focusing attention on the positives as well as the negatives.

The dysfunctional thought processes that are much in evidence with depressed clients also figure prominently in the interactions of distressed spouses. For example in Figure 3 the client was jumping to conclusions (mind reading) that his/her partner thought more of work than the relationship. An arbitrary inference was made ('I don't count') and the distress was compounded by labelling the spouse as a 'workaholic'. A series of completed 'how I felt' diaries is necessary to help identify the most common cognitive distortion to which a partner is predisposed. Knowledge of a particular vulnerability can equip a spouse to take more speedy remedial action nearer to the onset of distress.

The diary material is normally reviewed in the session but it is extremely important to check with the writer of each diary which, if any, material they want to discuss. Completion by the spouses of the RBI can alert the therapist as to what particular dysfunctional attitudes may be operative in the situation described in the diary. Often a spouse will have been unable to complete the fourth section of the diary. The therapist's task is to share with the couple the silent assumptions that may have been operative. It is extremely important that such suggested interpretations are not imposed on the couple but rather canvassed as hypotheses. Having generated an agreed dysfunctional attitude as a working hypothesis it is examined and tested in the same manner as dysfunctional silent assumptions with depressed clients. Dealing with dysfunctional attitudes in the context of real life situations helps to ensure that modification of such attitudes will generalize to the natural settings; such may not be the case if the cognitive component of therapy consisted simply of an examination with the couple of their responses to the RBI.

COMMUNICATION TRAINING

Returning to Bob and Jane's difficulties the focus so far has been on behavioural exchanges and cognitive restructuring. However although Jane's criticism of Bob's fence mending was accepted in the session by both partners as being 'objectively' valid, and they agreed that he overreacted, the incident was perhaps indicative of communication deficits. Specifically Jane expressed her criticism without a positive context, making it unlikely that Bob would be receptive to her comments. Jacobson and Margolin (1979) have elaborated a set of Communication Guidelines for couples which are summarized in Table 4.

Table 4 Communication Guidelines

1. In stating a problem, always begin with something positive.
2. Be specific.
3. Express your feelings.
4. Admit to your role in the problem.
5. Be brief when defining problems.
6. Discuss only one problem at a time.
7. Summarize what your partner has said and check with them you have correctly understood them before making your reply.
8. Don't jump to conclusions, avoid mind reading, talk only about what you can see.
9. Be neutral rather than negative.
10. Focus on solutions.
11. Behaviour change should include give and take and compromise.
12. Any changes agreed should be very specific.

Jacobson and Margolin (1979) emphasize three sequential components to teaching the guidelines.

1) *feedback* – in which couples are given information about their maladaptive communication patterns. In Bob and Jane's case the therapist introduced the guidelines by reflecting back the impact of her monologue on himself 'Can you just hang on a second there Jane, I don't know about you but I am feeling bewildered. You have jumped from one problem to another and haven't settled on any one long enough to come up with possible solutions'. Jane replied 'Sorry I am always doing that'. The therapist commented, 'It's interesting, because one of the rules for effective communication is taking one problem at a time. There are other rules too, that I would like to go through with both of you in this final phase of therapy, and get you to practise discussing difficulties using them. Keeping to these rules will help you both win when there

is a problem to be tackled instead of both becoming distressed as in the past'.

2) *instruction* – in which the therapist provides alternative communication patterns for the couple. In Bob and Jane's case the therapist role played Jane's criticism of Bob but conformed to the guidelines thus, 'Thanks for having a go at mending the fence in such awful weather' (guideline 1). 'From where I am standing the two planks don't look level' (guideline 2), and 'I really would like to have it looking right in case anyone visits as a result of the estate agent's advertising' (guideline 3). 'Maybe I am fussing too much about what we have to do to sell the house' (guideline 4). Up to this point Jane has been both brief and kept to one problem thus observing guidelines 5 and 6. 'So you think that it is too difficult a job to do by yourself. It's impossible to hold the planks to the upright and check properly whether they are level at the same time, is that right?' (guideline 7). Up to this point Jane has made no arbitrary inferences so guideline 8 has been observed and so to has guideline 9 with the adoption of a neutral rather than a negative tone. 'Maybe I can hold the fence and you can stand back and tell me what to adjust until they are level and then you can come back and nail them' (guidelines 10 to 12).

3) *behaviour rehearsal* – where couples practise the communication patterns provided by the therapist. Couples may be asked in the session to practise the communication skills on a not too traumatic incident from the recent past. The therapist then provides feedback and if necessary instruction on their attempt at communication and problem solving. The three aspects of teaching communication skills are then interactive.

For homework the couple can be set two or three communication exercises between sessions. It is often important to specify in advance when these sessions will take place e.g. 'After the nine o'clock news and the kids have gone to bed'. The duration of the sessions should also be agreed in advance; if a problem is discussed for longer than twenty minutes extraneous matter tends to be introduced and arguments are likely to develop. The less highly charged problems should be tackled first, so that couples gain some success experience with the guidelines, moving on to more controversial subject matter as communication skills develop. Spouses need to be given explicit permission by the therapist to each act as referees as to whether the guidelines are being violated.

If one partner unilaterally takes on the business of being a referee this can cause deep resentment in a spouse, who sees the partner primarily as a fellow 'player'. Revision of how spouses fared with their between-session communication exercises constitutes an important part of a therapy session.

The broad shifts in this marital therapy programme are from behavioural exchange to cognitive restructuring then to communication training. As the therapist takes a couple through the programme the earlier phases are integrated with the later phases in the setting of homework assignments. It should be clear however that there is considerable interaction and overlap between the components. The basic programme can be covered in 12 to 16 sessions. In the present state of knowledge there seems to be no compelling reason to emphasize one component over another, though with a particular couple a therapist may place a differential emphasis depending on the receptivity of the partners. For example, a couple who continue to insist that the behavioural exchange procedures are too 'mechanical' and 'lacking in spontaneity' may lead a therapist to place more emphasis on the cognitive component. Alternatively a couple may find the cognitive restructuring 'too abstract' leading the therapist to place more emphasis on behavioural exchange.

However useful the programme may be in the short term it seems unlikely that such a brief programme will produce enduring changes in long-standing dysfunctional modes of interaction. A minimum requirement for the maintenance of treatment gains are probably follow-up booster sessions one, three, and six months after completion of the programme. Thereafter the therapist ought to be available on a consultancy basis. The booster sessions should involve trouble-shooting any unresolved problems that had arisen since completion of the programme. Specifically the appropriateness of skills already taught in the resolution of the 'new' difficulties should be underlined.

Chapter Ten

SOCIAL SKILLS

Social skill training of some variety has been applied to almost every client group imaginable. Nevertheless the principal focus has been on the socially anxious client. Programmes constituted for the socially anxious clients also have a relevance to adolescent offenders who have often been found to manifest social skill deficits. Spence (1981) in a videotaped comparison of matched offenders and non-offenders found that the offender group showed significantly less eye contact, appropriate head movements, and speech. Such a programme with offenders can fill the vacuum that is often left after they have been taught the anger control strategies described in Chapter 3. There is little evidence that social skills programmes can reduce recidivism and the case for running a programme can only realistically rest on the needs of the individual client. Whilst social skills programmes for socially anxious clients do generally result in more adept performers by the end of a programme compared to control groups, there is often a failure for gains made to generalize to the real life situation and for gains to be maintained over time. For example, Goldstein and Keller (1987) in reviewing approximately sixty investigations, half of which involved aggressive teenagers or adults, found that over 90 per cent of clients completing programmes acquired skills, however skill transfer only occurred with approximately 45–50 per cent of clients.

In this chapter a broad spectrum cognitive-behavioural social skills programme is described which takes particular account of the problems of generalization and maintenance. The programme is presented with a group format in mind though it can obviously be adapted to the needs of the individual client. Given that the effect of social skills training appears to be similar whether the clients are seen individually or in groups (see Linehan *et al.* (1979) for example), from a cost-efficiency point of view groups are to be preferred.

A COGNITIVE-BEHAVIOURAL PROGRAMME FOR SOCIALLY ANXIOUS CLIENTS

Possible assessment devices for use with socially anxious clients were described in Chapter 8. The key assessment device used in this programme is the Trower, Bryant, and Argyle Social Situations Questionnaire (SSQ) (see Appendix K). In this instrument clients are asked to rate their difficulty in coping with thirty situations and then indicate how often they had entered each situation. The nature of the SSQ serves as a reminder that the situations of concern to two socially anxious individuals may be quite different. Further the anxieties of any one individual will be specific to certain situations. Obviously all socially anxious clients would be expected to score highly on global measures such as the Social Avoidance and Distress Scale and the Fear of Negative Evaluation Scale (Watson and Friend 1969).

Clients are seen individually for an assessment interview at which they complete the SSQ and are asked in addition to tick those situations that are of major importance to them. The prime focus in the programme is to help clients cope better in the highly relevant but problematic situations. Perception of a given situation as being very difficult and therefore acting as a stimulus for social anxiety can arise for three reasons: a) the goals in a particular situation are unrealistic, b) the client is in fact closer to the goal than he or she perceives, and c) the client has inadequate skills to achieve the goal. Thus socially anxious clients are not an homogeneous group and may include highly skilled performers whose deficits are more of a cognitive nature, and lowly skilled performers whose deficits may include an inability or lack of knowledge of the behavioural skills of non-verbal communication and conversational interaction. It is important then that this group programme is adapted to the needs of individual group members.

The assessment interview itself furnishes the therapist with information on deficits in verbal and non-verbal communication, for example, whether the client makes eye contact, or makes

138

monosyllabic replies to questions. Sometimes the deficits are difficult to pinpoint exactly and may involve 'meshing skills' whereby the client fails to encourage the therapist, show interest in him, or control the interaction in a flexible way. To gauge any cognitive deficits it is useful to have the client recount the most recent episode of a relevant and difficult situation. Much of the client's description tends to be about their anxious symptoms in the situation; although listening to this material is off-task, active listening is to be encouraged at this early stage in the interests of establishing rapport. Asking the client what they hoped to get out of their difficult social encounter underlines the goal-directed nature of social interaction whilst at the same time helping the client to make explicit their destination. Stating their 'destination' makes possible an examination of the evidence that they did not 'arrive'. Later in the programme the inherent impossibility of arriving at certain destinations is examined; they are locations literally off the map. For example, to cope with a particular situation without anxiety because 'anxiety is "dangerous"'.

To take an example, at the assessment interview G.E. had indicated on the SSQ that he had great difficulty in meeting strangers and this was a major problem for him. In the session he was asked by the therapist to 'play a mental video for me of the most recent occasion that meeting strangers caused you problems'. G.E. cited an instance from the week before in which his counterpart from the southern branch of his firm came to visit him about the firm's new procedures for testing the strength of materials. He had felt almost sick in anticipation of the meeting. In the event he had found it much easier to converse about the procedures than he had thought. When it came to lunch time however and they went for a meal G.E. found it unbearable: 'I just couldn't stand the long silences'. The therapist asked how his colleague had seemed over lunch. G.E. replied 'Well I don't know really, he took ages eating, at the end he gave the waitress a much bigger tip than I would give'. In the circumstances it seemed unlikely that G.E. had been particularly socially unskilled. A more likely hypothesis was that he had set himself on a course to an impossible destination of almost constant chatter. In the session G.E. had described his difficulties in general in a socially skilful way, apart from a tendency to mumble and sit in a slightly hunched fashion. The therapist concluded that G.E.'s deficits seemed to be primarily

cognitive rather than behavioural. In the ensuing group programme the therapist ensured that, as far as G.E. was concerned,
the cognitive-behavioural balance was tipped in favour of cognitive
strategies.

Situations which are of major importance to the client but on
the SSQ are indicated as being 'avoided if possible' are targeted
for approach using systematic desensitization-graded exposure. For
example, to tackle G.E.'s fear of meeting strangers a hierarchy
was constructed. The ultimate challenge to be attempted near the
end of the group programme was to go on the Ramblers' Association Regional Holiday; the first step was to approach the bank
for a loan – something he had done on previous occasions.
Intermediate steps in order of increasing difficulty were to visit a
shop and discuss with an assistant the rival merits of different
videos; go for a walk with the local Ramblers on a Sunday, and
attend the Friday evening social gathering of the local Ramblers.
It was explained to G.E. that the five steps were only by way of
a suggestion and that it was difficult to know in advance the right
size steps. Further if any particular step proved too difficult it was
simply a question of creating an appropriate intermediate step; the
ultimate goal would still be realized, it would just take a little
longer. In this way failure experiences are anticipated and the
momentum developed already through the programme is hardly
reduced. The shift in such a hierarchy is inevitably from situations
in which the client feels he knows what is expected of him to more
ambiguous situations in which the social rules seem less clear.

Several treatment procedures are conjointly used in this
programme because on balance the research seems to indicate that
this produces a larger effect than would result from their separate
application (e.g. Kazdin and Mascitelli 1982). The group
programme has three overlapping phases: training in basic social
skills, training in specific social responses, and training in
cognitive restructuring. The programme can be conducted over
sixteen sessions of 1½ hours once a week, with monthly booster
sessions for three months. It is useful to start with 5 to 8
participants, with an anticipated loss of between a quarter and a
third of group members. A co-leader is necessary to ensure sufficient tailoring of the group programme to individual needs and to
participate in the role plays. Each component of the programme
is described in turn:

Training in basic social skills

The first phase of the programme covers non-verbal aspects of behaviour – eye contact, smile, etc., observing, listening, giving and receiving feedback. The first group session begins with the teaching of non-verbal skills. Typically clients have expended much energy in trying to identify the 'right' thing to say in social situations. It comes as both a relief and a surprise for many clients to be told that in everyday social encounters body language may be more important than what they say. For example, McFall *et al.* (1982) found that non-verbal was more important than verbal behaviour in communicating assertiveness. Assertiveness was found to be associated with smooth, steady, and purposive movement as opposed to shifting, fidgeting, activity. In order to better appreciate the relevance of non-verbal skills group members can be asked to think of three people they like and who are popular and ask themselves is it actually the precision of what they say that makes the difference? Group members then split in pairs and for five minutes discuss between them what it is about their chosen 'popular' people that attracts them. This also serves as an ice-breaker for group members.

A useful mnemonic to teach core non-verbal skills is the word SOFTEN:

> S – smile
> O – open posture
> F – forward lean
> T – touch
> E – eye contact
> N – nod

The significance of a smile can be emphasized by suggesting that just as group members feel fragile in social interactions so too, but to a lesser and more manageable extent, do members of the general public. Consequently all people are seeking approval in interactions. The most common and useful vehicle for conveying approval is a smile or a nod. Those who rarely smile or give others positive feedback by nodding are likely to be avoided. To illustrate the role of posture, the co-leader adopts three postures in turn whilst the therapist talks to him/her: a) head down, shoulders dropped, b) sitting back with arms folded, and c) leaning forward, making eye contact but pulling each finger in turn. The group is then asked what message the co-leader was sending out at each of the three stages. The correct responses are obviously depression/sadness, aloofness, and anxiety. Group members are then asked their likely response to each of the three signals. Typically the response these signals evoke is withdrawal. By way of contrast the group is asked to note before the next session the posture and mannerisms of a famous TV interviewer.

Touching and moving closer to someone are powerful vehicles for signalling increasing intimacy. However to use such strategies if there is any doubt about the recipient's positive regard is likely to have precisely the opposite effect to the one intended. Moving closer than three feet is usually taken to signal a close personal relationship. To move within three feet of a relative stranger or someone with whom there is a formal relationship may be resented as an invasion of personal space. At the other extreme, moving beyond six feet usually effectively sabotages personal discussion. A forward lean in discussions when seated is usually taken by the recipient as indicating a particular interest in what is being said.

Failure to make adequate eye contact is usually the social skill deficit that people notice most readily in the socially unskilled. As a general rule the socially skilled person might make eye contact about 90 per cent of the time when speaking and 60 per cent of the time when listening. Many socially anxious clients seem unaware of the impact of their usually minimal eye contact on others, yet an appreciation of this is often a precondition for rectifying the deficit. This lack of awareness reflects the socially anxious client's preoccupation with their own internal dialogue. A first step in generating awareness is to have the group members again split into pairs and tell each other how they feel if someone makes insufficient eye contact with them. In this conversation they are to try and observe the 'rule' about eye contact.

The conversation about 'eye contact' is repeated again after the group has been taught the skills of giving and receiving feedback. All aspects of SOFTEN are legitimate targets for feedback. The leader and co-leader should circulate around the pairs and troubleshoot any special problems as well as encourage the participants. Any problems common to dyads should lead the leader and co-leader to role play another scene themselves. Then invite the group members to do the same. Giving feedback involves a number of elements: 1) immediacy – providing feedback as soon as possible after performance of a behaviour, 2) praising – finding something positive to say before providing criticism. It can be explained that the justification for this is that people will not take on board criticism, however valid, unless they are first assured of their worth, 3) specificity – that which is being criticized has to be expressed in concrete behavioural terms, so that the recipient of the criticism is clearly aware of what would need to be done to remedy the difficulty.

If the person providing feedback is observing the guidelines it makes it less likely that the recipient of the criticism will reject it. But there can obviously be no guarantees about the recipient's response. Coping skills and cognitions for aggressive or depressive responses are discussed in the next section under assertion training. The prime requisites for receiving criticism are an immediate owning of the criticisms if they are thought to be valid. If criticisms are not thought to be valid a reply of the form 'I can see that if you thought A then you would feel that I should do B, however I think X is more accurate and so I feel I should do Y'. In this way the receiver of the criticism is not alienated yet the divergence of thinking is made apparent.

If it is felt that members have not yet grasped the rudiments of the non-verbal skills and feedback, further role plays by the leaders are necessary. It is important that the role plays reflect the situations encountered by group members. Group members who seem least to have grasped the material can be asked to recall the last situation in which they were unhappy either about their giving or receiving of criticism, and invited to outline the particular situation for the group. This scene can then be re-enacted by the group leader and co-leader to illustrate both feedback and non-verbal skills. The recipient of the feedback should, for the sake of the group, verbalize any pertinent cognitions that would normally be part of an internal dialogue, as well as expressing the usually vocalized replies. The role play is repeated by the group leader and co-leader, but this time violating the feedback guidelines, and group members are invited to comment on and specify the contraventions. The intention is to ensure that skills taught generalize to the real life situation by illustrating new coping skills within the context of what is actually experienced by group members. Further role plays involving the leaders and relevant group members are then required to underline the skills taught.

Homeworks should be set at the end of each of the sessions and in this, the first phase of the programme, they should begin with practice and observation of non-verbal skills. Assignments set in sessions three to five should also include practice of feedback skills. It is assumed throughout the programme that clients will be monitored for progress in tackling the steps of any hierarchies constructed to tackle avoided but important real life situations. Accordingly, part of each session's homework will be encouragement to take 'the next step' in one of the hierarchies; alternatively, if the previous step had proved too difficult, an intermediate step is introduced. Clearly, however, not all items on the SSQ lend themselves to being approached in a hierarchical fashion and some can only be tackled when the appropriate stage in the programme is reached, for example, 'Taking the initiative in keeping a conversation going'. Failure to attempt homework assignments bodes ill for long-term benefits of the programme no matter how adept a group member might become during the sessions. It is therefore important that homeworks are as specific as possible, e.g. 'to watch the non-verbal skills of Wogan on TV twice in the week'.

Training in specific social responses

The second phase of the programme covers initiating and continuing a conversation, talking oneself, being assertive, and ending social interaction. The essential skill of continuing a conversation is to summarize what the other person has said, turn it into a question and reflect it back. Thus the exchange is of the form 'Are you seriously saying they should abolish the offside rule in football, so the game flows more freely?' The group leaders should role play two or three scenes using this format and then split the group into pairs with one partner as the speaker and the other as practitioner of the new skill; roles are then reversed. Possible subject areas might include holidays, hobbies, and 'Where I grew up'. Partners should provide each other with feedback on their performance. The leaders likewise should endeavour to provide group members with feedback. Each group member should role play at least two scenes to ensure adequate appreciation of the skill involved. Some group members find summarizing of what the other person has said too difficult at this stage, and they can be advised to simply repeat the last few words the other person says and turn that into a question; thus 'I think I will go away for Christmas' becomes 'For Christmas?'

The second important skill for keeping a conversation going surrounds the art of asking open-ended questions rather than ones that admit of monosyllabic replies. 'What sort of music do you like?' is better for conversation purposes than 'Do you prefer pop or classical music?' Once again this skill is taught by role play. Homework should be set that involves the practice of these continuance of conversation skills on at least two or three occasions before the next session. The following session would begin with a review of the homework. Often the roadblocks to practice of a homework assignment are cognitive in nature and would need to be addressed in the session. The mechanics of unblocking the cognitive roadblocks are discussed in the next session.

A slightly more advanced way of teaching clients to keep a conversation going is to teach the general-specific-feeling format for asking questions. Essentially clients are taught to ask a general question, e.g. 'Are you going away on holiday this year?' If there is more than a monosyllabic reply a more specific question follows, e.g. 'Where are you going exactly?' The final question in the trio is a feeling question, e.g. 'Do you like going there?' Once again these skills are best taught by group leaders role playing interactions first performing the skills competently then repeating the exercise with a less than competent performance and inviting feedback from the group. Next, leaders would conduct role plays with group members and invite feedback.

After group members seem to have acquired a competence in the use of the general-specific-feeling format, attention should shift to ensuring that this strategy is not implemented in a rote manner. This is in many ways the more difficult part of the exercise – teaching a responsiveness to cues. One of the cues for a discontinuance of the interaction, monosyllabic replies, has already been mentioned. Another might be the body language of the person, perhaps they are turning away, or not making eye contact, or looking past you. Sometimes the cues are less obvious; perhaps something in the person's tone of voice. As a general rule it seems better to teach clients to attend to the more obvious cues; the more subtle ones, such as perhaps tone of voice, leave greater room for cognitive distortions, e.g. 'I withdrew because he didn't really like me, nobody does, he talked to me with his lips almost closed'. Nevertheless it should be borne in mind that a socially anxious person may not lack behavioural interaction skills so much as misperceive cues. Operationalizing the cues for interaction has proved extremely difficult. The paradox is, as Curran (1979) has noted, 'everyone seems to know what good and poor social skills are, but no one can define them adequately'. The role plays for teaching the general-specific-feeling format should be repeated with the added attention of group members paid to the body language of the questioner.

The general-specific-feeling format can also be used to teach clients themselves how to talk in conversation. To continue the example of the client who has successfully engaged someone in conversation using his trio of questions; simply to ask questions of another without some self disclosure runs the risk of being seen as intrusive or as a possible threat because something is being held back. The questioner would thus switch the focus onto himself with a reply like, 'I was thinking of going away at Christmas myself, down to South Wales to see the family, we always have a good time over the holiday'. This exchange once again follows the general-specific-feeling format. To illustrate the strategy, group leaders engage in a dialogue that involves each of them taking a questioning and disclosure role. The interaction is repeated but this time including some deliberate mistakes which the group are asked to identify. The group is then split into pairs for further role plays of the skills, using content areas such as food, the school I went to as a child, TV programmes, etc. Again the leaders circulate and provide feedback. The session ends with the setting of relevant homework assignments.

Initiating a conversation is perhaps more difficult than continuing it. The starting point is to teach the client to focus on something innocuous, an ice-breaker. An exchange at a bus stop with a new neighbour to whom the client had not been previously introduced might start with 'It's freezing today and it's only September'. If the neighbour responded in like manner the client might say 'Sorry for being nosey but haven't you just moved in somewhere along . . .'; anything more than a monosyllabic reply would lead the client to introduce themselves with 'Oh, by the way I am . . . I live along . . .'. This information would probably be reciprocated by the neighbour. Group leaders should role play a number of scenes in which ice-breakers are required, such as meeting a stranger at a party or meeting a distant relative at a wedding or funeral; then group members, in pairs, are asked to engage in similar exchanges. A related skill is introducing people to each other. This skill starts with a focus on the person to whom the client wishes to introduce a friend or colleague, e.g. 'Have you got a minute Paul?' (pause for a verbal or non-verbal reply). If the reply is one of openness, for example, a smile accompanied by a comment such as 'Yes sure', the client continues 'Pete this is Paul, renowned for his speedy completion of crosswords, occasionally he actually fixes the lights in the building!' 'Paul this is Pete, he is going to be working on the heating system in the building, so you will be both working on stopping the place grinding to a halt'. Group leaders should first role play this skill. Other possible scenes might include introducing a new friend to old friends in a pub, or introducing a new club member to other club members.

The verbal and non-verbal social skills discussed so far are essentially those for helping clients make initial contacts. Historically, little attention has been paid to the skills needed to maintain relationships. Yet many socially anxious clients report an ongoing problem of 'loneliness', and it may be that for a sub-group the deficits are more to do with the maintenance rather than the initiation of relationships. Continued failure to maintain relationships may lead to decreased confidence and thereby to a subsequent impairment of the ability to initiate relationships. It is suggested that the socially anxious clients are a heterogeneous group and will require treatment strategies at least along an axis initiation-maintenance. Numerous studies (e.g. Billings and Moos 1982) have shown that it is the reported adequacy or quality of support that is a better predictor of adjustment than is the sheer availability of interactions. It may be that some of the 'lonely' clients are lonely because they are unskilled support elicitors and therefore do not get the suport they wish for.

Winefield (1984) has suggested four areas of importance for support-elicitation skills training. These are discussed in turn, together with appropriate strategies for teaching the skills:

a) Understanding the social norms re intimacy and its reciprocation.
It is common for lonely or depressed clients to prematurely

disclose negative information about themselves. This often results in subsequent avoidance of the client despite an initial show of sympathy and concern (for details of the interpersonal model of depression see Chapter 5). Such behaviour serves to confirm the client's sense of isolation. This sets up a vicious circle in which the client becomes even more desperate for intimacy with an increased likelihood that he or she will forgo the preliminaries of making a relationship. Little attention is paid to setting a positive tone for and gauging the potential of the relationship. In a dating context the client is likely to become too serious too quickly, more attached to the idea of 'being in love' than with what is realistically feasible given the resources of both parties. Initially, having fun is likely to be seen as trivial and superficial. Yet without some prior history of positive interactions there is little likelihood of being able to address negative aspects without one of the partners withdrawing.

There are no hard and fast rules about what should be disclosed when, but a necessary condition for the continuance of a relationship is probably matching levels of self-disclosure. The attentive but low self-disclosing person may be experienced by others as almost as aversive as the non-attentive high-discloser. If the problem for the lonely/depressed sub-group is usually too much disclosure too soon, the major difficulty for the remaining socially anxious clients is likely to be the withholding of personal information. Group members should be asked to reflect on previous intimate relationships and assess the style of interaction, asking themselves 1) did they seem to make initial contact and the partner 'suddenly' withdraw, or 2) were they accused of being a 'clam' or 'withdrawn'. The former would suggest a lonely/depressed client for whom the appropriate strategy is slowing the pace of disclosure. The latter would suggest an increased pace of disclosure.

b) Knowing how and when to complain.
Deciding pragmatically whether it is 'worth' expressing a complaint is a necessary first step in the assertive process. It may be that the short-term advantages for a client of 'getting something off my chest' are more than offset by the long-term consequences of becoming unable to pursue a chosen goal. In most cases clients can be advised to perform a cost-benefit analysis to aid the

decision-making process. In making this analysis account has to be taken of differences in power between the client and those he or she would interact with. Nevertheless there are occasions when the moral 'rightness' of a client's position will dictate expression of a complaint even if the overall consequences would appear negative for the client. Only the client can decide whether a particular instance does fall in this special category.

The mechanics of expressing a complaint have been summarized by Goldstein and Keller (1987):

(1) Define what the problem is, and who is responsible.
(2) Decide how the problem might be solved.
(3) Tell the person what the problem is and how it might be solved.
(4) Ask for a response.
(5) Show you understand his or her feelings.
(6) Come to agreement on the steps to be taken by each of you.

The first step in the procedure calls for specificity on the client's part in terms of who, did what, when. The second step involves the generation of as many solutions as possible. Each solution is weighed for its merits and a tentative solution is proposed. The client then asks for feedback on the proposed solution. Step 5 requires the development of empathy, a capacity to put oneself in another person's shoes and view a problem from their point of view. The egocentrism of the socially anxious or depressed person often militates against assuming the role of the other person. In the long term this may lead to a series of unproductive interactions in which other people feel literally not understood, complaints are not voiced, and avoidance ensues. Step 6 requires agreed solutions to be concretely expressed and the areas of responsibility precisely defined. There are clear overlaps here between this strategy and the communication training strategies used with distressed couples discussed in the previous chapter. In terms of maintenance of relationships it is the continued use of such strategies that determines eventual outcome. Such modes of interaction need to become the norm, and where this is the case the relationship will be strong enough to withstand the occasional violation of the strategies. The 'occasional violations' can then be conceptualized as 'part of being human' and pose little threat to the integrity of the relationship. In the group, the mechanics for expressing complaints should be

149

role played in the usual way, using examples from an intimate relationship and from a work situation.

However, it should be stressed to group members that ultimately it is much less important that they can demonstrate an understanding of the complaint strategy in the session, or indeed as a homework assignment, than that they construct something which would act as a long-term prompt for instigating such strategies. To this end group members should be asked to construct cards which on one side summarize the complaint procedure; the other side should recall relationships which were sabotaged by the client's lack of awareness of or non-use of the strategies. The form of the recall should be such that it acts as a stimulus for action rather than a dwelling on past 'failures'. A useful proforma might be 'When I was with . . . I often (mention specific violation of complaint guidelines) . . . Looking back maybe I could have played it differently by . . . The only real mistake is one you don't learn from. In future I'll make sure that, at least more often than not, I . . . then there is a better chance of being just reasonably content'. These cards should be placed in strategic places so that client has regular reminders long after the group has finished. Such cards can be constructed for each area of maintenance skills, as necessary. Clients may wish to elaborate their cards further after they have learnt the assertive strategies discussed in the next section. The importance of these cards is that they are 'home made', a synthesis of the client's experiences in relationships and the strategies taught in the sessions. They encourage generalization of skills taught, partly because they act as physical reminders, but probably also because the examples used are highly pertinent to the particular client.

c) Attending to and displaying interest in the other person.
Long-term maintenance of relationships may be sabotaged because the client pays insufficient attention to the role of everyday pleasantries or small talk in demonstrating appreciation of the other person. If communication is restricted to the client's high-agenda concerns the other person can come to feel devalued. Often clients have come to see small talk as 'superficial', 'trivial' and discussion about matters such as 'the weather today' as 'inane'. In the group, clients are asked to reconsider the meaning of such communications and to consider an alternative interpretation that

such exchanges are for the most part simply a socially sanctioned vehicle for telling someone that you are both aware and glad they exist. It is a question of clients learning to appreciate that just as they need affirmation so do other people.

An important way of displaying interest in another person is by asking them questions about their prime concerns. In order to do this however, it is necessary to first of all have paid attention to the lifestyle and comments of the other person. To some extent, by this stage of the group's life, members will be aware of each other's interests. It is useful to have members split into pairs and practise showing interest in each other. As a homework assignment clients should be asked to identify three prime concerns of someone they are currently interacting with, or would like to interact with, on a long-term basis. If the opportunity to interact occurs or can be arranged the client should attempt to focus discussion on the other person's major concerns. Remembering the responses to questions constitutes a particularly powerful demonstration of attention and this material should form the starting point for subsequent interaction.

d) Rewarding helping behaviour by responding positively.
Possibly the most common malaise in long-term relationships is that people can come to take each other for granted. Usually initial helping behaviour is perceived as a deliberate decision on the part of the 'helper' and appropriately rewarded. As time goes on the 'helpful' behaviour may become attributed to external factors beyond the motivation of an individual, specifically a necessary product of the role in which a person is cast. This means the 'helping' behaviour is not reinforced and as a consequence will probably be extinguished. A belief in the volitional nature of 'helping behaviours' seems to be a prerequisite of a positive response. To help group members appreciate this it is useful to have members discuss how much latitude people with whom they have (or would like to have) long-term relationships with in fact have in the way they respond. Essentially clients are made aware that a continuum of responses is possible from helpful to unhelpful. Further the price to be paid for not rewarding helpful behaviour is that it will cease.

Training in cognitive restructuring

The final phase of the programme covers assertion training, and developing an awareness of and challenges to ideas that interfere with the exhibition of social skills.

Assertiveness training is probably the aspect of social skills given the highest public profile. The essence of assertion training is teaching the client to balance his or her needs against the needs of others. Many clients seem to alternate between two poles, doormat-aggressive. For most of the time the client dwells at the doormat pole, operating on the silent assumption 'I have got no rights, I am better off putting other people before myself'. This tends to fuel resentment and eventually the client swings 'violently' to the opposite pole and makes an aggressive response, in effect saying 'I have got rights, blow others' rights'. The aggressive response is usually short-lived, a debilitating sense of guilt soon sets in and the client resolves to reside permanently at the doormat pole and so the pendulum continues to swing. It is useful to teach clients that being a doormat and being aggressive are at opposite ends of a continuum and that there is the mid-way alternative of being assertive. This helps to challenge the dichotomous thinking characteristic of many neurotic clients. The assertive person is then portrayed as working on the assumption 'I have got needs, you have got needs, let's try and balance them'.

It is often a relatively simple matter to teach clients to make a one-off assertive response to someone who has become particularly troublesome of late. For example, Sue was the only female in a room of four other male colleagues. They had taken to jibing her for the speed at which she processed letters even though they and she knew she always met her quota. Sue was taught the broken record technique, which essentially involves a repetition of the same few words without any explanation. In Sue's case she decided to look her colleagues straight in the eye when they were teasing her and calmly say 'get lost' or words to that effect! It was as important what Sue didn't say as what she did say; she totally refused to try and justify how many letters she had processed. To have given an explanation would have given her colleagues ammunition. In explaining the broken record strategy to group members it is useful to use the imagery of 'making yourself like a hedgehog in a curled up ball; prickly, but you just can't be got at'. Clients should be warned however that if they use this strategy initially the actions of the 'transgressors' are likely to be intensified as they sense they are losing control. Things worsening before they improve is often the price to be paid for utilizing the broken record strategy.

The problems that are particularly debilitating for the unassertive client are likely to be fairly enduring and often involve other family members. In such circumstances the broken record technique will probably make only a minor contribution to the resolution of the difficulties. Pat was married with three adult children living at home. As the time for the evening meal approached she would become very frayed in an attempt to cater for all family members' preferences. Inevitably some family member would pass a caustic remark about the evening meal. Pat then thought 'I am at home all day, I don't work, the least I can do is to provide them with a decent meal. I am just not up to anything', and she would be in a depressed mood for the rest of the evening. Pat's difficulties were used to teach the group how to identify an appropriate role model and to break the false dichotomy between an aggressive and doormat response. Pat agreed that she fitted the description of a doormat and was asked to think of someone who was 'just the opposite' and she chose her sister whom she disliked intensely. The group leader then drew a line on a board with the two poles at either end and Pat and her sister residing at them. Pat was then asked for someone 'not quite as bad as your sister' and came up with her husband. He was accordingly allotted a place along the continuum. The next step was to ask for someone 'not quite as doormat like as yourself' and she chose her sister-in-law. Finally she was asked for someone in between her husband and sister-in-law. Pat volunteered a neighbour she was good friends with. So the neighbour was accorded the mid-point on the continuum.

This procedure helps clients clarify what their assertive goals are; they can be visualized concretely in terms of the sort of thinking and behaviours engaged in by someone at the mid-point of the continuum. Importantly, it graphically illustrates to the client that in changing he or she is not heading to become the very sort of person they most abhor. A further benefit of this procedure is that it makes clear that to approach the goal the client must use stepping stones. In Pat's case she would strive first of all to become more like her sister-in-law. Pat regarded her sister-in-law as less distressed than herself, so that to move along the doormat-aggressive continuum even as far as her would be a definite gain. Group members for whom assertion was a particular problem then each have to construct their own continuum. Initially it is simpler to ask for the specification of just three intermediate points. In practice clients can specify as many 'stepping stones' as they wish; the important point is that they grasp that it is a question of 'becoming' assertive rather than 'being' assertive. The standards they are trying to realize are only those of the person located at the particular point in the continuum that they have reached; as such there is an implicit antidote to perfectionist standards. Clients are encouraged to praise themselves for how far they have come along the continuum rather than berate themselves for how far they have to go to be like their ideal person. To return to Pat, she felt it was too much initially to act like her neighbour and to say to her family 'You are all going to have the same meal. If you do not like it cook your own!' She decided in the first instance that she would act more like her sister-in-law, and for homework it was agreed that she would tell her family that she wasn't cooking at all on Friday nights, and one of them would have to either cook or bring the meal home from the local fish-and-chip shop.

Clients are advised to watch their role models carefully for their behaviours and attitudes, and when confronted by situations demanding an assertive response to act 'as if I was . . .'. Homework assignments based on these fixed roles should be carefully monitored and non-compliance should be investigated at the next session. A common roadblock to the completion of such assignments is the belief that 'It's OK for them to do that but it's not right for me'. This double standard should be made explicit and questioned. For example, 'What are you saying is so different about you that makes one rule for other people and another for yourself?' A typical reply from a client would be 'Well, I just feel I am'. The leader might continue, 'Because you feel something is true, does it thereby make it truth? I might feel strongly that the earth is flat but would that make it true?'

A key principle of assertion training is that the sender of an assertive response may suggest or advise the recipient to make a less distressing interpretation of the message sent, but ultimately choice of interpretation is in the hands of the recipient. The implication of this principle is that the assertive actor cannot assume total responsibility for the recipient's response. This confers a degree of freedom on the would-be assertive client and a lessened vulnerability to emotional blackmail. Assertion training as described above can be viewed as implicitly challenging a set of dysfunctional silent assumptions which clients might hold, including 'I am responsible for other people's feelings', 'I have got to make sure I am liked all the time', and 'I must always put everyone else's needs before my own'. Non-assertive clients are often only dimly aware that they are operating on such assumptions. Indeed, these assumptions expressed in such a bald manner are initially liable to be disowned by clients. Prior to discussion of such assumptions, it is a useful homework assignment to have clients record incidents in which they felt an assertive response was called for. A simple ABCD pro forma can be used where: A describes the external event (e.g. boss asked me to work overtime again); C describes the emotions and behaviour in response to A (e.g. felt helpless, depressed but agreed to come in anyway); B describes the thoughts or beliefs about A (e.g. It's not fair, why me? but I suppose I must); D represents the rational responses to B (e.g. I have done my stint, tough if he doesn't like it). Clients can often have difficulty initially identifying B; for most it seems that their own particular situations produce the feelings of being 'squashed'. Pointing out that there is an intermediary between situations and feelings that they can exercise some control over of itself generates hope even if they are having difficulty identifying quite what their self-talk is. After completion of a series of such pro formas the identified B's are usually found to be traceable to a small set of dysfunctional silent assumptions. Knowing that any early manifestations of non-assertive behaviour are likely to be attributable to one or other of the silent assumptions, each of the set can be tried on for size as it were, to see if it accounts for the emotional response in the particular situation. This then allows a more speedy generation of a rational response, D, than would otherwise be the case. In this way non-assertive behaviours can be nipped in the bud. (For a more detailed discussion of how rational responses to negative automatic thoughts can be generated, see Chapter 6.)

In the final 4 to 6 sessions of the programme members should be asked to use the ABCD pro forma across the range of situations they encounter which make them socially anxious. Some of the more common automatic thoughts include: 'Anxiety is dangerous',

'People are put off by my anxiety', 'It would be dreadful if I said the wrong thing', and 'They will find out how awful I am if I talk'. Such thoughts can be challenged in terms of: their validity, 'Is this really wholly true, partially true, or untrue?'; utility, 'How far does it actually get me believing . . .? Would it be better acting as if I believed . . . and see how far that gets me?'; consistency, 'Am I applying one standard for myself and another for other people? If it's OK, acceptable, for . . . to . . ., then why not for me?' Any particular negative automatic thought may be tested via an appeal to either validity, utility, or consistency, or some judicious combination.

Finally, given the difficulty of social skills programmes in general to demonstrate generalizability, monthly booster sessions for at least three months are necessary to check that skills taught are still being utilized, and to deal with any new problems that have arisen. However, the onus in these sessions should be on the group to distil the material already taught and suggest solutions to problems. In this way the social skills group can become self supporting with minimal professional involvement, the therapist acting more as a consultant.

Part 4

A COGNITIVE-BEHAVIOURAL APPROACH TO DISORDERS OF SELF-REGULATION

Chapter Eleven

SELF-REGULATORY DISORDERS: THEORY AND ASSESSMENT

Disorders of self-regulation present therapists with perhaps the greatest therapeutic challenge. Outcome studies on the long-term effects of various treatment modalities make dismal reading, at least at first glance. Hunt *et al.* (1971) compared relapse rates across a range of addictions including heroin, smoking, and alcohol addiction. Independent of the particular addiction, two thirds of treated clients had relapsed within three months, and 80 per cent within twelve months. However, these figures present a slightly over-pessimistic picture in that they do not distinguish between single slips and full-blown relapses. Nevertheless the therapeutic efficacy of treatment modalities is more questionable than with, say, the treatment of depression or child behaviour problems. There are, however, a handful of treatment studies across various areas that have demonstrated a treatment effect and perhaps point the way forward.

Hunt and Azrin (1973) compared the effects of a community reinforcement programme in helping alcoholics modify their post discharge environment with the functioning of a control group. Follow up over a six-month period indicated that the community reinforcement patients remained more sober than the controls, spent more time in employment, with their families, and out of institutions. The reinforcement programme was wide ranging including teaching job finding skills and contingency contracting for those with marital or family difficulties. In addition, for those who were isolated attempts were made to arrange a foster family, and a self-supporting social club for clients was developed. Essentially external sources of reinforcement were manipulated with a decreased opportunity to engage in a drinking lifestyle. This study is particularly instructive as it suggests that modifying a client's specific dissatisfactions with his/her environment, that is modifying the 'psychological environment' as Lewin (1951) put it, is potentially of key importance in any relapse prevention programme.

In Chapter 13 a cognitive-behavioural programme to prevent relapse is described in which there is an explicit focus on modifying the psychological environment. Cognitive-behavioural programmes for bulimia nervosa have yielded positive results, but it is not clear whether the active ingredients for change in the programmes were actually derived from a cognitive-behavioural theoretical base. Bulimics are usually 5 to 15 per cent underweight and their behaviour is characterized by phases of binge eating and severely restricted dieting accompanied by at least weekly and often daily self-induced vomiting. The bulimic becomes predisposed to renal damage, although usually the only obvious health problems in the short term are dental, menstrual, and a chronic hoarseness. Kirkley *et al.* (1985) have undertaken a controlled trial of group-conducted cognitive-behavioural treatment. Twenty-eight bulimics were assigned to a group cognitive-behavioural treatment package or to a controlled condition. The latter involved sixteen weekly group meetings in which participants admitted to and shared their bulimic experiences, reflecting on the consequences of their addiction and the situations in which they would binge eat and vomit. A detailed description of the cognitive-behavioural treatment programme used is provided by Fairburn (1984).

The core programme is in two phases. The first phase involves prescription of a regular pattern of eating and avoidance or re-arrangement of situational causes to vomit. Health information is also provided on the effects of bulimic behaviour. Sessions in the first phase are twice weekly for four weeks. The second phase involves eight weekly sessions focusing around problem solving and cognitive restructuring procedures. Kirkley *et al.* (1985) found that there was a 95 per cent reduction in binge eating and vomiting for the cognitive-behavioural group during the sixteen weeks of treatment, significantly greater than the reduction in the control group. However the control group did also show sizeable reductions in binge eating and purging, and by the three months' follow-up session had attained similar results to the CB group. Nevertheless the CB programme had exerted an immediate impact over and above the impact of group support. More recently

Fairburn (1987) has conducted a comparison of cognitive behaviour therapy, behaviour therapy, and interpersonal therapy; and the preliminary findings are that clients in each group are responding equally well. Interestingly, the interpersonal therapy condition involves no mention of food at all. This raises the possibility that there is some shared characteristic between the therapies that is responsible for change. Fairburn's study calls into question an exclusive focus on a cognitive-behavioural approach. Cooper and Fairburn (1984) have used a modified form of their CB programme for bulimics with anorexics, and the response has been mixed. A major difficulty was that these clients were often poorly motivated, seeing no need of treatment. The problem of motivation also arises in a particularly acute way in the treatment of opiate abuse. Typically, drug agencies 'fail' to engage the opiate addict in treatment, most agencies in the community reporting an average two to three contacts per addict. Motivation is also often a problem with the alcoholic. In the next chapter the issue of motivation is addressed in detail and strategies for enhancing motivation are discussed.

Controlled studies of the treatment of opiate abuse are conspicuous by their absence. In part this arises because of the methodological difficulties involved, not the least of which is keeping trace of the addict in order to perform assessments. In one study of the determinants of relapse amongst opiate users (Phillips 1989) the researchers had to make an average of six attempts to make contact with an addict; the record was held by one worker who made nineteen attempts to make contact with a particular addict! The use of heroin to relieve depression is quite common (Taintor and D'Amanda 1973). This suggests that a therapy that is effective in relieving depression such as cognitive therapy might, in suitably modified form, constitute an important ingredient of an effective treatment programme for substance abuse. Negative emotional states are, however, only one of the determinants of relapse across the addictions. Cummings, Gordon, and Marlatt (1980) in an analysis of 311 initial relapse episodes obtained from clients with a variety of addictions, identified the factors in Table 5.

Table 5 Analysis of Relapse Situations with Alcoholics, Smokers, and Heroin Addicts

Relapse situation	Alcoholics (n = 70)	Smokers (n = 64)	Heroin addicts (n = 129)
Intrapersonal determinants			
Negative emotional states	38%	37%	19%
Negative phsyical states	3%	2%	9%
Positive emotional states	–	6%	10%
Testing personal control	9%	–	2%
Urges and temptations	11%	5%	5%
TOTAL	61%	50%	45%
Interpersonal determinants			
Interpersonal conflict	18%	15%	14%
Social pressure	18%	32%	36%
Positive emotional states	3%	3%	5%
TOTAL	39%	50%	55%

Three-quarters of all relapsers across each addiction are accounted for by three factors: interpersonal conflict, negative emotional status, and social pressure. The relative importance of the three factors varies somewhat from addiction to addiction. Nevertheless it is clear that a cognitive-behavioural programme to prevent relapse amongst substance abusers must go beyond a narrow focus on negative emotional states, and embrace coping with conflicts and social pressure. Drawing on the positive results of Hunt and Azrin (1973) any such programme must also attend to modification of the psychological environment. The programme described for giving up addictions in Chapter 13 is accordingly a broad-spectrum cognitive-behavioural approach, but one still in need of empirical evaluation.

Tuchfield (1981) studied the recovery process of a sample of alcoholics who recovered without formal treatment. On the basis of this work he proposed a two-stage model of recovery. This model has considerable utility across the addictions, though given the origins of the model it must be viewed as tentative.

The first stage is concerned with the recognition by the individual that his/her addiction has become problematic. Tuchfield's (1981) work suggests that the decision to abstain is often arrived at in an idiosyncratic way, with relatively trivial incidents often acting as the spear. For example, 'It was the start of a new term at school, so I just decided to stop'. In some cases the decision to stop is arrived at after a long period of weighing the costs and benefits of the addiction, whilst in others it is a more instantaneous response. The second stage of the model is concerned with maintenance of the resolution. In this stage external factors such as relationships and employment appear to have influenced the scope an addict had to modify his/her lifestyle in such a way as to maintain the initial resolution. Some success in maintaining the resolution enhances psychological well-being, which in turn makes maintenance of the resolution more likely.

Prochaska and DiClimente (1983) have produced what seems to be a more fine-grained version of Tuchfield's model. It should be noted however that Prochaska and DiClimente's model of the self-change process related to cigarette smokers, and though it is convenient to apply it to other addictions it is nevertheless an extrapolation. Applied to, say, opiate abuse one may well encounter deficiencies in the use of model and further refinements might be necessary. There are five stages in Prochaska and DiClimente's model:

1 *Precontemplation* In this phase clients are not aware of the fact that they have problems.
2 *Contemplation* In this stage clients start realizing that there are personal problems but have not yet made a decision to change.
3 *Action* The act of quitting. This is perhaps the most obvious stage.
4 *Maintenance* The maintenance stage begins the moment after initiation of abstinence or control. In this phase the task is to retain changes made.
5 *Relapse* If maintenance is unsuccessful, relapse is experienced and the cycle of stages is begun again, i.e. back to Stage 1 and onwards. Typically, escape from the cycle is possible after cumulative trials, eventually exiting at Stage 4.

Prochaska and DiClimente's model captures the dynamic features of giving up addictions rather than the rather static conceptualization of Tuchfield's. There are clear overlaps between the two models however; Stages 1 and 2 of Prochaska and DiClimente's model correspond to the first, the decision-making phase, of Tuchfield's model. Stages 3 to 5 of Prochaska and DiClimente's model have been collapsed into a single stage in Tuchfield's maintenance phase.

Historically, the focus of treatment for addictive behaviours has been on Prochaska and DiClimente's Stage 3, the act of quitting. This tends to be matched by a client focusing on the mechanics of quitting. Such a narrow focus frequently means that both client and therapist can quickly become frustrated by engaging in a treatment programme before the client has thoroughly considered the implications of embarking on this course. Not surprisingly, many clients who enter treatment default. Mark Twain succinctly underlined the problems of an exclusive Stage 3 focus: 'Quitting smoking is easy – I've done it a hundred times'. This suggests that Stages 4 and 5 (maintenance and relapse) are of key importance in overcoming an addiction. Learning the specific cognitive and behavioural skills needed to cope with the situation and cues that were hitherto the springboard into an addictive lifestyle is an important determinant of maintenance of the resolution to abstain or control the behaviour. Naturalistic (without formal treatment) studies of cigarette smokers and overeaters (Schachter 1982) have shown that 60–70 per cent of those intent on changing their habits 'ultimately' did so. This can be contrasted with the high relapse rate after single formal treatments mentioned earlier (Hunt *et al.* 1971). The implication for treatment programmes is that clients probably will relapse (Stage 5 of Prochaska and DiClimente's model); but if the therapist encourages learning from the mistake or slip, and nudges the client in the direction of further attempts then ultimate success is more likely. Chapter 12 is concerned with Stages 1 and 2 of Prochaska and DiClimente's model, motivation, whilst Chapter 13 is concerned with the actual treatment of addictive behaviour.

ASSESSMENT

Assessment for the 'treatment' of drug addiction requires first of all a clarification of goals. Is the client seeking to abstain from the particular substance? seeking controlled use of the substance? seeking controlled use after a period of abstinence? or, alternatively, not wishing to alter their usage of drugs but wanting a 'supportive' relationship in which to discuss his/her general life problems? The spread of AIDS is facilitated by the sharing of needles and syringes and the consequent injection of infected blood. Many addicts however will not countenance abstinence, and other options devoted to containment of AIDS rather than abstaining from opiate abuse may become viable goals. Stallard *et al.* (1987) suggest a hierarchy of levels of outcome with respect to opiate abuse as follows:

Abstinence
Using but not injecting
Using but injecting with sterile equipment
Using but not sharing equipment
Using and still sharing

She suggests that any movement to a 'higher' level of use could be seen as a successful outcome, while relapse could be described in terms of moving to more dangerous use, the worst being needle sharing. There are clearly a wide range of options for substance abusers and, particularly since the advent of AIDS, problem opiate abusers. The decision-making process can be extremely brief and clear-cut, or it can involve protracted contact with a therapist and/or a supportive group. Facilitating the decision-making process is discussed in the next chapter, on motivation.

Possibly the most comprehensive assessment device for substance abuse is the Addiction Severity Index (ASI, Erdlen *et al.* 1978). The ASI takes a therapist 20 to 30 minutes to complete, and is in the form of a semi-structured interview covering six domains:

1. Substance abuse 4. Legal
2. Medical 5. Family/Social
3. Psychological 6. Employment/Support

The first section in each of the problem areas focuses on objective information pertaining to problem symptoms. In the second section of each problem area using a five-point scale, the client is requested to rate the extent to which he/she has been bothered or troubled by problems in the area of function and the extent to which he/she feels treatment for those problems is important. The data from the objective information and client report sections of each problem area are integrated by the interviewer to produce a ten-point severity rating in each domain. The ASI covers the previous thirty days and is a useful way of taking monthly snap-shots of clients' drug and drug-related behaviours, and thereby gauging the impact of decision-making and/or relapse prevention programmes.

In practice, semi-structured interviews such as the ASI are likely to be forsaken in favour of less time-consuming self-report measures, though they ought to be seen as complementary and not as alternatives. One particularly useful self-report measure to assess the degree of a client's alcohol dependence is the Short Alcohol Dependence Data (SADD, Davidson and Raistrick 1986) Questionnaire. The SADD consists of fifteen items answered on a four-point scale (never, sometimes, often, nearly always). Sample items include 'Do you drink as much as you want irrespective of what you are doing next day?' and 'Do you find difficulty getting the thought of drink out of your mind?' The instrument seeks to measure the degree of alcohol dependence rather than classify a client as alcoholic or not. As such it reflects the rejection of the term 'alcoholism' in the International Classification of Diseases (WHO 1979) and its replacement by alcohol dependence syndrome. Dependence is seen on a continuum ranging from 'mild' to 'severe' with mild dependence being a statistically normal condition. According to the ICD the elements of the syndrome are: i) repeated withdrawal symptoms; ii) relief drinking; iii) narrowing of drinking repertoire – the time and context of drinking becoming invariable; iv) giving priority to drink-seeking behaviour over previously regarded important behaviours; v) increasing tolerance – having to take more alcohol to achieve the same effect; vi) subjective awareness of a compulsion to drink – impaired control; vii) rapid reinstatement of all the other elements if drinking takes place after a period of abstinence. From a relapse prevention point of view an instrument which helps pin-point the situations in which a client would likely slip is at a premium. The Relapse Precipitants Inventory (RPI) (Litman *et al.* 1983) does just this. The RPI consists of twenty-five items answered on a seven-point scale from 'certainly will' to 'not at all'. Sample items include: 'when I pass a pub or off-licence', 'when I feel tense', 'when there are rows and arguments at home', and 'when there are special occasions, like Christmas, birthdays, etc.' Responses to some of these items carry fairly straightforward treatment implications; for example, the therapist might suggest to a client who had indicated he is easily 'lured' into a pub on his way home from work that initially he avoid the pub and travel home a different way. However response to other items suggests wider enquiry into the social and cognitive domains. (The instrument can easily be adapted for use with other substance abusers but the instrument's psychometric properties are then unknown.)

Corney and Clare's (1985) Social Questionnaire (Appendix B) assesses clients' satisfaction with various aspects of their environment; as already mentioned these are often crucial determinants of relapse. This instrument is particularly useful in keeping the therapist mindful of the clients' pressing concerns so that therapy continues to be seen by the client as relevant to his or her whole lifestyle. The client's ability to avoid relapse will also probably depend on the modification of salient dysfunctional drug-related attitudes.

In the absence of a drug instrument encapsulating such attitudes the author has developed the Drug Related Attitude Questionnaire (DRAQ) (Scott 1986, see Appendix L). It has been found a useful adjunct to therapy but its psychometric properties have only just begun to be examined. Preliminary analysis suggests a Cronbachs alpha = 0.82 and significant correlations of 0.5 and 0.52 with Beck Depression and Hopelessness Scales. The DRAQ contains eighteen items answered on a seven-point scale from 'totally agree' to 'totally disagree'. Sample items include 'If I slip and take drugs it is useful to try to control myself after that', 'I have got to do just what I feel', 'I have nothing to look forward to', and 'If you cannot do something well there is little point in doing it at all'.

Chapter Twelve

MOTIVATION

Problems of 'motivation' are not peculiar to addictive behaviours. Question marks are often raised variously about the 'motivation' of couples who drop out of marital therapy, parents who drop out of parent training programmes, and depressed clients who fail to complete homework assignments. Non-compliance can be viewed as a continuum from dropping out of a programme at one extreme to not completing a particular homework assignment at the other. So the problem of 'motivation' is at least a minor issue in all therapeutic endeavours. However with the addictive behaviours the 'unmotivated clients' seem often to be in the majority and seem to threaten to sabotage the whole therapeutic enterprise.

Motivation, or rather the lack of it, has traditionally been viewed as an integral characteristic of the client, first manifested when he/she fails to follow through the therapist's edicts. In this conceptualization the client is easily blamed. The participation or non-participation in the treatment plan is viewed as the client's responsibility. Neither the therapist nor the agency accepts responsibility for either providing what the client wants or seeing that the client receives what is wanted elsewhere. The fact that, in drug agencies in particular, there is often a steady through-put of clients can blind therapist and agency to the fact that the clients simply do not like what is on offer! To use an analogy, they soon go off to shop elsewhere only to find that the other shops are much the same. What may be needed is a wider range of goods on sale in the shops, and perhaps also more diversity and communication between the businesses. Viewing the clients, and in particular the addicts, as customers affords them greater respect, and the onus shifts to therapists and agencies to see that they are offering what is actually wanted rather than the particular form of service delivery to which they are attached. This suggests that client evaluation of programmes in agencies, using instruments such as Larsen *et al.* (1979), ought to be obligatory.

Kelly (1955) has suggested that clients will only move in a direction that makes life more meaningful. Given the choice, for example, between smoking and non-smoking a person might continue to smoke because they know exactly what the implications are and it is at least a predictable lifestyle, whilst to become a non-smoker means entering uncharted territory with few landmarks, and the implications of making this choice seem by comparison shrouded in mystery. From this vantage point, clients are seen as making 'purposeful' decisions, though it often may not seem like that to the therapist. The therapist's first task is to attempt to make sense of the 'purposeful' thinking and behaviour of the client.

A client's refusal to travel the road advised by the therapist may arise either because they believe they do not have the ability to make the journey (Bandura's (1977) efficacy expectations), or because they anticipate the journey will be unrewarding (Bandura's (1977) outcome expectations). (Both efficacy expectations and outcome expectations are part of Bandura's concept of self-efficacy.) Much of an addict's current behaviour can be understood by the catastrophic anticipations he/she has of embarking on any other road. Within a cognitive-behavioural framework, motivation is not seen as a personality trait – a something which some clients have and some don't. Rather it is a product of the interaction with the therapist. If the therapist can help generate goals that are 'meaningful' to the client then 'compliant' behaviours are likely.

The process of helping clients make decisions about treatment goals is now elaborated. This constitutes the first stage of the two-stage process of recovery outlined by Tuchfield (1976). First the general conditions for enabling effective decision making are discussed, then specific strategies for decision making with addictive behaviours are considered. Finally the techniques of motivational interviewing are described.

CONDITIONS FOR DECISION MAKING

According to Janis (1983) people will weigh the benefits of a recommended course of action against the costs only when their dominant coping pattern is vigilance. The vigilance pattern occurs *only* when three conditions are present: 1) the person is aware of serious risks for whichever alternative is chosen (that is, conflict is aroused); 2) the person is hopeful or optimistic about finding a satisfactory solution, and 3) the person believes that there is adequate time to search and deliberate before a final decision is required. Janis suggests further that variables that have hitherto been found to be linked to adherence to professional recommendations – such as whether the client has social support at home and whether there is supportive interaction with the therapist – only exert their marked effect in the context of the vigiliance coping pattern being elicited. The implication of Janis's (1983) work is that the decision-making phase of treatment of addictive behaviours should have as its focus shifting the client from non-vigilant to vigilant coping pattern. At one extreme the client who minimizes experienced symptoms might be challenged with more accurate information about the particular symptoms. At the other extreme the client who has become hypervigilant – searching for and trying every quack remedy – might be challenged about his beliefs concerning the efficacy of a long-term systematic programme. Janis's third condition for vigilance suggests that this first phase in the treatment of addictive behaviours cannot be rushed. The engagement/decision-making phase may well be a protracted affair depending on the needs and circumstances of a particular client. Janis has suggested a number of essential ingredients for a positive motivating relationship between the therapist and client. These involve: 1) becoming a dependable enhancer of the client's self-esteem, giving consistently positive feedback conveying acceptance, and eliciting a moderate level of self-disclosure rather than a very low or a very high level; 2) avoiding impairment of the supportive relationship when making recommendations (or endorsing clients' expressed goals) by making it clear that any demands being made are very limited in scope and that failure to live up to those demands following an attempt to do so will not change the therapist's basic attitude of acceptance.

TWO STRATEGIES FOR DECISION MAKING

a) *Decision balance sheet* Janis and Mann (1977) have constructed a decision balance sheet procedure illustrated in Figure 4.

Figure 4 Balance Sheet Procedure; after Janis and Mann (1977)

	'If I continue the addictive behaviour'	'If I give up/control the addictive behaviour'
1. Practical gains and losses for myself		
2. Practical gains and losses for people important to me.		
3. Self-approval disapproval		
4. Approval or disapproval of people important to me		

The pro-forma in Figure 4 asks the client to contrast the continuance of the addictive behaviour with cessation (or controlled used) in four areas. The first two are the utilitarian gains and losses for themselves and significant others. The last two areas relate to the client's own self-esteem and that of significant others. It should be noted that the pro forma anticipates the client will see both gains and losses arising from each alternative course of action. Janis and Mann hypothesize that a client who, for example, omits to specify the losses accruing from giving up an addictive behaviour has probably made an unstable decision to quit an addiction. Similarly a client who is over-optimistic about what will be gained from cessation of the addictive behaviour may well be making a short-lived decision. The more complete and accurate the balance sheet, the more likely it is that a stable decision has been reached. Having a client complete a 'balance sheet' at intervals can help chart the stability of decisions being made and allow the client's 'readiness' for a withdrawal/relapse prevention programme to be gauged.

Marlatt and Gordon (1985) have produced a refinement of Janis and Mann's (1977) Balance Sheet in the form of a decision matrix.

The most important difference is that Marlatt and Gordon's matrix makes a further distinction between immediate consequences and delayed consequences. This refinement can be easily integrated into the pro forma of Figure 4, by splitting each of the eight cells into two, one part of each cell describing immediate consequences and the second part of each cell the delayed consequences. The amalgamated pro forma then has sixteen instead of eight cells.

b) *Ultimate consequences technique* A major problem in overcoming addictive behaviours is that any negative consequences of the behaviour tend to be in the long term, with positive consequences reinforcing the addictive behaviour in the short term. The Ultimate Consequences Technique (Horan 1971) attempts to surmount this difficulty. Essentially the strategy involves pairing a long-term negative consequence of continuing the addictive behaviour (i.e. 'I'll lose the wife and kids, the only ones I can trust') with a positive long-term consequence of overcoming the behaviour (e.g. 'I'll be pleased with myself for keeping in good shape again'). The client is helped to generate a list of such positive and negative pairs. The client then repeats the list of positive and negative consequences in response to certain regularly occurring cues in the day, e.g. when he makes a cup of tea or coffee or sits down. The procedure is enhanced if the client is encouraged vividly to imagine each of the consequences. For example, the client might be asked to imagine the dejected look on his face if his wife and children left him, and try and feel the churning of the stomach he would probably experience. Likewise he would be asked to imagine the healthy glow and feeling of well-being he would experience from being fit again.

It would be a gross oversimplification of intervention in the decision-making phase to suggest that use of either of the two strategies described above would of themselves 'propel' clients into treatment. Rather, such techniques have to be embedded in the context of a supportive therapeutic relationship. Motivational interviewing as described by Miller (1983) makes explicit the essential components of such a relationship.

MOTIVATIONAL INTERVIEWING

The strategies of motivational interviewing (MI) were developed initially with problem drinkers in mind (Miller 1983), but have been subsequently adapted for use with heroin addicts in the context of motivational milieu therapy (MMT) (van Bilsen 1987). From what follows it will be clear that MI can also be easily adapted to other addictive behaviours such as eating disorders, or cigarette smoking. With some modification the strategies presented here could be applied to behaviour change areas beyond the addictive behaviours. For example, for a client distressed about his marriage, undecided whether to separate or not, and too hurt to countenance marital therapy, Miller (1983) has suggested the following sequence of intervention strategies in MI.

i) *Eliciting self-motivational statements* This strategy is based on the principle that stable decisions are more likely to be made by clients as a result of their own reasoning or experience than on the advice of other people. The role of the therapist is then simply to underline and reflect back the clients' expressed concerns about their addictive behaviour. This requires the therapist to summarize what a client says in a very specific way and reflect it back. For example, 'Have I got this right, are you saying that if you continue your present behaviour there is a fair chance of you losing your job?' The client would probably respond 'It's not just a fair chance I'll lose my job if I continue going on as I have been doing, there's a good chance'. In this exchange the therapist is concerned not to import what he would see as other negative consequences of the client's drinking; thus he would refrain from saying 'You're going to lose everything, job *and family*'. The importation of the therapist's perception of 'other' negative consequences, or the exaggeration of the stated negative consequences, is likely to be seen by the client as a ploy and moralizing, resulting in alienation. Reflecting back the client's concerns encourages the client to reiterate them; in this way the client's awareness of what he/she believes about the negative consequences of his/her addictive behaviour is increased. This strategy follows the basic psychological principle that you learn what you believe by verbalizing it.

Paradox may also be used to elicit self-motivational statements.

For example, 'The only problem drink seems to create for you is with the job; is it really worth the effort of changing?' Playing the devil's advocate in this way usually produces a look of astonishment from the client and the expression of a catalogue of other reasons for changing the addictive behaviour. The client tends to argue in the opposite direction to the therapist. A response from the therapist such as 'So you are saying, it is absolutely impossible to manage your addictive behaviour, because you have tried before and failed'. This will be likely to bring a retort of the form 'Well no, I have always tried to give up staying in this area, maybe if I went down south, to my sister's it could be different.' The therapist's summaries and reflections of the client's conversation are selective focusing on the expressed concerns. In the reflection process the therapist can shift the discussion away from red herrings. For example, a key principle of MI is that labelling is not important; what matters are the problems the person is having in relation to the addictive behaviour. Labelling is actively de-emphasized. Thus a client who says 'I can't be an alcoholic because . . .' may be reflected with 'I imagine that's confusing for you. On the one hand you can see that there are serious problems developing around your alcoholism, and on the other it seems like the label "alcoholic" does not quite fit because things don't look that bad'. The underlying strategy in eliciting self-motivational statements is to leave the client with the responsibility of elaborating the case for changing their addictive behaviour.

The effect of eliciting self-motivational statements from the client is to set up a state of cognitive dissonance. On the one hand, clients are increasingly aware of the negative consequences of their actions, but on the other there is the attraction of current drinking behaviour. This state of internal conflict is a necessary precondition for clients to contemplate making a decision about their addictive behaviour. The first stage of motivational interviewing is concerned with moving clients from what Prochaska and DiClemente (1982) term the precontemplation stage, in which there is little awareness of the negative consequences, to a contemplation stage in which negative consequences are increasingly acknowledged. It should be clear however that the way of effecting this transition is very different to the traditional confrontational mode of interaction with the addicted person. Such confrontation may indeed induce cognitive dissonance in the client but there is a danger that it will be resolved in unhelpful ways. The client may well seek to reduce the conflict by denial, effectively saying 'The negative consequences are not that bad at all'. Equally unhelpful is the possibility that the client may see the therapist's implied disapproval as yet further confirmation of his or her negative self-image; the client is then able to effectively resolve the dissonance by saying 'Yes, I know I am a bum, but what more can you expect of a bum than to continue to drink?' Similarly the therapist may unwittingly aid the resolution of the dissonance in an unhelpful direction by proclaiming life-long and total abstinence as the only meaningful goal. Such a proclamation lowers the client's sense of self-efficacy, 'I just have not got what it takes for that'. The client resolves this internal conflict by deciding 'I have just got no other option but to continue drinking as I have been doing, it is outside my control'. In MI the therapist has to be extremely careful that, having induced the necessary internal conflict (cognitive dissonance) in the client, he or she does not in any way short circuit the effective resolution of this conflict.

To take a further example, A. was complaining and saddened that his adult children had neither contacted him nor sent him a card over the Christmas period. He felt they had just grown tired of him and his drink problem. A. had himself already become painfully aware of the negative consequences of his drink problem. It would have been inappropriate for the therapist in such an instance to reply, 'Well, if you're going to drink you are going to lose your health as well'. Such a comment would have further diminished his self-esteem. Instead the therapist first acknowledged the client's pain and conflict and then went on to enhance A's self-esteem, 'Sounds like at the moment, you are at a crossroads, and in a lot of pain trying to decide which way to go. There is one sign to the family and another towards the same drinking behaviour. Whichever way you go, it is worth pausing at traffic lights to stop and think whether you are really as bad as you say you are. Okay, so you feel you've messed up the last five years for your wife and kids. But if you play the video in your mind of what you gave to them in the first fifteen years, that was pretty good. In fact you could say overall you've done pretty well only messing up a quarter of your marriage so far!'

Effective resolution of the cognitive dissonance can be enhanced by increasing the client's self-efficacy. With this in mind, at a later session with client A., the therapist commented, 'The picture you paint at least of the first ten years of marriage is pretty good, and it shows that you can really make life work for you and get on with people. In fact, maybe the only problem in the end was that you were too friendly, buying drinks for everyone in the pub, becoming too popular for your own good. It just became "If you want something ask A." To feel OK again it seems that for you it is just a question of regaining lost ground; you don't actually have to learn anything new except maybe how to avoid the "popularity" game'.

ii) *Objective assessment* In eliciting the client's concerns about a drug or drink problem the therapist is forming a model of the addictive behaviour and the context in which it operates. At a more formal level the instruments described in the previous chapter may be used to assess the severity of dependence. Such assessments can be made the subject of ongoing reviews.

iii) *Education* MI almost invariably involves some degree of education of clients and often their relatives also. These educational requirements vary greatly from client to client. Some of the more common points made by therapists in MI are:
- the addictive behaviour is learned and not a disease and can be unlearned.
- there is little physical inevitability about continued use of a drug after initial ingestion. Continued use is for the most part a decision.
- it is a fruitless endeavour classifying people as 'alcoholic' or 'not alcoholic'.

iv) *Summary* Periodically the therapist draws together the first three phases in a summary statement.

v) *Transition* A transition stage has been reached when a critical mass of motivation has been developed to usher in the determination stage. This is the third of Prochaska and DiClimente's (1982) stages of change following on from pre-contemplation and contemplation. Miller (1983) has commented that this stage is often an ephemeral state, 'as if a window has opened temporarily. The individual has a certain amount of time to get through the window into the next stage then the window closes again'. The determination phase may be followed by an action phase in which the individual attempts to modify the addictive behaviour. The breadth of options canvassed by the therapist may affect the likelihood of a client selecting an option which they see to be both meaningful and within their capacity. So that, for example, a therapist might discuss with a client the strengths and difficulties of controlled drinking. A too restricted focus may result in a client inappropriately adopting an action-change strategy, only to find that modification of addictive behaviour is short lived and they arrive back at Prochaska and DiClimente's (1982) pre-contemplation phase. Successful use of action-change strategies means that a client enters what Prochaska and DiClimente (1982) term the final maintenance phase. Strategies to both avoid and minimize the effects of slips are discussed in detail in the next chapter.

The time taken to move clients from pre-contemplation to action will be extremely variable. For example, van Bilsen (1987) has adopted MI for use with heroin addicts. When heroin addicts attended his clinic for methadone maintenance they had to spend an hour a day in what he terms a 'motivational milieu'. This consisted of a living-room setting in which clients shared their concerns in the presence of a social worker using MI strategies. No properly controlled trial has been conducted of the efficacy of such procedures. However, van Bilsen has reported impressive results of individual cases who had attended MMT for two to three years. Clearly, however, some clients may at referral already be at the contemplation stage and much less time will be required to move to the determination and action stages.

Chapter Thirteen

NEW HABITS FOR OLD

The focus of the previous chapter was on increasing clients' motivation for change. The goal was to move clients to Prochaska and DiClimente's (1982) Determination Stage – in which they are on the threshold of making active changes in their behaviour. The Active Change Stage and Maintenance Stages are the last two phases of Prochaska and DiClimente's (1982) model of change. These final two phases are the focus of this chapter. The relapse prevention programme described here consists of approximately eight individual sessions at weekly intervals with monthly follow-up for six months.

ENTERING ACTIVE CHANGE

Active change and maintenance strategies may be instigated by the addicted person with or without therapeutic help. Indeed probably most of those who recover from an addiction do so under their own steam! Both self-helpers and clients usually instigate change with a period of avoidance of the situations which act as cues for the addictive behaviour. A functional analysis of the addictive behaviour can serve to make explicit those situations which need handling differently. Having the clients complete a diary retrospectively about recent lapses and to continue to monitor the addictive behaviours provides valuable data on which to base change strategies. A useful format for the diary is shown in Table 6.

Table 6 Addiction Diary

Setting (Where were you? Who was present? What were you doing?)	Antecedents (What was happening? How were you feeling prior to using drug?)	Amount taken	Way in which taking (Drank?/ Injected?/ Smoked?)	Consequences (What happened after you had used/drank – How did you you feel?)

Such a diary can be complemented by use of the standardized assessment devices described in Chapter 11. In particular completion of Litman *et al.*'s (1983) Relapse Precipitants Inventory can provide information on the high risk situations for the client. For example, if a client indicates that he/she certainly will use drugs if he/she passes somewhere where they are available, then the treatment implications, at least initially, would be to arrange contingencies to avoid that particular setting. Whilst behavioural changes of this nature are a necessary condition for change in addictive behaviours, they may be facilitated and secured by cognitive changes.

Client A lived alone, and was a teacher. He was very concerned about the children he taught, because he saw them as being particularly disadvantaged. He demanded very high standards of his colleagues and was very perfectionist himself. On the way home from work he would feel drained and experience a sinking feeling about arriving home to an empty flat. As soon as he got home he would reward himself for putting so much into the day with a beer, each beer was followed by another beer. Of late he had found he had not prepared materials for school the next day and spent most mornings recovering from the excesses of the previous evening. His self-esteem had plummeted, he felt he was letting the children down, and he had become increasingly irritable with colleagues. He sought therapeutic help after his headmaster told him to 'pull yourself together or disciplinary action will be taken'. Completion of the Drug Related Attitude Questionnaire – DRAQ (see Appendix L) at assessment had revealed A's perfectionist attitudes and it was clear these had to be tackled in tandem with behavioural change. A. decided i) not to stock drink in his flat; ii) to have his evening meal at a cafe on his way home from work where he knew and could chat to the proprietor, and iii) to tell himself that as far as the children were concerned he was running a marathon not a sprint and he had to pace himself accordingly.

Such active change strategies are only advisable if the balance of client concerns is more with the pursuit of life goals to which the addictive behaviour constitutes a roadblock. Recommendation of active change strategies in the absence of life goals is likely to prove an ill-fated endeavour.

Probably all the 'motivated' clients will carry some degree of ambivalence to their addictive behaviour and the extent of this ambivalence will vary within an individual from time to time. The task of the therapist is to persistently tip the balance of motivation in the direction of overtly healthy motivations.

ROADBLOCKS TO ACTIVE CHANGE

In the early stages of active change the client may encounter two major roadblocks to the ongoing process of change, a debilitating sense of hopelessness and a low tolerance of frustration. These are discussed in turn.

i) Hopelessness
Attempts at active change are likely to be shortlived if a client is not more or less constantly 'hopeful' of a better lifestyle. Literally the problem becomes 'Why bother changing?' The generation of hope and its constant rekindling is then a major therapeutic endeavour. This process can be aided by a detailed specification of the 'destinations' to which the client wishes to travel. Positive outcome expectations can be encouraged by having the client

elaborate on the benefits of reaching the chosen 'destinations'. Such expectations serve as a motivator, prompting the client into action.

Continuing the metaphor of the client making journeys to various destinations it is necessary first of all to increase a client's belief that they have the capacity to make the journey, that is to buttress their efficacy expectations. Clients' confidence in their ability to make the journey is enhanced by the achievement of smaller sub-goals en route. This requires further specifications of some of the first stations to be met along the various routes. The steps have ideally to be seen by clients as manageable but presenting some difficulty. Clients are inoculated against failure to achieve the first step by the therapist explaining in advance that not achieving a goal was a distinct possibility, and an intermediate step might actually be a more realistic sub-goal at this stage. Clients' appraisals of their endeavours exert a crucial influence on their behaviour. For example to continue travelling in the early phases of treatment it is necessary that clients congratulate themselves on how far they have come rather than castigate themselves for how far they still have to travel.

The addictive behaviour is considered only in the context of the achievement of sub-goals and goals. So the discussion of the addictive behaviour becomes a less highly charged issue, and the behaviour itself comes to be regarded as an inefficient means of realizing goals which therefore requires modification.

The reduction of a client's sense of hopelessness may be begun by helping to map out the ultimate 'destinations' in some or all of the following six areas: work/unemployment, housing, finances, social life, marriage/living alone, and family.

Client B decided:
1) he would like to work outdoors preferably in forestry;
2) he would like a flat of his own away from his parents;
3) he would like to have enough money to travel to work in summer camps in the USA;
4) he wanted to make a new circle of friends;
5) he wanted to stop stammering when he talked to members of the opposite sex;
6) he wanted a better way of relating to his highly critical father. Each goal was broken down to sub-goals.

Within the first four sessions B had taken steps towards the following goals. Re goal 1 he enquired about helping conservation volunteers; goal 4 – he contacted an old school friend, and goal 6 – he decided to start painting the outside of the house to avert his father's criticism that he did not pay his way.

ii) Low Tolerance of Frustration

During the early sessions of the programme much of the clients' concern is usually focused on the distressing withdrawal symptoms they are experiencing. The client's sleep and concentration are usually impaired and much discussion can be taken up with whether, say, methadone is being reduced too fast, or whether they are being prescribed an inadequate dosage of tranquillizers. This ultimately can be a rather sterile discussion, as some discomfort during the withdrawal process is inevitable. It is usually more fruitful for the therapist to refocus the discussion in terms of making the discomfort more manageable. One way of managing the discomfort is by having the client prime themselves as to the time limited nature of the discomfort. Each time, the client engages in a high-frequency behaviour such as sitting down, they are asked to remind themselves that the discomfort will not last for ever. The use of imagery to deliberately exaggerate the extent of the discomfort tends to put existing unpleasantness into perspective.

Client C imagined each time he sat down that he was an old man of 100 with a long white beard and a walking stick. He listened to himself still complaining of his symptoms and that his arms and legs kept dropping off and he had to replace them. C made a drawing of 'me at 100' and carried it around with him to act as an enhancer of motivation.

Such imagery in effect challenges the cognitive distortion 'I just can't stand it without drugs'. The time limited nature of craving responses can also be usefully exploited by the therapist. Clients may be taught to simply postpone their use of the addictive substances and in the meantime to distract themselves with, say, a relaxation exercise or the completion of a puzzle. Craving responses tend to be at their peak for a matter of minutes, so any postponement of the satisfaction of the craving decreases the likelihood of relapse. Postponement of the addictive behaviour also has the advantage that such a behaviour does not become more appealing because it is the 'forbidden fruit'.

ROADBLOCKS TO MAINTAINING CHANGE

Mark Twain once remarked of cigarette smoking 'Quitting is easy . . . I've done it a hundred times'. His observation seems pertinent right across the addictions. Therapeutic endeavours have tended to focus almost exclusively on the stage of active change. However the maintenance stage is equally important and constitutes probably the more daunting challenge; as one addict put it 'It's not coming off, it's staying off that's the problem'.

Understandably, therapists tend to lavishly praise the client for his or her initial successes at abstinence. This however can make it difficult for the client to admit to lapses on subsequent occasions. In the client's mind therapist approval is associated with abstinence. From the client's perspective the therapist ceases to be a dependable enhancer of self esteem. Not surprisingly the client may avoid the therapist after lapses. To prevent avoidance the therapist must take a matter of fact, problem-solving stance about the client's endeavours, whether 'successful' or not.

The client's self-image after initial 'success' in modifying addictive behaviour may undergo a transformation 'I am a junkie' to 'I am no junkie!' The polarized either/or nature of this construing makes the client particularly vulnerable to an escalation of addictive behaviour subsequent to a lapse. Case D described below illustrates how this happens.

Client D was a heroin addict. He had withdrawn from heroin over a three-week period, tapering off his daily intake of methadone over this period. He was pleased with his progress, and encouraged by his improving relationship with his family. Walking along the road he met an old friend, X, recently released from a local remand centre. X had been placed on remand for a drugs offence. For old time's sake D went back to X's flat; after an exchange of pleasantries, X produced the materials for smoking heroin. The sight of the tin foil etc. proved too much for D and X readily agreed to share a bag of heroin with him. D felt so guilt-ridden after smoking that over the next few days he took more heroin to assuage his tremendous sense of guilt. In the scenario described above D had flipped successively from 'I am a junkie' to 'I am no junkie!' and back to 'Who are you trying to kid? You're just a junkie!' This last self-description makes it less likely that any active change strategies will be attempted but even if they are initiated the cycle of descriptions is likely to be repeated.

The term abstinence violation effect (AVE, Marlatt and Gordon 1980) is used to describe the way in which a sense of guilt arising out of use of a substance after abstinence can, if unchecked, act as a stimulus for further addictive behaviour. Therapeutically the task is to teach clients that a small amount of guilt is constructive and ushers in change but too much guilt simply immobilizes. With regard to lapses, the task is to encourage the client to learn from them, thereby hopefully making the gap to the next lapse even longer. In this way the dichotomous thinking surrounding addictions e.g. 'Am I or am I not an alcoholic?' is replaced by the notion of a journey towards less problematic behaviours. This journey may be slowed by lapses, but provided the client keeps moving (trying) arrival at the chosen destination is more or less guaranteed.

Returning to D, after discussion and role play with his therapist, he decided on the following routine for use with old addict friends. He would i) greet them and ask one or two questions of them; ii) then use one of a series of reasons to excuse himself at the earliest opportunity; these would include 'Sorry I have got to dash and sign on at the dole/meet a friend/get to a shop before it closes'. Case D also indicates the almost innocuous way addicts have lapses. Decisions are made which are apparently unconnected with the addictive behaviour, e.g. in D's case visiting an old friend. Making explicit to the client that lapses are often the consequence of apparently irrelevant decisions can help clients prevent relapse. In particular clients should be taught to pause and critically examine any justification for contact with a current drug user or with any situation that has served as one for drug abuse in the past. The apparent 'innocence' of some rationalizations makes them particularly insidious. It may often need the client to act on one of these justifications and observe the consequences before he/she can see it for what it is.

Maintenance of non-addictive behaviour is very much dependent upon how the client learns to handle the likely lapses. Rehearsal of coping strategies for lapses therefore assumes a particular importance. Such rehearsal is often actively resisted by clients who have already gone some time without using the drug. Their self description may have already become 'I am no junkie' and they can feel affronted when it is suggested that rehearsal of lapses is put on the agenda. Usually however by the time this topic is raised in the programme, the therapist has sufficient rapport with the client and can usually justify rehearsal of lapses along the lines of 'It's an insurance policy, you may well not need it, but it costs little and if it is needed, it's worth its weight in gold'. Rehearsal of a lapse involves the generation of a set of coping self-statements that the client would become familiar with and use in the event of a slip. These statements should be couched in the client's own language and put on cards he/she would regularly come across. The therapist can aid the construction of these cards by ensuring that the self-statements are comprehensive enough to cover: i) an antidote to excessive inward irritability (e.g. 'Don't get mad, play things cool'); ii) a decatastrophizing statement (e.g. 'It's not the end of the world'); iii) a statement which challenges any possible global description of inadequacy (e.g. 'I only slipped'); iv) challenges to the belief that the situation is totally irredeemable (e.g. 'Using more would be a *decision*. I don't *need* to make that decision even though I might *want* to'); v) a statement that projects the client forward in time and away from the cravings of the moment (e.g. 'Maybe there is already something that I could learn from this that might be useful in the future'); and vi) a statement to enhance self-esteem (e.g. 'At least I am keeping my cool this time'). The intent of the set of self-statements is to effectively inoculate the client against full blown relapses.

The client's addictive behaviour takes place in a social context and it's often clients' dissatisfactions with aspects of that environment that are cited as precipitants of relapse. The monitoring of such precipitants can be facilitated by periodic administration of Corney and Clare's (1985) Social Questionnaire (see Appendix B). The identified social concerns may pre-date or be a consequence of the addiction.

Client E was a student when he started using heroin. Completion of the Social Questionnaire indicated that he was severely dissatisfied with being alone. Further enquiry revealed that as a student he was very shy, particularly so with girls and found it a great strain interacting. After six weeks of abstinence from heroin his libido had returned but so did the fears and anxieties he had not experienced whilst on heroin. This all came as a surprise to E and he became down-hearted.

Drug abuse can serve to nullify the discomfort of pre-existing emotional disorders and interpersonal problems. Where present these underlying problems will probably need tackling in their own right if the client is to obtain long-term control of the addiction. The underlying problems tend to become most in evidence when the client is already well into the maintenance phase of change, perhaps the fifth or sixth session of the seven-week core programme. In such cases it is appropriate to add a module to the end of the programme dealing with the particular difficulty. In E's case, a six-week social skills module constituted the extra input; particular cognitive foci were the 'superficial' meaning he assigned to every day chit-chat with females, and the catastrophic meaning he attached to his advances being rejected. Behaviourally the focus was on the skills needed to break the ice. During the course of the extra modules the client's drug-related behaviour continues to be monitored as it does during the suggested monthly follow-ups for six months. Likely areas in need of extra remedial treatment are depression, anxiety, interpersonal problems, and assertion. (For the construction of the extra modules the reader is advised to consult the relevant sections of this volume.)

Modules may also need to be constructed for deficiencies that seem more a consequence of addictive behaviour than a cause. For example a client's difficulties in being assertive can be specifically related to drug use and are not necessarily an enduring trait manifested in diverse areas. With a client for whom this was the case a social skill module focusing primarily on assertion would usefully complement the core addiction programme. This would probably include: i) teaching the client to make eye contact and speak audibly when refusing a drink; ii) challenging the idea that he/she needs the approval of all his/her friends; and iii) the generation and rehearsal of a set of coping self-statements.

SUPPORTING CHANGE

Many of the more traditional interventions with addicted clients have relied heavily on the support provided by groups such as Alcoholic Anonymous and Narcotics Anonymous. Some clients clearly appear to benefit from the safety net such groups provide; others do not. There is a general consensus that 'support' is important in overcoming addictions. At the present time the key question 'What type of support is required by what type of client under what set of circumstances?' goes largely unanswered, at least as far as the addictions are concerned. It is probably therefore most fruitful to experiment with various forms of support. Providing support to the client by involving a client chosen, non-addict relative or friend as quasi-therapist helps to tackle the problem of generalization of treatment effects. The non-addict relative or friend is admitted to the last fifteen minutes of the session and is presented with a potted version of the session together with information on any homework assignments. Most therapists are not usually available to the client at times of crises between sessions but the quasi-therapist is. In this way the quasi-therapist can take the treatment programme into the community. An added bonus of having a quasi-therapist is that they can liaise between clients and their families. This latter advantage can be exploited where core relationships between the addict and his family have become so highly charged as to prevent meaningful dialogue. The quasi-therapist can, for example, negotiate how much the client's family check up on his/her whereabouts.

PRACTICAL ISSUES

The range of alternative 'positive' addictions and goals that therapists and clients can generate differs greatly with social context. Working with an adolescent drug abuser in the inner city it is often very difficult to help map out appropriate goals. Prospects of employment in some areas are virtually nil and there is little prospect of 'legitimately' attaining the sort of lifestyle portrayed on the media. To some extent therapists may find that their hands are tied. In such circumstances one of the roles of the therapist is to make it clear that therapeutically there may be little room for manoeuvre. To the extent that the therapist and client

187

are confronted with negative realities the solutions may be political and social more than psychological.

Therapeutic efforts have focused primarily on helping the drug abuser rather than the family of the abuser. Yet drug abuse often has devastating consequences for other family members. Parents, and mothers in particular, often present as clinically depressed. The parents often blame themselves for their son or daughter's drug abuse. The depressed parent may see evidence of their negative influence, when they reflect on how they spoilt their child when he or she was very young, perhaps in an attempt to compensate for their own harsh upbringing. Other parents may berate themselves for a marriage that 'failed' and see this as greatly contributing to their child's substance abuse. The cognitive therapy strategies discussed in Chapter 5 can be very useful in such cases. Specifically, the degree of the parents' responsibility can be re-examined and compared with the influence of myriad other factors. Even where parents remain convinced that they were a major negative influence on their offspring, overwhelming guilt may still be inappropriate because of the absence of intent. Often parents remain with a debilitating sense of guilt because they see other actions as incompatible with the role of a 'good mother' or 'good father'. A parent may have informed the police of their son/daughter's drug abuse in the desperate hope that if they were 'out of action' for a time something might change. Or parents may insist their abusing son or daughter takes a separate flat rather than disrupting the parental home by stealing items, continually lying stretched out on the settee, eyes rolling, etc. Draconian measures such as these can produce great guilt even though there is often no alternative course of action. The guilt of a parent is initially considerably exacerbated if a partner seems to take a less involved attitude to their child. If the depressed parent can be helped to see his/her partner's less involved response to their child as not inconsistent with 'caring', then a new mode of interaction can be opened up. The depressed parent can experiment with acting and thinking 'as if' they were the other partner. Ideally parents should arrive at an agreed approach so that they can support each other. The strategies of motivational interviewing (Chapter 12) can be used to help parents make decisions such as whether the abusing child should be allowed to stay in the parental home.

Part 5

NEW PASTURES

Chapter Fourteen

NEW HORIZONS IN COGNITIVE-BEHAVIOUR THERAPY

The last decade has witnessed an explosion of interest in the application of cognitive-behavioural therapy, principally in the realm of emotional disorders and to a lesser extent in the areas of interpersonal problems, child behaviour problems, and addictive behaviours. It can be confidently anticipated that research in these areas will continue apace. Important questions still remain unanswered. Cognitive-behavioural therapy is in fact a broad church, embracing rational emotive therapy (RET), cognitive therapy (CT), and self-instruction training (SIT) as its largest groups. It remains to be demonstrated whether the different consti-tuents would be equally effective in the treatment of a given disorder. Such studies present considerable methodological problems, not the least of which would be ensuring that the activities of therapists stayed strictly within the confines of one constituent. Whether RET, CT, and SIT are sufficiently different to allow meaningful comparison to be made is open to debate.

Not all forms of cognitive-behaviour therapy have been sub-jected to the same level of empirical evaluation. For example, cognitive therapy has been much more critically evaluated than rational emotive therapy in the treatment of depression. It is important that the fervour of the proponents of existing and future cognitive-behaviour therapies soon gives way to rigorous scientific examination. To rephrase Paul's (1967) famous dictum, the important question is 'What form of cognitive-behaviour therapy, by whom, is most effective for this individual with that specific problem under which set of circumstances?' There is still a considerable way to go before this can be answered. Care has to be taken in posing the above question however, lest it be taken to imply that a cognitive-behavioural perspective contains the 'whole truth'. Perhaps one of the most important features of the cognitive-behavioural approach is that it can act as a possible bridge between behaviourist and psychodynamic perspectives. The behavioural aspects of, say, cognitive therapy are readily apparent from Beck's own description of CT. However, his description of the scheme (the template with which the individual processes incoming information) involving the activation of latent silent assumptions sounds sufficiently like a description of the unconscious as to awaken the interest of those from a psychodynamic perspective. Moving from Beck's automatic thoughts to schemata parallels movement from surface problems to underlying conflicts within a psychodynamic framework. The fruits of such a dialogue (rapprochement?) are very much something for the future. However, the dialogue will be enriched if greater account is taken of academic psychology, and cognitive psychology in particular, with its propensity for a stricter definition of terms than is common amongst therapists. Mathews and MacCleod (1987) have already reported on the way in which threatening stimuli in the environment may be processed, leading to an increase in anxiety, without the individuals concerned being able to report on their presence.

If cognitive-behavioural therapy comes to increasingly act as a bridge between the behaviourist and the more psychodynamic therapist, then information processing will move to centre stage. This will have important implications not only for how therapists treat their clients, but also may profoundly alter conceptualizations of the whole therapeutic enterprise. It will be acknowledged that distortions of information processing are not the exclusive preserve of distressed clients; therapists too can process information in ways that lead to faulty treatment decisions. For example, a therapist may have very speedy recall of how a particular client benefited from a 'pet' form of therapy. This can lead to the therapist seeing this client as an exemplar of what the favoured treatment achieves; cases which do not respond are less easily recalled, and if recalled are quickly discarded on various grounds e.g. '. . . he just wasn't motivated'. Because all therapists are prone to such distortions Nisbett and Ross (1980) have suggested the use of self-statements along the lines of:

1. 'I don't know whether my treatment works unless it has been demonstrated empirically'.
2. 'Is X claiming too much? She is citing a particular case that did well but is it representative of all the cases X has treated this way? Have the exceptions been forgotten?'
3. 'What is the evidence that people like X treats, treated in some other way, improve?'
4. 'Is X fervently holding on to his 'favourite' cases because of the difficult position he is in rather than being deliberately awkward?'

The upshot of such considerations is to move therapists to think statistically, rather than individually, with regard to outcome so helping in minimizing biasing effects.

CARE IN THE COMMUNITY

Over the last decade a consensus has emerged that care in the community is the 'ideal' for the majority of sufferers with schizophrenia, persons with a mental handicap, and aged persons. Whilst few would dissent from the 'ideal' (to do so would be rather like being against 'love' or 'peace') considerable concern has been expressed about whether the quality of care in the community actually constitutes an improvement on the previous residential modes of care. Doubts are expressed about care in the community simply being seen as the cheap economic option. In the next decade the cognitive-behavioural perspective may be increasingly used to help explicate what constitutes support in the community. The types of support that will be required by three groups of clients, the schizophrenic sufferer, the person with a mental handicap, and the aged, are briefly considered in turn.

Schizophrenia

Schizophrenia can most usefully be viewed as an interaction between a genetic predisposition and social stressors. There remains considerable uncertainty however about the precise nature of the genetic or biochemical excess or deficiency. Raised levels of the neurotransmitter dopamine in the brain mean that thoughts run through the chain in too rapid a fashion producing schizophrenia-like symptoms. Yet not all the symptoms of schizophrenia are manifested, leading to a certain caution about the dopamine hypothesis. More success has been achieved in identifying the environmental stress to which schizophrenic clients are vulnerable. The likelihood of relapse is predicted by the level of expressed emotion (EE) in the schizophrenic client's family (Kuipers 1979). EE is a composite of the number of critical comments made by the family and over-involvement of family members. Over-involvement is a complex measure comprising over-anxiety, over-protectiveness, and symbiosis – the inability of the relative to separate his or her life from the client's. Unfortunately the training to rate EE is very time-consuming (Vaughn and Leff 1976) but it is likely that clients who seem to require recurrent admissions to hospital, despite being maintained on medication, are probably from high EE families and certainly ones in which there are high tensions. Effective 'support' for the schizophrenic client can therefore be operationalized as the lowering of EE. This may be achieved by reducing the amount of face to face contact between schizophrenic clients and their carers, and/or by family intervention programmes. In a study by Leff *et al.* (1982) one of the goals was to reduce the amount of mutual social contact to less than thirty-five hours a week. Such a reduction may be achieved on the client's side by altering leisure activities, or utilizing day hospitals, day centres, group homes, hostels, or lodgings. On the relatives' side the reduction in mutual contact may be achieved by altered leisure activities or finding a job. Relapse rates using family intervention programmes have typically been 10 per cent or less; whereas interventions solely with the schizophrenic client have shown relapse rates of the order of 50 per cent (Goldstein 1984). These findings have been confirmed in a later study by Falloon *et al.* (1985). This family-based, problem-solving approach involved treating the schizophrenic client merely as one member of the family unit. His particular needs were catered for within the context of the overall functioning of the family. The main aim of the intervention was to teach the family problem-solving skills – defining a problem precisely, generating a wide range of possible solutions, and agreeing on a detailed plan to implement the best solution (see Chapter 6 for more details of problem solving). Roadblocks to the practice of problem solving skills – which might include parental conflict, anxiety, or depression – were treated within a cognitive-behavioural perspective. The family sessions were an hour long over a nine-month period, and conducted in the home. More recently Hogarty *et al.* (1986) have compared four groups for the extent to which they prevent schizophrenic relapse:

1. Family treatment and medication.
2. Social skills and medication.
3. Family treatment, social skills, and medication.
4. Drugs alone in a standard dose.

The family treatment consisted of an education workshop followed by sessions at home. The aims of the latter were to increase information about the illness, to augment social networks, and reduce isolation. The social skills training was aimed at helping clients improve their social perceptions and to be more assertive with their families. This was conducted with the clients alone. The drugs alone group had a 41 per cent relapse rate over the next year, the family treatment/medication group had a 19 per cent relapse rate; the social skills/medication group a 20 per cent relapse rate; and no relapses were reported for the family treatment/social skills/medication group, making a case for the most wide-ranging approach. A particularly interesting finding of this study was that though family treatment and social skills training both independently reduced relapse, they did not appear to have reduced EE. The majority of the 'medication plus' families remained high in EE. It may be that the intervention programmes are not so much preventing relapse as delaying it.

Whilst EE has been the stimulus for intervention programmes that are bearing fruit, doubts are being expressed about the concept itself. Birchwood *et al.* (1987) see a concentration on 'high EE' families as too narrow, being liable to exclude other families with problems from effective help. They also argue that families do not possess high EE as an enduring trait, but rather that it develops as the response of some relatives to the burdens of living with someone who has schizophrenia. Whatever the ultimate status of EE the cognitive-behavioural intervention programmes are of sufficiently proven worth as to merit wider application and research in the community.

Mental handicap

Learning theory has been used extensively as a method of behaviour change with mentally handicapped persons. In many ways intervention programmes to manage difficult behaviour or to teach new skills have been similar to the behavioural programme outlined in Chapter 1, except on a more extended time scale. The Portage model is an early intervention scheme in which training personnel visit family homes weekly. The child is assessed using a developmental check-list and a small number of target behaviours are selected from a Curriculum Guide which consists of 580 cards of behavioural objectives and teaching methods. A recording chart is drawn up with the parent and the teaching approach is demonstrated. For the more severely mentally handicapped child smaller step sizes between behavioural objectives have been required (Barna *et al.* 1980).

One disadvantage of a purely behavioural approach is that it is unable to consider the experience of people with handicaps or the communications between them and people such as parents and professionals who work with them. As the policy of community care is translated into practice more people with a mental handicap are encountering novel social situations, either living with foster parents or within a small group home in the community. The self-image and self-confidence of adults with at least a mild mental handicap will crucially affect their ability to cope and adjust. Aggression and self-injury are the most frequently cited reasons for the breakdown of community placements (Intagliata and Willer 1982) and the major contributor to stress experienced amongst carers (Pahl and Quine 1984). The cognitive-behavioural framework has already been addressed to the problems of low self-image and aggressive behaviour manifested by non-mentally handicapped people, the next step is the adaptation of such strategies to the needs of the person with a mental handicap. From within a cognitive-behavioural perspective Self-Instruction Training (SIT; Meichenbaum 1977) and Personal Construct Theory (Kelly 1955) are probably the two frameworks most readily applicable to the needs of persons with a mental handicap. The cornerstone of SIT is that anxieties and performance difficulties are maintained by negative self-statements. Importantly, SIT does not assume that individuals are aware of their self-statements, and this can frequently be the case with people with mental handicaps who may not even have formed the thoughts linguistically. The therapist can help make explicit what it sounds 'as if' an individual has said to themselves. These thoughts may then be modified or replaced by positive self-statements. Lindsay and Kasprowicz (1987) have used a general social skills training plus SIT package in working with groups of adults with mental handicaps. The group they described met weekly for six months and important changes seem to have occurred. This case study highlights some of the particular adaptations necessary in using a cognitive-behavioural programme with people with a mental handicap. These include:

i) taking into account the client's non-verbal language to compensate for linguistic deficiencies;
ii) making allowance for the limited concentration of the client by switching the focus regularly from one client to another in the group, and
iii) checking that the client is not making the same monosyllabic reply to questions irrespective of their content, i.e. that the client has not developed a response set.

Personal Construct Theory (PCT) sees the person with a mental handicap as someone attempting to make sense of events in order to anticipate and therefore adjust to them. He/she is seen as operating like all other people and not qualitatively differently. The implications of this perspective are that people with a mental handicap are not there simply to be 'educated' or worse still patronized. In this context it is much more likely that people with mental handicap will have their self-acceptance enhanced. Nooe (1977) has shown self-acceptance to correlate more highly than IQ with the degree of independent living achieved. The practical import of PCT is that therapists and parents pause before labelling as a 'nuisance' a particular behaviour of a person with a mental handicap. For example, a therapist was visiting the home of Mr and Mrs X to discuss the development of their child with a severe mental handicap. Mid-way through the therapist-parent exchange the child had crawled away and was pulling at the cable to the stereo. Somewhat embarrassed and frustrated this mother retrieved the child and sat him on her knee. Whereupon the child duly wriggled frantically to get down. The therapist became more frustrated, she had her list of behavioural objectives to get through! At this point the father simply said 'Maybe he wants his nursery rhymes tape on'. The illustration opens up the possibility that parents who are in difficulty with their child with a mental handicap are those who are unable to construe their behaviour meaningfully and usefully. Myatt (1983) has used PCT to examine the way in which professionals construed their clients in a Portage scheme. Interestingly the children were not construed in terms of their own characteristics but in terms of their diagnostic category, the programme success, and the mother's attributes such as her understanding, motivation, and ability related to the treatment programme. This is not to castigate behavioural approaches but simply to suggest that they may possibly be better integrated into a PCT framework. Ultimately, the issue is not whether people with a mental handicap are helped to achieve as near normal behaviour as they can manage (important though the normaliza-tion process is), but whether they are respected as being not qualitatively different human beings. PCT can contribute to furthering the latter.

The elderly

Numerically, pehaps the group most affected by 'Care in the Community' policies are the elderly, with boarding-out and befriending increasingly used as an alternative to residential accommodation. However, the level of psychopathology amongst the elderly is much greater than in the younger age groups. The incidence of depression amongst older adults has been conserv-atively estimated at 13 per cent (Gurland et al. 1980). Much depression in the elderly probably goes under-reported because the negative feelings experienced are taken as a natural part of the ageing process and therefore not worth reporting. Given the ubiquity of the problem in the elderly it is perhaps strange (or simple age-ism!) that cognitive-behavioural therapists have paid comparatively little attention to it. A recent study by Beutler et al. (1987) showed that patients treated with group cognitive therapy plus or minus antidepressants did better than patients prescribed just antidepressants plus support, and better than patients prescribed a placebo plus support. Medication did not potentiate the effects of cognitive therapy. The groups met for ninety minutes each week for twenty weeks. The programme consisted of four phases (and is described fully in Yost *et al.* 1986) each building on the previous one. Treatment begins with a preparation or orientation phase, which takes place independent of the group experience. The preparation phase is followed by the identification and collaboration phase which is designed to assist clients to define problems within a cognitive-behavioural framework as an aid to subsequent change. The middle phase of treatment (sessions 3 to 17 approximately) is directed to changing dysfunctional cognitions. During this phase the client learns to categorize and challenge dysfunctional thoughts with *in vivo* practice of new behaviours and thought patterns. The final termination phase (sessions 12 to 15) is aimed at consolidation. These sessions are also used to anticipate future stresses and develop change plans.

Fry (1984) has evaluated the efficacy of an individually based cognitive behaviour package for use with elderly clients. This involved the therapists in three sessions of therapy a week per client for four weeks making a total of twelve sessions. Each session was an hour long with fifteen minutes of that time spent just in getting to know the client. An interesting feature of the package was the encouragement of clients to take on fixed roles, and practise these for at least an hour a day noting other people's reactions. The roles were first discussed with the therapist, rehearsed by the client, and modelled by the therapist. Clients' dysfunctional attitudes focused chiefly around issues of dependence, self-blame, incapacity, and difficulties in eliciting support. They were encouraged to rehearse positive self-reinforcing statements in these areas as follows:

1. Cognitions of independence e.g. 'I have my own opinions about this matter and I am not going to worry about what X thinks about me.'
2. Cognitions of self-respect e.g. 'I must not let others push me around, hurry me up, or get impatient with me because I am slow in deciding.'
3. Cognitions of self-efficacy e.g. 'I must not dwell on things at which I have failed, or things that were a disappointment. I must concentrate on the number of things I have accomplished.'

4. Cognitions for eliciting support e.g. 'I want others to take an interest in me, which means I must try to be cheerful, energetic, and pleasant in talking with others.'

EYBERG CHILD
BEHAVIOUR INVENTORY

Reproduced by permission of Professor Sheila Eyberg, University of Florida.

Date ....

Child's name ....

Child's age .... Birth date ....

EYBERG CHILD BEHAVIOUR INVENTORY

Directions: Below are a series of phrases that describe children's behaviour. Please (1) circle the number describing *how often* the behaviour currently occurs with your child and (2) circle 'yes' or 'no' to indicate whether the behaviour is *currently a problem* for you.

	How often does this occur with your child?							Is this a problem for you?	
	Never	Seldom	Sometimes		Often	Always			
1. Dawdles in getting dressed	1	2	3	4	5	6	7	Yes	No
2. Dawdles or lingers at mealtimes	1	2	3	4	5	6	7	Yes	No
3. Has poor table manners	1	2	3	4	5	6	7	Yes	No
4. Refuses to eat food presented	1	2	3	4	5	6	7	Yes	No
5. Refuses to do chores when asked	1	2	3	4	5	6	7	Yes	No
6. Slow in getting ready for bed	1	2	3	4	5	6	7	Yes	No

APPENDICES

	How often does this occur with your child?							Is this a problem for you?	
	Never	Seldom	Sometimes		Often	Always			
7. Refuses to go to bed on time	1	2	3	4	5	6	7	Yes	No
8. Does not obey house rules on their own	1	2	3	4	5	6	7	Yes	No
9. Refuses to obey until threatened with punishment	1	2	3	4	5	6	7	Yes	No
10. Acts defiant when told to do something	1	2	3	4	5	6	7	Yes	No
11. Argues with parents about rules	1	2	3	4	5	6	7	Yes	No
12. Gets angry when doesn't get their own way	1	2	3	4	5	6	7	Yes	No
13. Has temper tantrums	1	2	3	4	5	6	7	Yes	No
14. Cheeky to adults	1	2	3	4	5	6	7	Yes	No
15. Whines	1	2	3	4	5	6	7	Yes	No
16. Cries easily	1	2	3	4	5	6	7	Yes	No
17. Yells or screams	1	2	3	4	5	6	7	Yes	No
18. Hits parents	1	2	3	4	5	6	7	Yes	No
19. Destroys toys and other objects	1	2	3	4	5	6	7	Yes	No
20. Is careless with toys and other objects	1	2	3	4	5	6	7	Yes	No
21. Steals	1	2	3	4	5	6	7	Yes	No
22. Lies	1	2	3	4	5	6	7	Yes	No
23. Teases or provokes other children	1	2	3	4	5	6	7	Yes	No
24. Verbally fights with friends their own age	1	2	3	4	5	6	7	Yes	No
25. Verbally fights with sisters and brothers	1	2	3	4	5	6	7	Yes	No
26. Physically fights with friends of their own age	1	2	3	4	5	6	7	Yes	No

	How often does this occur with your child?							Is this a problem for you?	
	Never	Seldom	Sometimes		Often	Always			
27. Physically fights with sisters and brothers	1	2	3	4	5	6	7	Yes	No
28. Constantly seeks attention	1	2	3	4	5	6	7	Yes	No
29. Interrupts	1	2	3	4	5	6	7	Yes	No
30. Is easily distracted	1	2	3	4	5	6	7	Yes	No
31. Has short attention span	1	2	3	4	5	6	7	Yes	No
32. Fails to finish tasks or projects	1	2	3	4	5	6	7	Yes	No
33. Has difficulty entertaining themselves alone	1	2	3	4	5	6	7	Yes	No
34. Has difficulty concentrating on one thing	1	2	3	4	5	6	7	Yes	No
35. Is overactive or restless	1	2	3	4	5	6	7	Yes	No
36. Wets the bed	1	2	3	4	5	6	7	Yes	No

SOCIAL QUESTIONNAIRE

Reproduced by permission of Dr Roslyn Corney and Professor Anthony Clare, Institute of Psychiatry, London.

Social Questionnaire

Please underline the most appropriate answer

A. Housing (*Everyone answer*)

1. Are your housing conditions adequate for you and your family's needs?	Adequate	Slightly inadequate	Markedly inadequate	Severely inadequate
2. How satisfied are you with your present accommodation?	Satisfied	Slightly dissatisfied	Markedly dissatisfied	Severely dissatisfied

B. Work

For all men and women working outside the home

Tick box if not applicable ☐

3. How satisfied are you with your present job?	Satisfied	Slightly dissatisfied	Markedly dissatisfied	Severely dissatisfied
4. Do you have problems getting on with any of the people at your work?	No problems	Slight problems	Marked problems	Severe problems

For housewives with no outside work

Tick box if not applicable ☐

5. How satisfied are you with being a housewife?	Satisfied	Slightly dissatisfied	Markedly dissatisfied	Severely dissatisfied

For housewives with a full or part-time job outside the home

Tick box if not applicable ☐

6. How satisfied are you with working and running a home?

| Satisfied | Slightly dissatisfied | Markedly dissatisfied | Severely dissatisfied |

For those who are not working (retired, unemployed, or off sick)

Tick box if not applicable ☐

7. How satisfied are you with this situation?

| Satisfied | Slightly dissatisfied | Markedly dissatisfied | Severely dissatisfied |

C. Financial circumstances *(Everyone answer)*

8. Is the money coming in adequate for you and your family's needs?

| Adequate | Slightly inadequate | Markedly inadequate | Severely inadequate |

9. Do you have any difficulties in meeting bills and other financial commitments?

| No difficulties | Slight difficulties | Marked difficulties | Severe difficulties |

10. How satisfied are you with your financial position?

| Satisfied | Slightly dissatisfied | Markedly dissatisfied | Severely dissatisfied |

D. Social contacts *(Everyone answer)*

11. How satisfied are you with the amount of time you are able to go out?

| Satisfied | Slightly dissatisfied | Markedly dissatisfied | Severely dissatisfied |

12. Do you have any problems with your neighbours?

| No problems | Slight problems | Marked problems | Severe problems |

13. Do you have any problems getting on with any of your friends?

| No problems | Slight problems | Marked problems | Severe problems |

14. How satisfied are you with the amount of time you see your friends?

| Satisfied | Slightly dissatisfied | Markedly dissatisfied | Severely dissatisfied |

15. Do you have any problems getting on with any close relative? (including parents, in-laws or grown-up children)	No problems	Slight problems	Marked problems	Severe problems
16. How satisfied are you with the amount of time you see your relatives?	Satisfied	Slightly dissatisfied	Markedly dissatisfied	Severely dissatisfied

E. Marriage and boyfriends/girlfriends

17. What is your marital status? — Single   Married/ cohabiting   Widowed   Separated   Divorced

For all those who are married or have a steady relationship

Tick box if not applicable ☐

18. Do you have difficulty confiding in your partner?	No difficulty	Slight difficulty	Marked difficulty	Severe difficulty
19. Are there any sexual problems in your relationship?	No problems	Slight problems	Marked problems	Severe problems
20. Do you have any other problems getting on together?	No problems	Slight problems	Marked problems	Severe problems
21. How satisfied in general are you with your relationship?	Satisfied	Slightly dissatisfied	Markedly dissatisfied	Severely dissatisfied
22. Have you recently been so dissatisfied that you have considered separating from your partner?	No	Sometimes	Often	Yes, planned or recent separation

For all those who are not married/do not have a steady relationship

Tick box if not applicable ☐

23. How satisfied are you with this situation?	Satisfied	Slightly dissatisfied	Markedly dissatisfied	Severely dissatisfied

F. Domestic life

For those with children under 18

Tick box if not appropriate ☐

24. Do you have any difficulties coping with your children?	No difficulties	Slight difficulties	Marked difficulties	Severe difficulties

25. How satisfied do   Satisfied   Slightly   Markedly   Severely
    you feel with   dissatisfied dissatisfied dissatisfied
    your relationship
    with the
    children?

For those with children of school age

Tick box if not applicable ☐

26. Are there any   No   Slight   Marked   Severe
    problems   problems   problems   problems   problems
    involving your
    children at
    school?

For all those with other adults living with them (including relatives but
excluding spouse)

Tick box if not applicable ☐

27. Do you have any   No   Slight   Marked   Severe
    problems about   problems   problems   problems   problems
    sharing
    household tasks?

28. Do you have any   No   Slight   Marked   Severe
    difficulties with   difficulties difficulties difficulties difficulties
    the other adults
    in your
    household?

29. How satisfied are   Satisfied   Slightly   Markedly   Severely
    you with this   dissatisfied dissatisfied dissatisfied
    arrangement?

G. Legal matters *(Everyone answer)*

30. Do you have any   No   Slight   Marked   Severe
    legal problems   problems   problems   problems   problems
    (custody,
    maintenance,
    compensation,
    etc.)?

H. For those who are living alone

Tick box if not applicable ☐

31. Do you have any   No   Slight   Marked   Severe
    difficulties living difficulties difficulties difficulties difficulties
    and managing
    on your own?

32. How satisfied are   Satisfied   Slightly   Markedly   Severely
    you with living   dissatisfied dissatisfied dissatisfied
    on your own?

I. Other *(Everyone answer)*

33. Do you have any   No   Slight   Marked   Severe
    other social problems problems   problems   problems   problems
    or problems?

If so, please specify . . .

Appendix C:

THE DYSFUNCTIONAL ATTITUDE SCALE

Reproduced by permission of Professor Aaron T. Beck, Center for Cognitive Therapy, Philadelphia.

DAS – FORM A

This Inventory lists different attitudes or beliefs which people sometimes hold. Read EACH statement carefully and decide how much you agree or disagree with the statement.

For each of the attitudes, show your answer by placing a tick (✔) under the column that BEST DESCRIBES HOW YOU THINK. Be sure to choose only one answer for each attitude. Because people are different, there is no right answer or wrong answer to these statements.

To decide whether a given attitude is typical of your way of looking at things, simply keep in mind what you are like MOST OF THE TIME.

Example:

Attitudes	Totally agree	Agree very much	Agree slightly	Neutral	Disagree slightly	Disagree very much	Totally disagree
1. Most people are O.K. once you get to know them.			✔				

Look at the example above. To show how much a sentence describes your attitude, you can tick any point from totally agree to totally disagree. In the above example, the tick at 'agree slightly' indicates that this statement is somewhat typical of the attitudes held by the person completing the inventory.

Remember that your answer should describe the way you think MOST OF THE TIME.

NOW TURN THE PAGE AND BEGIN

DAS

Attitudes	Totally agree	Agree very much	Agree slightly	Neutral	Disagree slightly	Disagree very much	Totally disagree
Remember: Answer each statement according to the way you think MOST OF THE TIME							
1. It is difficult to be happy unless one is good looking, intelligent, rich and creative.							
2. Happiness is more a matter of my attitude towards myself than the way other people feel about me.							
3. People will probably think less of me if I make a mistake.							
4. If I do not do well all the time, people will not respect me.							
5. Taking even a small risk is foolish because the loss is likely to be a disaster.							
6. It is possible to gain another person's respect without being especially talented at anything.							
7. I cannot be happy unless most people I know admire me.							
8. If a person asks for help, it is a sign of weakness.							

Attitudes	Totally agree	Agree very much	Agree slightly	Neutral	Disagree slightly	Disagree very much	Totally disagree
9. If I do not do as well as other people, it means I am an inferior human being.							
10. If I fail at my work, then I am a failure as a person.							
11. If you cannot do something well, there is little point in doing it at all.							
12. Making mistakes is fine because I can learn from them.							
13. If someone disagrees with me, it probably indicates he does not like me.							
14. If I fail partly, it is as bad as being a complete failure.							
15. If other people know what you are really like, they will think less of you.							
16. I am nothing if a person I love doesn't love me.							
17. One can get pleasure from an activity regardless of the end result.							
18. People should have a reasonable likelihood of success before undertaking anything.							

Attitudes	Totally agree	Agree very much	Agree slightly	Neutral	Disagree slightly	Disagree very much	Totally disagree
19. My value as a person depends greatly on what others think of me.							
20. If I don't set the highest standards for myself, I am likely to end up a second-rate person.							
21. If I am to be a worthwhile person, I must be truly outstanding in at least one major respect.							
22. People who have good ideas are more worthy than those who do not.							
23. I should be upset if I make a mistake.							
24. My own opinions of myself are more important than other's opinions of me.							
25. To be a good, moral, worthwhile person, I must help everyone who needs it.							
26. If I ask a question, it makes me look inferior.							
27. It is awful to be disapproved of by people important to you.							
28. If you don't have other people to lean on, you are bound to be sad.							

Attitudes	Totally agree	Agree very much	Agree slightly	Neutral	Disagree slightly	Disagree very much	Totally disagree
29. I can reach important goals without slave driving myself.							
30. It is possible for a person to be scolded and not get upset.							
31. I cannot trust other people because they might be cruel to me.							
32. If others dislike you, you cannot be happy.							
33. It is best to give up your own interests in order to please other people.							
34. My happiness depends more on other people than it does on me.							
35. I do not need the approval of other people in order to be happy.							
36. If a person avoids problems, the problems tend to go away.							
37. I can be happy even if I miss out on many of the good things in life.							
38. What other people think about me is very important.							
39. Being isolated from others is bound to lead to unhappiness.							
40. I can find happiness without being loved by another person.							

DAS SCORING

1. Every item on the DAS (Form A) is scored from one to seven. Depending on the content, either totally agree or totally disagree will be the anchor point of one and each category from that point will be one more, i.e., if totally agree = +1 then the next category, agree very much, will be = +2, etc. to totally disagree which will be = +7.

2. The following items are scored in the adaptive way if a 'Totally Agree Response' is given:

FORM A

#2	#29
#6	#30
#12	#35
#17	#37
#24	#40

That is, Totally Agree = +1; Agree very much = +2; Agree Slightly = +3; Neutral = +4; Disagree Slightly = +5; Disagree Very Much = +6; Totally Disagree = +7.

3. All the other items on Form A of the DAS are scored in the reverse direction of what was stated in number 2 above; i.e. Totally Disagree = +1; . . . Totally Agree = +7.

4. The Total Score on DAS-A is obtained by summing the item scores for each individual.

5. Omits have been coded as zero (missing data). However, if by some chance, the individual omits a large proportion of the items, the test should be ignored.

THERE'S HOPE

THERE'S HOPE

If you are feeling at the end of your tether, thinking there is nothing to look forward to, unhappy about yourself and feeling that nobody cares, then your feelings are very like those of the three clients below when they first came for help. Read in their own words how they felt and how they were taught to master their depression and begin a new life, you too can probably make similar gains if you are prepared to WORK on your problem; with us over the next THREE MONTHS . . .

Case No. 1 . . . 25-year-old. Female clerical supervisor

'Early on in life I felt I had to put up a front to cover my defects, blotchy skin, big hands, I forced myself to go out, get qualifications and meet people. Three years ago I took a new job, the office staff didn't want me, I was unsure of the job, I was told I was trying too hard and everything was wrong, became ratty at home and lost a stone in weight when I got married. Because I was depressed I caught flu's and allergies, the valium and diazepam a doctor gave me liberally were not helpful – I didn't want to meet other people. I worried about the smallest details at home and at work. I thought I couldn't be helped – felt everybody was talking about me.

I was assigned projects to do each week including writing down upsetting situations and was taught that in these situations I was saying things to myself that made me depressed. I didn't understand this at first but on reflection gradually saw what he was getting at – when someone told me off at work I couldn't stand up for myself. It was as though I believed I should be a carpet for people to walk over. I used to say I must be awful if someone finds fault in me. Another technique I learnt was rewarding myself with coffee or biscuits for tackling a problem. I applied for other jobs, more able to project the positive aspects of myself, my confidence was renewed, I had learnt things like making eye contact. My next six months appraisal was very good. I still need to use the skills I had learnt as they are not quite automatic yet. I can laugh at myself now when I see myself intolerant of minor frustrations. If I had not had help I would certainly be in a mental hospital now. I wasn't keen on putting my problems on paper and analysing them – it was hard graft but worth it in the end.'

Case No. 2 . . . 27-year-old unemployed man with a long history of depression

'Depression is like falling down a hole and you can't climb out, it's very easy to lose nearly all your self respect when you get depressed. I have had depression a number of times in my life but this is the only treatment that's made me feel I am back in control of the situation again, it's given me a way of fighting it, that none of the other treatments have ever done including electric shock. After seeing various professionals I felt better on the day I had seen them but then it was back to the same old thing but with cognitive therapy you feel armed with a way of fighting it yourself. The most important thing is that it is the only treatment that's made me feel I can do something about it. I am not at the mercy of other people, it gives you your pride and self respect back. You've got to continue to challenge your depression producing thoughts, you mustn't get overconfident, you must apply it when-ever you begin to feel down. It's amazing, in the past I just didn't see my own irrational thoughts – nothing but praise for the idea. Nothing better than feeling you're helping yourself.'

Case No. 3 . . . 42-year-old male teacher

'Matters came to a head late last year, I got to a point where I couldn't carry on, I felt threatened by people, I was turning away from situations, and crying a lot at home. I tried not to at work but it was almost uncontrollable and I wasn't sure what was wrong. I didn't want to get dependent on any drug. There isn't social acceptance of depression. From the reading material I was given in therapy I realised I was perpetuating my depression – this was hope because it meant I could control my emotional state, that was the first ray of sunshine – it was going to be me who solved my own condition – the possibility of an independent cure was really inviting. The first thing I learnt to accept was that I am not perfect and second that the world isn't perfect, these were the cornerstones of my getting better. I had to get rid of self blame and self pity, stop doing myself down, e.g. if something didn't go right, then I would conclude I am not right as a person. I had to learn that the world wouldn't fit into my pattern and it was conceited to expect it to. I had to make an act of faith in myself, to give myself permission to enjoy myself, allow myself to get things wrong. I had to stop rating myself and begin forgiving myself. It took a lot of putting this into practice – under pressure I tended to go to the old responses and it takes time to bring in the rational responses.

I have a new-found confidence based on more healthy premises, I really do feel a new person – it couldn't have been achieved without cognitive therapy, I was introduced to tactics of survival like taking a lunch break. It has been four months now since completing cognitive therapy and I have had only one downer in that time and I got out of it quickly using cognitive therapy techniques. I was able to stop taking medication at the end of cognitive therapy which I was very grateful for.'

HOW TO OVERCOME YOUR DEPRESSION

Overcoming your depression will almost certainly involve changing some of your behaviours and some of the ways you look at things.

To get started
Try thinking of something you used to do and enjoy but probably haven't done lately e.g. go to a football match, visit an old friend or eat an orange. It doesn't have to be anything big.

Do an experiment
Do at least one of these old enjoyable activities some time this

week and see how much you actually enjoy it. You might be predicting you won't but you don't know until you actually try!

Regular upsets
If there's some event that regularly upsets you – write it down – in just three or four lines – what it is and how you feel about it.

Ask yourself
Then ask yourself, 'would everybody else in this same situation feel the same?' Try and guess how many out of ten people you know would feel one way, how many another way and how many yet another way.

Other ways
You might think that your way of looking at the situation is the only way, but it seems to produce great distress – have a look at how some of the less distressed people would be looking at the same situation.

Be realistic
Ask yourself if it would be more realistic to begin changing how you look at the situation, to be more in line with that of those you think might be less distressed in the same situation.

Below are some of the self-defeating thought patterns which depressed people often have need to chip away at:

1. All or nothing thinking sees everything in black and white.
2. Over-generalization expects constant bad luck.
3. Mental filtering seizes upon negative parts and broods.
4. Automatic discounting brushes aside compliments.
5. Jumping to conclusions assumes that others look down on us.
6. Magnification and minimization enlarges our imperfections and decreases our strengths.
7. Emotional reasoning makes us think bad of ourselves because we feel bad.
8. 'Should' statements make us feel guilty instead of getting us to do something.
9. Labelling and mislabelling make us think of failure

instead of mistakes.

10. Personalization makes us blame ourselves for whatever happens or whatever others do.

It's not easy to change the behaviours and thoughts that lead on to depression, that's why the therapy takes three months – but – reading this today, you are making a start – well done.

Appendix E:

DYSFUNCTIONAL THOUGHT RECORD

DAILY RECORD OF DYSFUNCTIONAL THOUGHTS

DATE	SITUATION Describe: 1. Actual event leading to unpleasant emotion, or 2. Stream of thoughts, daydream, or recollection, leading to unpleasant emotion.	EMOTION(S) 1. Specify sad, anxious/angry, etc. 2. Rate degree of emotion, 1–100.	AUTOMATIC THOUGHT(S) 1. Write automatic thought(s) that preceded emotion(s). 2. Rate belief in automatic thought(s), 0–100%.	RATIONAL RESPONSE 1. Write rational response to automatic thought(s). 2. Rate belief in rational response, 0–100%.	OUTCOME 1. Re-rate belief in automatic thought(s), 0–100%. 2. Specify and rate subsequent emotions, 0–100%.

EXPLANATION: When you experience an unpleasant emotion, note the situation that seemed to stimulate the emotion. (If the emotion occurred while you were thinking, daydreaming, etc., please note this.) Then note the automatic thought associated with the emotion. Record the degree to which you believe this thought: 0% = not at all; 100% = completely. In rating degree of emotion: 1 = a trace; 100 = the most intense possible.

221

PROBLEM SOLVING

SOLVING PROBLEMS

STEP 1: WHAT IS THE PROBLEM?

Talk about the problem, listen carefully, ask questions, get everybody's opinion. Then write down *exactly* what the problem is.

_____

_____

_____

STEP 2: LIST ALL POSSIBLE SOLUTIONS.

Put down *all* ideas, even bad ones. Get everybody to come up with at least one possible solution.

1. _____

2. _____

3. _____

4. _____

5. _____

6. _____

STEP 3: DISCUSS EACH POSSIBLE SOLUTION.

Go down the list of possible solutions and discuss the advantages and disadvantages of each one.

STEP 4: CHOOSE THE BEST SOLUTION OR COMBINATION OF SOLUTIONS.

_____

_____

_____

STEP 5: PLAN HOW TO CARRY OUT THE BEST SOLUTION.

Step 1: _____

Step 2: _____

Step 3: _____

Step 4: _____

STEP 6: REVIEW IMPLEMENTATION AND PRAISE _ALL_ EFFORTS.

Appendix G:

RELAXATION EXERCISE

Reproduced by permission Methuen Publications 1978.

RELAXATION TECHNIQUE

Pause ten seconds for each series of ellipses (. . .) in recording this exercise.

Think for a few moments about your breathing . . . Notice how you draw each breath in and then let it out . . . Notice now what happens if you don't try to breathe – it just takes care of itself . . . So much of life is spent in working at things that just take care of themselves . . . If I just let it happen, my breath flows in, flows out, flows in, flows out, like the tide of the sea . . . I have nothing to do but relax . . .

Now I think of my toes . . . When I am tense and anxious, I clench my toes, but now I relax them completely, just letting go of them . . . It feels so good to relax . . . As my toes relax, a warm and comfortable feeling spreads from them through my feet, so that all of the tiny muscles in my feet relax and let go . . . I am becoming warm and comfortable . . . Now I loosen my ankles, I can feel that sense of warmth and comfort spreading from my feet into my calves . . . Those big muscles in my calves just become limp, so that my legs feel weak as a kitten's legs . . . I am warm and comfortable. Now I loosen all of the muscles in my thighs . . . the big muscles on the tops of my thighs . . . the muscles on the insides of my thighs . . . Now my legs feel very heavy . . . so heavy it would take a major effort to move them . . . My legs are as limp and limber as the legs of a rag doll . . .

I am warm and comfortable . . . Now I let go of all tension in my buttocks . . . At the same time, my abdomen relaxes, so that I suddenly feel like I've taken off a tight pair of pants . . . I'm much more comfortable now . . . I feel like yawning or sighing . . . (pause) . . . When I do, I sigh out all the tightness of my chest. My breathing is now very quiet, and my chest hardly moves at all . . . Now I can feel the loosening of my back muscles, and as they loosen I can feel my back sink into the chair or bed . . . I feel so relaxed . . . My shoulders drop and loosen . . . My arms feel relaxed and heavy . . . I could lift them if I tried, but they're so heavy . . . Now the muscles of my neck just . . . let . . . go . . . and my head comes to rest in its most natural position . . . All of the tiny muscles in my face relax . . . My cheeks sag . . . My mouth feels as if it wants to drop open . . . My eyes are closed and the lids feel very heavy . . .

While my body is very relaxed, my mind is open and alive and focused . . . I am concentrated only on the thoughts I have chosen to think . . . I am ready . . . I am at peace . . . I am relaxed and comfortable . . . I am warm and comfortable.

DYADIC ADJUSTMENT SCALE

DYADIC ADJUSTMENT SCALE

Most persons have disagreements in their relationships. Please indicate below the approximate extent of agreement or disagreement between you and your partner for each item on the following list.

	Always agree	Almost always agree	Occasionally disagree	Frequently disagree	Almost always disagree	Always disagree
1. Handling family finances	5	4	3	2	1	0
2. Matters of recreation	5	4	3	2	1	0
3. Religious matters	5	4	3	2	1	0
4. Demonstrations of affection	5	4	3	2	1	0
5. Friends	5	4	3	2	1	0
6. Sex relations	5	4	3	2	1	0
7. Conventionality (correct or proper behaviour)	5	4	3	2	1	0
8. Philosophy of life	5	4	3	2	1	0
9. Ways of dealing with parents or in-laws	5	4	3	2	1	0
10. Aims, goals, and things believed important	5	4	3	2	1	0
11. Amount of time spent together	5	4	3	2	1	0
12. Making major decisions	5	4	3	2	1	0
13. Household tasks	5	4	3	2	1	0
14. Leisure-time interests and activities	5	4	3	2	1	0
15. Career decisions	5	4	3	2	1	0

	All the time	Most of the time	More often than not	Occasionally	Rarely	Never
16. How often do you discuss or have you considered divorce, separation, or terminating your relationship?	0	1	2	3	4	5
17. How often do you or your mate leave the house after a fight?	0	1	2	3	4	5
18. In general, how often do you think that things between you and your partner are going well?	5	4	3	2	1	0
19. Do you confide in your mate?	5	4	3	2	1	0
20. Do you ever regret that you married (or lived together)?	0	1	2	3	4	5
21. How often do you and your partner quarrel?	0	1	2	3	4	5
22. How often do you and your mate "get on each other's nerves"?	0	1	2	3	4	5

	Every day	Almost every day	Occasionally	Rarely	Never
23. Do you kiss your mate?	4	3	2	1	0

	All of them	Most of them	Some of them	Very few of them	None of them
24. Do you and your mate engage in outside interests together?	4	3	2	1	0

How often would you say the following occur between you and your mate:

	Never	Less than once a month	Once or twice a month	Once or twice a week	Once a day	More often
25. Have a stimulating exchange of ideas	0	1	2	3	4	5
26. Laugh together	0	1	2	3	4	5
27. Calmly discuss something	0	1	2	3	4	5
28. Work together on a project	0	1	2	3	4	5

These are some things about which couples sometimes agree and sometimes disagree. Indicate if either item below caused differences of opinions or were problems in your relationship during the past few weeks. (Check yes or no.)

	Yes	No	
29.	0	1	Being too tired for sex
30.	0	1	Not showing love

31. The dots on the following line represent different degrees of happiness in your relationship. The point, 'happy', represents the degree of happiness of most relationships. Please circle the dots that best describes the degree of happiness, all things considered, of your relationship.

0	1	2	3	4	5	6
●	●	●	●	●	●	●
Extremely unhappy	Fairly unhappy	A little unhappy	Happy	Very happy	Extremely happy	Perfect

32. Which of the following statements best describes how you feel about the future of your relationship:

5 I want desperately for my relationship to succeed and would go to almost any lengths to see that it does.

4 I want very much for my relationship to succeed and will do all that I can to see that it does.

3 I want very much for my relationship to succeed and will do my fair share to see that it does.

2 It would be nice if my relationship succeeded, and I can't do much more than I am doing now to help it succeed.

1 It would be nice if it succeeded, but I refuse to do any more than I am doing now to keep the relationship going.

0 My relationship can never succeed, and there is no more than I can do to keep the relationship going.

229

Appendix I:

AREAS OF CHANGE
QUESTIONNAIRE

AREAS OF CHANGE QUESTIONNAIRE

Instructions

In every relationship there are behaviors one or both partners seek to change. Behaviors may occur either too often or not often enough. For example, a partner may be dissatisfied because the other takes out the rubbish only once a week. The desired change would be for this behavior to occur *more often*. On the other hand, one might be dissatisfied because too much time was being spent cleaning up the house; in this case the desired change would be for this behavior to occur *less often*. In other words, a person's dissatisfaction with partner performance of a particular behavior can be expressed as a desire for a behavior to occur either more or less often.

The following pages list typical behaviors which can cause relationship dissatisfactions. As you read each item, decide whether you are *satisfied* with your partner's performance described in that item. If you are satisfied with your partner's performance or if an item is not relevant to you, tick the zero point on the scale, meaning "NO CHANGE DESIRED".

If you are *not satisfied* with your partner's performance in a particular item, indicate the direction of change in behavior you would like to see. Use the rating scale accompanying each item. If you would prefer to see a particular behavior occur *less often*, make a tick ($\checkmark$) on the 'minus' half of the rating scale and indicate how much less you would like this behavior to occur. If you would prefer to see a particular behavior occur *more often*, make a check mark on the 'plus' half of the rating scale to indicate how much more you would like this behavior to occur. Finally, as you go through the list, please indicate which items you consider to be of major importance in your relationship.

Please note that the scales change direction, so that *much less* is sometimes on the left, and at other times on the right.

PART I

I want my partner to:

								Major Item
1 . . . participate in decisions about spending money.	− 3 much less	− 2 less	− 1 some what less	0	+ 1 some what more	+ 2 more	+ 3 much more	☐
2 . . . spend time keeping the house clean.	+ 3 much more	+ 2 more	+ 1 some what more	0	− 1 some what less	− 2 less	− 3 much less	☐
3 . . . have meals ready on time.	− 3 much less	− 2 less	− 1 some what less	0	+ 1 some what more	+ 2 more	+ 3 much more	☐
4 . . . pay attention to his/her appearance	− 3 much less	− 2 less	− 1 some what less	0	+ 1 some what more	+ 2 more	+ 3 much more	☐
5 . . . hit me.	+ 3 much more	+ 2 more	+ 1 some what more	0	− 1 some what less	− 2 less	− 3 much less	☐
6 . . . get together with my friends	+ 3 much more	+ 2 more	+ 1 some what more	0	− 1 some what less	− 2 less	− 3 much less	☐
7 . . . pay the bills on time.	− 3 much less	− 2 less	− 1 some what less	0	+ 1 some what more	+ 2 more	+ 3 much more	☐

I want my partner to:

8 . . . prepare interesting meals.	− 3 much less	− 2 less	− 1 some what less	0	+ 1 some what more	+ 2 more	+ 3 much more	☐
9 . . . start interesting conversations with me.	+ 3 much more	+ 2 more	+ 1 some what more	0	− 1 some what less	− 2 less	− 3 much less	☐
10 . . . go out with me.	− 3 much less	− 2 less	− 1 some what less	0	+ 1 some what more	+ 2 more	+ 3 much more	☐
11 . . . show appreciation for things I do well.	+ 3 much more	+ 2 more	+ 1 some what more	0	− 1 some what less	− 2 less	− 3 much less	☐
12 . . . get together with my relatives.	− 3 much less	− 2 less	− 1 some what less	0	+ 1 some what more	+ 2 more	+ 3 much more	☐
13 . . . have sexual relations with me.	+ 3 much more	+ 2 more	+ 1 some what more	0	− 1 some what less	− 2 less	− 3 much less	☐
14 . . . drink.	+ 3 much more	+ 2 more	+ 1 some what more	0	− 1 some what less	− 2 less	− 3 much less	☐
15 . . . work late.	− 3 much less	− 2 less	− 1 some what less	0	+ 1 some what more	+ 2 more	+ 3 much more	☐
16 . . . get together with our friends.	− 3 much less	− 2 less	− 1 some what less	0	+ 1 some what more	+ 2 more	+ 3 much more	☐
17 . . . help with housework when asked.	− 3 much less	− 2 less	− 1 some what less	0	+ 1 some what more	+ 2 more	+ 3 much more	☐

I want my partner to:

Major Item

	+3	+2	+1	0	-1	-2	-3	
18 . . . argue with me.	much more	more	some what more		some what less	less	much less	☐
19 . . . discipline children.	-3 much less	-2 less	-1 some what less	0	+1 some what more	+2 more	+3 much more	☐
20 . . . engage in extra-marital sexual relationships.	+3 much more	+2 more	+1 some what more	0	-1 some what less	-2 less	-3 much less	☐
21 . . . spend time in outside activities.	+3 much more	+2 more	+1 some what more	0	-1 some what less	-2 less	-3 much less	☐
22 . . . pay attention to my sexual needs.	-3 much less	-2 less	-1 some what less	0	+1 some what more	+2 more	+3 much more	☐
23 . . . spend time with children.	-3 much less	-2 less	-1 some what less	0	+1 some what more	+2 more	+3 much more	☐
24 . . . to give me attention when I need it.	+3 much more	+2 more	+1 some what more	0	-1 some what less	-2 less	-3 much less	☐
25 . . . assume responsibility for finances.	-3 much less	-2 less	-1 some what less	0	+1 some what more	+2 more	+3 much more	☐
26 . . . leave me time to myself.	+3 much more	+2 more	+1 some what more	0	-1 some what less	-2 less	-3 much less	☐
27 . . . agree to do things I like when we go out together	-3 much less	-2 less	-1 some what less	0	+1 some what more	+2 more	+3 much more	☐

I want my partner to:

Major
Item

28 . . . accept praise.	+3 much more	+2 more	+1 some what more	0	−1 some what less	−2 less	−3 much less	☐
29 . . . accomplish his/her responsibilities promptly.	+3 much more	+2 more	+1 some what more	0	−1 some what less	−2 less	−3 much less	☐
30 . . . help in planning our free time.	−3 much less	−2 less	−1 some what less	0	+1 some what more	+2 more	+3 much more	☐
31 . . . express his/her emotions clearly.	−3 much less	−2 less	−1 some what less	0	+1 some what more	+2 more	+3 much more	☐
32 . . . have non-sexual relationships with men/women.	+3 much more	+2 more	+1 some what more	0	−1 some what less	−2 less	−3 much less	☐
33 . . . spend time with me.	−3 much less	−2 less	−1 some what less	0	+1 some what more	+2 more	+3 much more	☐
34 . . . come to meals on time.	+3 much more	+2 more	+1 some what more	0	−1 some what less	−2 less	−3 much less	☐

PART II

It would please my partner if I:

Major
Item

1 . . . participated in decisions about spending money.	−3 much less	−2 less	−1 some what less	0	+1 some what more	+2 more	+3 much more	☐
2 . . . spent time keeping the house clean.	−3 much less	−2 less	−1 some what less	0	+1 some what more	+2 more	+3 much more	☐

It would please my partner if I:

**Major
Item**

3 . . . had meals ready on time.	+3 much more	+2 more	+1 some what more	0	−1 some what less	−2 less	−3 much less	☐
4 . . . paid attention to my appearance.	−3 much less	−2 less	−1 some what less	0	+1 some what more	+2 more	+3 much more	☐
5 . . . hit him/her.	+3 much more	+2 more	+1 some what more	0	−1 some what less	−2 less	−3 much less	☐
6 . . . got together with his/her friends.	−3 much less	−2 less	−1 some what less	0	+1 some what more	+2 more	+3 much more	☐
7 . . . paid the bills on time.	+3 much more	+2 more	+1 some what more	0	−1 some what less	−2 less	−3 much less	☐
8 . . . prepared interesting meals.	+3 much more	+2 more	+1 some what more	0	−1 some what less	−2 less	−3 much less	☐
9 . . . started interesting conversations with him/her.	+3 much more	+2 more	+1 some what more	0	−1 some what less	−2 less	−3 much less	☐
10 . . . went out with him/her.	−3 much less	−2 less	−1 some what less	0	+1 some what more	+2 more	+3 much more	☐
11 . . . show him/her appreciation for things he/she does well.	+3 much more	+2 more	+1 some what more	0	−1 some what less	−2 less	−3 much less	☐
12 . . . got together with his/her relatives.	−3 much less	−2 less	−1 some what less	0	+1 some what more	+2 more	+3 much more	☐

It would please my partner if I: **Major Item**

13 . . . had sexual
relations with
him/her.

| −3 much less | −2 less | −1 some what less | 0 | +1 some what more | +2 more | +3 much more | ☐ |

14 . . . drank.

| −3 much less | −2 less | −1 some what less | 0 | +1 some what more | +2 more | +3 much more | ☐ |

15 . . . worked late.

| +3 much more | +2 more | +1 some what more | 0 | −1 some what less | −2 less | −3 much less | ☐ |

16 . . . got together
with our friends.

| +3 much more | +2 more | +1 some what more | 0 | −1 some what less | −2 less | −3 much less | ☐ |

17 . . . helped with
housework when
asked.

| −3 much less | −2 less | −1 some what less | 0 | +1 some what more | +2 more | +3 much more | ☐ |

18 . . . argued with
him/her.

| +3 much more | +2 more | +1 some what more | 0 | −1 some what less | −2 less | −3 much less | ☐ |

19 . . . disciplined
children.

| −3 much less | −2 less | −1 some what less | 0 | +1 some what more | +2 more | +3 much more | ☐ |

20 . . . engaged in
extra-marital
relationships.

| +3 much more | +2 more | +1 some what more | 0 | −1 some what less | −2 less | −3 much less | ☐ |

21 . . . spent time in
outside activities.

| +3 much more | +2 more | +1 some what more | 0 | −1 some what less | −2 less | −3 much less | ☐ |

22 . . . paid attention
to his/her sexual
needs.

| −3 much less | −2 less | −1 some what less | 0 | +1 some what more | +2 more | +3 much more | ☐ |

It would please my partner if I:

23 . . . spent time with children.	− 3 much less	− 2 less	− 1 some what less	0	+ 1 some what more	+ 2 more	+ 3 much more	☐
24 . . . gave him/her attention when he/she needs it.	+ 3 much more	+ 2 more	+ 1 some what more	0	− 1 some what less	− 2 less	− 3 much less	☐
25 . . . assumed responsibility for finances.	− 3 much less	− 2 less	− 1 some what less	0	+ 1 some what more	+ 2 more	+ 3 much more	☐
26 . . . left him/her time to himself/herself.	− 3 much less	− 2 less	− 1 some what less	0	+ 1 some what more	+ 2 more	+ 3 much more	☐
27 . . . agreed to do things he/she likes when we go out together.	+ 3 much more	+ 2 more	+ 1 some what more	0	− 1 some what less	− 2 less	− 3 much less	☐
28 . . . accepted praise.	− 3 much less	− 2 less	− 1 some what less	0	+ 1 some what more	+ 2 more	+ 3 much more	☐
29 . . . accomplished my responsibilities promptly.	+ 3 much more	+ 2 more	+ 1 some what more	0	− 1 some what less	− 2 less	− 3 much less	☐
30 . . . helped in planning our free time.	+ 3 much more	+ 2 more	+ 1 some what more	0	− 1 some what less	− 2 less	− 3 much less	☐
31 . . . expressed my emotions clearly.	+ 3 much more	+ 2 more	+ 1 some what more	0	− 1 some what less	− 2 less	− 3 much less	☐
32 . . . had non-sexual relationships with men/women.	+ 3 much more	+ 2 more	+ 1 some what more	0	− 1 some what less	− 2 less	− 3 much less	☐

It would please my partner if I:

Major
Item

33 . . . spent time with him/her.	− 3 much less	− 2 less	− 1 some what less	0	+ 1 some what more	+ 2 more	+ 3 much more	☐
34 . . . came to meals on time.	− 3 much less	− 2 less	− 1 some what less	0	+ 1 some what more	+ 2 more	+ 3 much more	☐

RELATIONSHIP BELIEF
INVENTORY

Reproduced by permission of Professor Norman Epstein, University of Maryland.

SCORING OF RELATIONSHIP BELIEF INVENTORY

The subscales are as follows:

D	=	Disagreement is Destructive
M	=	Mindreading is Expected
C	=	Partners cannot Change
S	=	Sexual Perfection
MF	=	The Sexes are Different

Compute a total for each subscale as follows:
For positively keyed items, leave the subject's response as it is.
For negatively keyed items, reverse the response scale, so that

SUBJECT'S RESPONSE	becomes	SCORE
5		0
4		1
3		2
2		3
1		4
0		5

Then compute the sum for the 8 items on the scale.

Name _____ Date _____

Relationship Belief Inventory

(Roy J. Eidelson and Norman Epstein, 1981)

The statements below describe ways in which a person might feel about a relationship with another person. Please mark the space next to each statement according to how strongly you believe that it is true or false for you. *Please mark every one.* Write in 5, 4, 3, 2, 1, or 0 to stand for the following answers.

> 5: I *strongly* believe that the statement is *true.*
> 4: I believe that the statement is *true.*
> 3: I believe that the statement is *probably true,* or more true than false.
> 2: I believe that the statement is *probably false,* or more false than true.
> 1: I believe that the statement is *false.*
> 0: I *strongly* believe that the statement is *false.*

D + ____ 1. If your partner expresses disagreement with your ideas, s/he probably does not think highly of you.

M − ____ 2. I do not expect my partner to sense all my moods.

C + ____ 3. Damages done early in a relationship probably cannot be reversed.

S + ____ 4. I get upset if I think I have not completely satisfied my partner sexually.

MF − ____ 5. Men and women have the same basic emotional needs.

D + ____ 6. I cannot accept it when my partner disagrees with me.

M − ____ 7. If I have to tell my partner that something is important to me, it does not mean that s/he is insensitive to me.

C + ____ 8. My partner does not seem capable of behaving other than s/he does now.

S − ____ 9. If I'm not in the mood for sex when my partner is, I don't get upset about it.

MF + 10. Misunderstandings between partners generally are due to inborn differences in psychological makeups of men and women.

D + ____ 11. I take it as a personal insult when my partner disagrees with an important idea of mine.

M + ____ 12. I get very upset if my partner does not recognize how I am feeling and I have to tell him/her.

C − ____ 13. A partner can learn to become more responsive to his/her partner's needs.

S + ____ 14. A good sexual partner can get himself/herself aroused for sex whenever necessary.

MF + 15. Men and women probably will never understand the opposite sex very well.

D − ____ 16. I like it when my partner presents views different from mine.

M + ____ 17. People who have a close relationship can sense each other's needs as if they could read each other's minds.

C − ____ 18. Just because my partner has acted in ways that upset me does not mean that s/he will do so in the future.

S + ____ 19. If I cannot perform well sexually whenever my parter is in the mood, I would consider that I have a problem.

MF − 20. Men and women need the same basic things out of a relationship.

D + ____ 21. I get very upset when my partner and I cannot see things the same way.

__M +__ ___ 22. It is important to me for my partner to anticipate my needs by sensing changes in my moods.

__C +__ ___ 23. A partner who hurts you badly once probably will hurt you again.

__S −__ ___ 24. I can feel OK about my lovemaking even if my partner does not achieve orgasm.

__MF −__ ___ 25. Biological differences between men and women are not major causes of couples' problems.

__D +__ ___ 26. I cannot tolerate it when my partner argues with me.

__M +__ ___ 27. A partner should know what you are thinking or feeling without you having to tell.

__C −__ ___ 28. If my partner wants to change, I believe that s/he can do it.

__S −__ ___ 29. If my sexual partner does not get satisfied completely, it does not mean that I have failed.

__MF +__ ___ 30. One of the major causes of marital problems is that men and women have different emotional needs.

__D +__ ___ 31. When my partner and I disagree, I feel like our relationship is falling apart.

__M +__ ___ 32. People who love each other know exactly what each other's thoughts are without a word ever being said.

__C −__ ___ 33. If you don't like the way a relationship is going, you can make it better.

__S −__ ___ 34. Some difficulties in my sexual performance do not mean personal failure to me.

__MF +__ ___ 35. You can't really understand someone of the opposite sex.

__D −__ ___ 36. I do not doubt my partner's feelings for me when we argue.

__M +__ ___ 37. If you have to ask your partner for something, it shows that s/he was not "tuned into" your needs.

__C +__ ___ 38. I do not expect my partner to be able to change.

__S +__ ___ 39. When I do not seem to be performing well sexually, I get upset.

__MF +__ ___ 40. Men and women will always be mysteries to each other.

241

SOCIAL SITUATIONS QUESTIONNAIRE

Reproduced by permission of Dr Peter Trower.

SOCIAL SITUATIONS QUESTIONNAIRE

This questionnaire is concerned with how people get on in social situations, that is, situations involving being with other people, talking to them, etc.

PAGE ONE: HOW DIFFICULT?

The first page deals with how much difficulty, if any, you have in these situations. Having difficulty means that the situation makes you feel ANXIOUS or UNCOMFORTABLE, either because you don't know what to do, or because you feel frightened, embarrassed or self-conscious.

1. Across the top of page 1 you will see five different choices of difficulty, each with a number underneath (e.g. 'no difficulty' = 0).
2. Down the left-hand side of the page are listed 30 situations you might encounter which some people have said they find difficult. If some of these situations are ones in which you have never found yourself, please imagine how you would feel if you did.
3. Down the right-hand side of the page are two columns which refer to two different points in time. They are headed (a) the present time; (b) this time a year ago.

For each situation, and for each point in time, select the choice or difficulty which most clearly fits how you feel, and write the number of your choice in the appropriate column.

Examples:

	Present time	Year ago
A. Going to a public meeting	3	1
B. Going to the cinema	0	0

Example A means that someone had great difficulty (3) at the present time, and slight difficulty (1) a year ago. Example B means that someone had no difficulty (0) at either of these points in time.

Please note: Choice 'avoidance if possible' should only be used if you find the situation so difficult that you would avoid it whenever you could. It should NOT be used for situations you avoid because they are not to your taste — e.g. not going to concerts because you dislike music.

PAGE TWO: HOW OFTEN?

The second page deals with how often you have found yourself in each of the 22 situations listed on the left-hand side of the page. The procedure is exactly the same as that for page 1.

1. Across the top of page 2 are seven different 'how often' choices, each with a number underneath it (e.g. 'at least once a week' = 2).
2. Down the right-hand side of the page are two columns referring to two three-month periods; (a) the last three months; and (b) the same three months a year ago.

For each situation, and for each three-month period, select a 'how often' choice and write the number in the appropriate column.

Please note: Choice 'never' (7) means that you have never in your life been in that particular situation. It should therefore be used in both columns.

PAGE ONE

Date: .... Sex: .... Name: ....

No difficulty 0	Slight difficulty 1	Moderate difficulty 2	Great difficulty 3	Avoidance if possible 4

	At the present time	This time a year ago
1. Walking down the street	_____	_____
2. Going into shops	_____	_____
3. Going on public transport	_____	_____
4. Going into pubs	_____	_____
5. Going to parties	_____	_____
6. Mixing with people at work	_____	_____
7. Making friends of your own age	_____	_____
8. Going out with someone you are sexually attracted to	_____	_____
9. Being with a group of the same sex roughly the same age as you	_____	_____
10. Being with a group containing both men and women of roughly the same age as you	_____	_____
11. Being with a group of the opposite sex of roughly the same age as you	_____	_____
12. Entertaining people in your home, lodgings, etc.	_____	_____
13. Entertaining people in your home, lodgings, etc.	_____	_____
14. Going to dances, dance halls or discotheques	_____	_____
15. Being with older people	_____	_____
16. Being with younger people	_____	_____
17. Going into a room full of people	_____	_____
18. Meeting strangers	_____	_____
19. Being with people you don't know very well	_____	_____
20. Being with friends	_____	_____
21. Approaching others — making the first move in starting up a friendship	_____	_____
22. Making ordinary decisions affecting others (e.g. what to do together in the evening)	_____	_____
23. Being with only one other person rather than a group	_____	_____
24. Getting to know people in depth	_____	_____
25. Taking the initiative in keeping a conversation going	_____	_____
26. Looking at people directly in the eyes	_____	_____
27. Disagreeing with what other people are saying and putting forward your own views	_____	_____
28. People standing or sitting very close to you	_____	_____
29. Talking about yourself and your feelings in a conversation	_____	_____
30. People looking at you	_____	_____

PAGE TWO

Every day or almost every day	At least once a week	At least once a fortnight	At least once a month	Once or twice in three months	Not at all in three months	Never
1	2	3	4	5	6	7

	Last three months	Three month period a year ago
1. Walking down the street	_____	_____
2. Going into shops	_____	_____
3. Going on public transport	_____	_____
4. Going into pubs	_____	_____
5. Going to parties	_____	_____
6. Mixing with people at work	_____	_____
7. Making friends of your own age	_____	_____
8. Going out with someone you are sexually attracted to	_____	_____
9. Being with a group of the same sex roughly the same age as you	_____	_____
10. Being with a group containing both men and women of roughly the same age as you	_____	_____
11. Being with a group of the opposite sex of roughly the same age as you	_____	_____
12. Entertaining people in your home, lodgings, etc.	_____	_____
13. Going to restaurants or cafes.	_____	_____
14. Going to dances, dance halls or discotheques	_____	_____
15. Being with older people	_____	_____
16. Being with younger people	_____	_____
17. Going into a room full of people	_____	_____
18. Meeting strangers	_____	_____
19. Being with people you don't know very well	_____	_____
20. Being with friends	_____	_____
21. Approaching others — making the first move in starting up a friendship	_____	_____
22. Making ordinary decisions affecting others (e.g. what to do together in the evening)	_____	_____

Comments: If you wish to add any comments about your ratings of difficulty or frequency, please do so below and continue overleaf if necessary.

DRUG RELATED ATTITUDE QUESTIONNAIRE

SCORING

Responses are scored on a scale 1 to 7:

Totally Agree	7
Agree Very Much	6
Agree Slightly	5
Neutral	4
Disagree Slightly	3
Disagree Very Much	2
Totally Disagree	1

The response to each item is then summed to give a total response in the range 18–126.

ATTITUDES

For each of the attitudes, show your answer by placing a tick (✔) under the column that BEST DESCRIBES HOW YOU THINK. Be sure to choose only one answer for each attitude.

To decide whether a given attitude is typical of your way of looking at things, simply keep in mind what you are like MOST OF THE TIME.

ATTITUDES	Totally Agree	Agree Very Much	Agree Slightly	Neutral	Disagree Slightly	Disagree Very Much	Totally Disagree
1. I cannot be happy unless most people I know admire me.							
2. If a person asks for help, it is a sign of weakness.							
3. If I do not do as well as other people it means I am an inferior human being.							
4. If I slip and take drugs it is useless to try to control myself after that.							
5. If you cannot do something well, there is little point in doing it at all.							
6. If I fail partly, it is as bad as being a complete failure.							
7. I have got to do just what I feel.							
8. If I am to be a worthwhile person, I must be truly outstanding in at least one important respect.							
9. I'm too weak to control myself.							

ATTITUDES	Totally Agree	Agree Very Much	Agree Slightly	Neutral	Disagree Slightly	Disagree Very Much	Totally Disagree
10. To be a good, moral, worthwhile person, I must help everyone who needs it.							
11. I can't go without drugs when I'm down.							
12. I take drugs because nobody cares about me.							
13. I cannot trust other people because they might be cruel to me.							
14. Difficult issues in life are best handled by being avoided as long as possible.							
15. I have nothing to look forward to.							
16. Being isolated from others is bound to lead to unhappiness.							
17. Other people make me take drugs.							
18. I have got to have what is enjoyable now.							

REFERENCES

INTRODUCTION

Bandura, A. (1977) *Social Learning Theory*, Engelwood Cliffs, New Jersey: Prentice Hall.

Bandura, A. (1978) 'The self system in reciprocal determination', *American Psychologist*, 33: 444–58.

Beck, A.T. (1976) *Cognitive Therapy and the Emotional Disorders*, New York: International Universities Press.

Beck, A.T., Rush, A.J., Shaw, B.F., and Emery, G. (1980) *Cognitive Therapy of Depression*, New York: Wiley.

Beck, A.T., Emery, G., and Greenberg, R.L. (1985) *Anxiety Disorders and Phobias: A cognitive perspective*, New York: Basic Books.

Blackburn, J.M., Bishop, S., Glen, A.I.M., Whalley, L.G., and Christie, J.E. (1981) 'The efficacy of cognitive therapy in depression. A treatment trial using cognitive therapy and pharmacotherapy each alone and in combination', *British Journal of Psychiatry*, 139: 181–9.

Blackburn, I.M. (1986) 'The cognitive revolution: an ongoing evolution', *Behavioural Psychotherapy*, 14, 4: 274–7.

Braceland, F.J. and Griffin, M.E. (1950) 'The mental changes associated with multiple sclerosis (an interim report)', *Proceedings of the Association for Research in Nervous and Mental Diseases*, 28: 450–5.

Brown, G. and Harris, T. (1978) *Social Origins of Depression – a study of psychiatric disorder in women*, London: Tavistock.

Eidelson, R.J. and Epstein, N. (1982) 'Cognitive and relationship maladjustment: Development of a measure of dysfunctional relationship beliefs', *Journal of Consulting and Clinical Psychology*, 50: 715–20.

Ellis, A. (1962) *Reason and Emotion in Psychotherapy*. New York: Lyle Stuart.

Epstein, N. (1982) 'Cognitive therapy with couples', *American Journal of Family Therapy*, 10: 5–16.

Friedberg, F. (1985) 'Overcoming obstacles to real-life generalisation in exposure treatments in agoraphobia', *British Journal of Cognitive Psychotherapy*, 3, 2: 10–22.

REFERENCES

Fry, P.S. (1984) 'Cognitive training and cognitive-behavioural variables in the treatment of depression in the elderly', *Clinical Gerontologist*, 3: 25–45.

Garner, D.M. and Bemis, K. (1982) 'A cognitive-behavioural approach to anorexia nervosa', *Cognitive Therapy and Research*, 6: 1–7.

Jacobsen, N., Follette, W., Revensdorf, D., Hahlweg, K., Baucom, D., and Margolin, G. (1984) 'Variability in outcome and clinical significance of behavioural mental therapy: a re-analysis of outcome data', *Journal of Consulting and Clinical Psychology*, 52: 497–504.

Jansson, L. and Ost, L.G. (1982) 'Behavioural treatments for agoraphobia: an evaluative review', *Clinical Psychology Review*, 2: 311–36.

Kelly, G.A. (1955) *The Psychology of Personal Constructs*, New York: Norton.

Larcombe, N.A. and Wilson, P.H. (1984) 'An evaluation of cognitive-behaviour therapy for depression in patients with multiple sclerosis', *British Journal of Psychiatry*, 145: 366–71.

Lindsay, W.R., Gamsu, C.V., McLaughlin, E., Hood, E.M., and Epsil, C.A. (1987) 'A controlled trial of treatments for generalised anxiety', *British Journal of Clinical Psychology*, 26: 3–15.

Marshal, P.D., Palmer, R.L., and Bothelo, R.J. (1986) 'Is there a place for a specific cognitive therapy of anorexia nervosa?', *British Journal of Cognitive Psychotherapy*, 4: 48–56.

Meichenbaum, D. (1977) *Cognitive Behaviour Modification*, New York: Plenum.

Morris, T. (1979) 'Psychological adjustment to mastectomy', *Cancer Treatment Review*, 6: 41–61.

Paul, G.L. (1967) 'Strategy of outcome research in psychotherapy', *Journal of Consulting Psychology*, 31: 109–18.

Ross, M. and Scott, M. (1985) 'An evaluation of individual and group cognitive therapy in the treatment of depression in an inner city health centre', *Journal of the Royal College of General Practitioners*, 35: 239–42.

Rush, A.J., Beck, A.T., Kovacs, M., and Hollon, S. (1977) 'Comparative efficacy of cognitive therapy and pharmacotherapy in the treatment of depressed outpatients', *Cognitive Therapy and Research*, 1: 17–37.

Salkovskis, P.M. (1986) 'The cognitive revolution: new way forward, backward, somersault or full circle?', *Behavioural Psychotherapy*, 14, 4: 278–82.

Scott, M.J. and Stradling, S.G. (1987) 'The evaluation of a group parent training programme', *Behavioural Psychotherapy*, 15: 224–39.

Silverman, J.A. and Eardley, B.A. (1984) 'Do maladaptive attitudes cause depression?', *Archives of General Psychiatry*, 41: 28–30.

Simons, A.D., Garfield, S.L., and Murphy, G.E. (1984) 'The process of change in cognitive therapy and pharmacotherapy for depression', *Archives of General Psychiatry*, 41: 45–51.

Simons, A.D., Murphy, G.E., Levine, J.L., and Wetzel, R.D. (1986) 'Sustained improvement one year after cognitive and/or pharmacotherapy of depression', *Archives of General Psychiatry*, 43: 43–8.

Skinner, B.F. (1938) *The Behaviour of Organisms*, New York: Appleton-Century-Crofts.
Skinner, B.F. (1963) 'Behaviourism at fifty', *Science*, 40: 951–8.

CHAPTER 1

Bandura, A. (1969) *Principles of Behaviour Modification*, New York: Holt, Rinehart & Winston.
Beck, A.T. (1976) *Cognitive Therapy and the Emotional Disorders*, New York: International Universities Press.
Becker, W.C. (1960) 'The relationship of factors in parental ratings of self and each other to the behaviours of kindergarten children as rated by mothers, fathers and teachers', *Journal of Consulting Psychology*, 24: 507–27.
Bell, R.Q. and Harper, L. (1977) *Child Effects on Adults*, New York: Wiley.
Berkley, R.A. and Cunningham, C.E. (1979) 'The effects of Ritalin on the mother-child interaction of hyperactive children', *Archives of General Psychiatry*, 36: 201–8.
Cameron, J.R. (1977) 'Parental treatment, children's temperament and the risk of childhood behavioural problems', *American Journal of Orthopsychiatry*, 47: 568–76.
Cox, K. (1982) 'Pregnancy and Parenthood in School-age Pupils', paper given at National Children's Bureau Conference.
D'Zurilla, T.J. and Nezu, A. (1982) 'Social problem solving in adults', in *Advances in Cognitive-Behavioural Research and Therapy*, vol. 1, New York: Academic Press.
Ellis, A. (1982) 'Psychoneurosis and anxiety problems', in R. Grieger and J. Grieger (eds) *Cognitive and Emotional Disturbance*, New York: Human Sciences Press.
Eyberg, S.M. and Ross, A.W. (1978) 'Assessment of child behaviour problems. The validation of a new inventory', *Journal of Clinical Child Psychology*, 7: 113–16.
Graham, P. (1973) 'Temperamental characteristics as predicators of behavioural disorders in children', *American Journal of Orthopsychiatry*, 43: 328–33.
Humphries, T., Kinsbourne, M., and Swanson, J. (1978) 'Stimulant effects on co-operation and social interactions between hyper-active children and their mothers', *Journal of Child Psychology and Psychiatry*, 19: 13–22.
Hutchings, B. and Madnick, S.A. (1975) 'Registered criminality in the adoptive and biological parents of registered male criminal adoptees', in R. Fiere, D. Rosenthal, and H. Brill (eds) *Genetic Research in Psychiatry*, Baltimore: Johns Hopkins University Press.
Kendall, P.C. and Wilcox, L.E. (1979) 'Self-control in children: development of a rating scale', *Journal of Consulting and Clinical Psychology*, 47: 1020–9.

REFERENCES

Lobitz, G.K. and Johnson, S.M. (1975) 'Normal versus deviant children: a multi-method comparison', *Journal of Abnormal Child Psychology*, 3: 353–74.

Luria, A. (1961) *The Role of Speech in the Regulation of Normal and Abnormal Behaviours*, New York: Liveright.

Meichenbaum, D. (1977) *Cognitive Behaviour Modification*, New York: Plenum.

Newson, J. (1982) 'Bringing up children in a changing world: disciplinary styles and moral outcomes', in G. Pugh (ed.), National Children's Bureau.

Orvaschel, H., Weissman, M.M., and Kidd, K.K. (1980) 'Children and depression', *Journal of Affective Disorders*, 2: 1–16.

Pavlov, I.P. (1927) *Conditional Reflexes: An Investigation of the Physiological Activity of the Cerebral Cortex*, London: Oxford University Press.

Peterson, D.R. and Quay, H.C. (1975) *Manual for the Behaviour Problem Checklist*, University of Miami.

Piaget, J. (1926) *The Language and Thought of the Child*, New York: Harcourt Brace.

Robins, L.N. (1979) 'Follow-up studies', in H.C. Quay and J.S. Werry (eds) *Psychopathological Disorders of Childhood*, New York: Wiley.

Rutter, M. (1964) 'Temperamental characteristics in infancy and later development of behaviour disorders', *British Journal of Psychiatry*, 110: 651–61.

Skinner, B.F. (1953) *Science and Human Behaviour*, New York: Free Press.

Thorley, G. and Yale, W. (1982) 'A role-play test of parent-child interaction', *Behavioural Psychotherapy*, 10: 146–61.

Thorndike, E.L. (1911) *Animal Intelligence: Experimental Studies*, New York: Macmillan.

Torgersen, A.M. and Kringlen, E. (1978) 'Genetic aspects of temperamental differences in infants', *Journal of Academic Child Psychiatry*, 17: 434–44.

Vygotsky, L. (1962) *Thought and Language*, New York: Wiley.

Walker, M.H. (1970) *Walker Problem Behaviour Identification, Checklist Manual*, Western Psychological Services.

Walkind, S.N. and De Salis, W. (1982) 'Infant temperament, maternal mental state and child behavioural problems', in R. Porter and G.M. Collins (eds) *Temperamental Differences in Infants and Young Children*, London: Pitman Books.

Wilson, H. (1980) 'Parental supervision: a neglected aspect of delinquency', *British Journal of Criminology*, 20: 203–35.

Zivin, G. (ed.) (1979) *The Development of Self-regulation through Private Speech*, New York: Wiley.

CHAPTER 2

August, G.J. (1983) 'A four-year follow-up of hyperactive boys with and without conduct disorder', *British Journal of Psychiatry*, 143: 192–8.

REFERENCES

Cantwell, D.P. (1977) 'Hyperkinetic Syndrome', in M. Rutter and L. Hervoz (eds) *Child Psychiatry: Modern Approaches*, London: Blackwell Scientific Publications.

Conners, C.K. (1978) 'Normative data on revised Conners parent and teacher rating scales', *Journal of Abnormal Psychology*, 6: 221–36.

Corney, R.H. and Clare, A.W. (1985) 'The construction, development and testing of a self-report questionnaire to identify social problems', *Psychological Medicine*, 15: 637–49.

Eyberg, S.M. and Ross, A.W. (1978) 'Assessment of child behaviour problems: the validation of a new inventory', *Journal of Clinical Child Psychology*, 7: 113–16.

Loney, J., Langhorne, J.E., and Paternite, C.S. (1978) 'An empirical basis of subgrouping: the hyperkinetic/minimal brain dysfunction syndrome', *Journal of Abnormal Psychology*, 87: 431–41.

McCauley, R. (1977) *Child Behaviour Problems*, London: Macmillan.

Peterson, D.R. (1961) 'Behaviour problems of middle childhood', *Journal of Consulting Psychology*, 25: 205–20.

Rutter, M., Shaffer, D., and Shepherd, M. (1975) *A Multi-social Classification of Child Psychiatric Disorder*, Geneva: World Health Organization.

Scott, M.J. and Stradling, S.G. (1987) 'Evaluation of a group programme for parents of problem children', *Behavioural Psychotherapy*, 15: 224–39.

Snaith, R.P., Constantopoulous, A.A., Jardine, M.Y., and McGuffin, P. (1978) 'Clinical scale for self-assessment of irritability (IDA)', *British Journal of Psychiatry*, 132: 164–71.

Thorley, G. and Yule, W. (1982) 'A role-play test and parent child interaction', *Behavioural Psychotherapy*, 10: 146–61.

CHAPTER 3

Ambrose, S., Hazzard, A., and Haworth, J. (1980) 'Cognitive-behavioural parenting groups for abusive families', *Child Abuse and Neglect*, 4: 119–24.

Dubey, D.R., O'Leary, S.G., and Kaufman, K.F. (1983) 'Training parents of hyperactive children in child management: A comparative outcome study', *Journal of Abnormal Child Psychology*, 11: 229–46.

Kempe, C. (1976) 'Approaches to preventing child abuse', *American Journal of Childhood Disease*, 133: 1124–8.

Nomellini, S. and Katz, R.C. (1983) 'Effects of anger control training on abusive parents', *Cognitive Therapy and Research*, 7: 57–68.

Novaco, R. (1976) 'The functions and regulation of the arousal of anger', *American Journal of Psychiatry*, 133: 1124–8.

Patterson, G.R., Ray, R.S., Shaw, D.A., and Ebb, J.A. (1969) 'Manual for coding family interaction', (6th edn), unpublished manuscript, University of Oregon.

Scott, M.J. and Stradling, S.G. (1987) 'Evaluation of a group programme for parents of problem children', *Behavioural Psychotherapy*, 15: 224–39.

CHAPTER 4

Beck, A.T. (1976) *Cognitive Therapy and the Emotional Disorders*, New York: International Universities Press.

Bernard, M.E. (1985) 'Enhancing the psychological adjustment of school-age children: a rational-emotive perspective', *British Journal of Cognitive Psychotherapy*, 3: 23–41.

Butler, R.J. (1985) 'Towards an understanding of childhood difficulties', in N. Beail (ed.) *Repertory Grid Techniques and Personal Constructs. Applications in Clinical and Educational Settings*, London: Croom Helm.

Campe, B.W. and Bash, M.A.S. (1981) *Think Aloud. Increasing Social and Cognitive Skills — Problem-Solving Programme for Children*, Champaign, Ill: Research Press.

Conners, C.K. (1978) 'Normative data on revised Conners parent and teacher rating scales', *Journal of Abnormal Child Psychology*, 6: 221–36.

Graziano, A.M., Deciovanni, I., and Garcia, K. (1979) 'Behavioural treatment of child's fear', *Psychological Bulletin*, 56: 804–30.

Graziano, A.M. and Mooney, N.B. (1980) 'Family self control instructions for children's night-time fear reduction', *Journal of Consulting and Clinical Psychology*, 48: 206–13.

Hartzenbuehler, L.C. and Schroeder, H.E. (1978) 'Desensitization procedures in the treatment of childhood disorders', *Psychological Bulletin*, 85: 331–44.

Jackson, S.R. and Bannister, D. (1984) 'Growing into Self', in D. Bannister (ed.) *Issues and Approaches in Personal Construct Therapy*, London: Academic Press.

Kovacs, M. and Beck, A.T. (1977) 'An empirical-clinical approach towards a definition of childhood depression', in J.G. Schulterbrandt and A. Rasking (eds) *Depression in Childhood: Diagnosis, Treatment and Conceptual Models*, New York: Raven Press.

Meichenbaum, D. and Turk, D. (1976) 'The cognitive-behavioural management of anxiety, anger and pain', in P.O. Davidson (ed.) *The Behavioural Management of Anxiety, Depression and Pain*, New York: Brunner/Mazel.

Nelson, W.M. (1981) 'A cognitive-behavioural treatment for disproportionate dental anxiety and pain. A case study', *Journal of Clinical Child Psychology*, 10: 79–82.

Reynolds, W.M. and Coats, K.I. (1986) 'A comparison of cognitive-behavioural therapy and relaxation training for the treatment of depression in adolescents,' *Journal of Consulting and Clinical Psychology*, 54: 653–60.

Waters, V. (1982) 'Therapies for children: Rational-emotive therapy', in C.R. Reynolds and T.B. Gutbein (eds) *Handbook of School Psychology*, New York: Wiley.

CHAPTER 5

American Psychiatric Asociation (1980) *Diagnostic and Statistical Manual of Mental Disorders* (3rd edn), Washington, DC: American Psychiatric Association.

Beck, A.T., Ward, C.H., Mendelson, M., Mock, J., and Erbaugh, J. (1961) 'An inventory for measuring depression', *Archives of General Psychiatry*, 4: 561–71.

Beck, A.T., Emery, G., and Greenberg, R. (1985) *Anxiety Disorders and Phobias: A Cognitive Perspective*, New York: Basic Books.

Beck, A.T. (1987) 'Cognitive models of depression', *Journal of Cognitive Psychotherapy*, 1: 1–37.

Blacker, C.V.R. and Clare, A.W. (1987) 'Depressive disorder in primary care', *British Journal of Psychiatry*, 150: 737–51.

Breslau, H. and Davis, G.C. (1986) 'Chronic stress and major depression', *Archives of General Psychiatry*, 43:309–14.

Murphy, J.M., Olivier, D.C., Sobol, A.M., Monson, R.S., and Leighton, A.H. (1986) 'Diagnosis and outcome: depression and anxiety in a general population', *Psychological Medicine*, 16: 117–26.

Snaith, R.P. and Zigmond, A.S. (1983) 'The Hospital Anxiety and Depression Scale', *Acta Psychiatrica Scandinavica*, 67: 361–70.

Snaith, R.P. (1987) 'The concepts of mild depression', *British Journal of Psychiatry*, 150: 387–93.

Wing, J.K., Cooper, J.E., and Sartorius, N. (1974) *The Measurement and Classification of Psychiatric Symptoms*, Cambridge University Press.

World Health Organisation (1978) *Mental Disorders: Glossary and Guide to their Classification in Accordance with the Sixth Revision of the International Classification of Disease*, Geneva.

CHAPTER 6

Beach, S.R.H. and O'Leary, K.D. (1986) 'The treatment of depression in the context of marital discord', *Behaviour Therapy*, 17: 43–9.

Beck, A.T. and Greenberg, R. (1976) *Coping with depression*. Copies from: Center for Cognitive Therapy, Room 602, 133 South 36th Street, Philadelphia, PA 19104, USA.

Beck, A.T., Ward, C.H., Mendelson, M., Mock, J., and Erbaugh, J. (1961) 'An inventory for measuring depression', *Archives of General Psychiatry*, 4: 561–71.

Burns, D.D. (1980) *Feeling Good: the new mood therapy*, New York: William Morrow & Co.

Corney, R.H. and Clare, A.W. (1985) 'The construction, development and testing of a self-report questionnaire to identify social problems', *Psychological Medicine*, 15: 637–49.

Fennell, M.J.V. and Teasdale, J.D. (1987) 'Cognitive therapy for depression. Individual differences and the process of change', *Cognitive Therapy and Research*, 11,2: 253–71.

REFERENCES

Murphy, G.E. (1985) 'A conceptual framework for the choice of interventions in cognitive therapy', *Cognitive Therapy Research*, 15,2: 127–34.
Ross, M. and Scott, M. (1985) 'An evaluation of the effectiveness of
individual and group cognitive therapy in the treatment of depressed
patients in an inner city health centre', *Journal of the Royal College of
General Practitioners*, 35: 239–42.
Weissman, A.N. and Beck, A.T. (1978) 'Development and validation of
of the Dysfunctional Attitudes Scale', paper presented at the American
Educational Research Association Annual Convention, Toronto,
Canada.

CHAPTER 7

Beck, A.T., Emery, G., and Greenberg, R.L. (1985) *Anxiety Disorders and
Phobias: A Cognitive Perspective*, New York: Basic Books.
Butler, G. (1987) 'Cognitive Conceptualisation in Generalised Anxiety',
paper presented at symposium, Cognitive Therapy with Adult
Psychological Disorders: A Clinical Update, University of Oxford.
Clark, D.M., Salkovskis, P.M., and Chalkley, A.J. (1985) 'Respiratory
control as a treatment for panic attacks', *Journal of Behaviour Therapy and
Experimental Psychiatry*, 16: 23–30.
Friedberg, F. (1985) 'Overcoming obstacles to real-life generalisation in
exposure treatments of agoraphobia', *British Journal of Cognitive
Psychotherapy*, 3, 2: 10–19.
Marlatt, G.A. and Gordon, J. (1985) *Relapse Prevention: Maintenance
Strategies in Addictive Behaviour Change*, New York: Guilford Press.

CHAPTER 8

Argyle, M. (1986) 'Social skills and the analysis of situations and
conversations', in C. Hollin and P. Trower (eds) *Handbook of Social
Skills Training: Clinical Applications and New Directions*, vol. 2, Oxford:
Pergamon.
Argyle, M. and Kendon, A. (1967) 'The experimental analysis of social
performance', in L. Berkowitz (ed.) *Advances in Experimental Social
Psychology*, vol. 3, New York: Academic Press.
Beck, A.T. (1987) 'Cognitive models of depression', *Journal of Cognitive
Psychotherapy*, 1: 5–38.
Coyne, J.C. (1985) 'Towards an interactional description of depression',
in J.C. Coyne (ed.) *Essential Papers on Depression*, New York University
Press.
Epstein, N. (1985) 'Depression and marital dysfunction: cognitive and
behavioural linkages', *International Journal of Mental Health*, 13 (3–4):
86–104.
Epstein, N. and Eidelson, R.J. (1981) 'Unrealistic beliefs of clinical
couples: their relationship to expectations, goals and satisfaction',
American Journal of Family Therapy, 9: 13–22.

REFERENCES

Epstein, N., Pretzer, J.L., and Fleming, B. (1987) 'The role of cognitive appraisal in self reports of marital communication', *Behaviour Therapy*, 18: 5-69.

Gottman, J.M. (1979) *Marital Interaction: Experimental Investigations*, New York: Academic Press.

Hops, H., Wills, T.A., Patterson, G.R., and Weiss, R.L. (1972) *Marital Interaction Coding System*, Eugene, OR: University of Oregon and Oregon Research Institute.

Jacobson, N.S., Waldren, H., and Moore, D. (1980) 'Toward a behavioural profile of marital distress', *Journal of Consulting and Clinical Psychology*, 48: 696-703.

Kern, J.M. (1982) 'The comparative external and concurrent validity of three role-plays for assessing heterosocial performance', *Behaviour Therapy*, 13: 666-80.

Kubler, A.L. and Stotland, E. (1964) *The End of Hope: A Social Clinical Study of Suicide*, New York: Free Press.

Newton, A., Kindness, K., and McFadgen, M. (1983) 'Patients and social skills groups: do they lack social skills?', *Behavioural Psychotherapy*, 11: 116-26.

Schlenker, B.R. and Leary, M.R. (1982) 'Social anxiety and self presentation: a conceptualization and model', *Psychological Bulletin*, 92: 641-69.

Spanier, G.B. (1976) 'Measuring dyadic adjustment: new scales for assessing the quality of marriage and similar dyads', *Journal of Marriage and the Family*, 38: 15-28.

Stravynski, A. and Shahar, A. (1983) 'The treatment of social dysfunction in non-psychotic psychiatric outpatients', A review *Journal of Nervous and Mental Diseases*, 171: 721-8.

Thibaut, J. and Kelly, H.H. (1959) *The Social Psychology of Groups*, New York: Wiley.

Trower, P., Bryant, B., and Argyle, M. (1978) *Social Skills and Mental Health*, London: Methuen.

Trower, P., O'Mahoney, J.F., and Dryden, W. (1982) 'Cognitive aspects of social failure: some implications for social skills training', *British Journal of Guidance Counselling*, 10: 176-84.

Trower, P. (1986) 'Social Skills Training and Social Anxiety', in C. Hollin and P. Trower (eds) *Handbook of Social Skills Training: Clinical Applications and New Directions*, vol. 2, Oxford: Pergamon.

Van Dam-Baggen, R. and Kraaimaat, F. (1986) 'A group social skills training program with psychiatric patients: outcome drop-out rate and prediction', *Behavior Research and Therapy*, 24: 161-9.

Weiss, R.L. (1978) 'The conceptualization of marriage from a behavioural perspective', in T.J. Paolino and B.S. McCrady (eds) *Marriage and Marital Therapy: Psychoanalytic, Behavioural and Systems Theory Perspectives*, (165-239), New York: Brunner Mazel.

Weiss, R.L., Hops, H., and Patterson, G.R. (1973) 'A framework for conceptualizing marital confliction', in L.A. Hamerlynck, L.C. Handy, and E.J. Marsh (eds) *Behaviour and Change: Methodology, Concepts and Practice* (309-42), Champaign, Ill: Research Press.

CHAPTER 9

Epstein, N. and Eidelson, R.J. (1981) 'Unrealistic beliefs of clinical couples: their relationship to expectations, goals and satisfaction', *American Journal of Family Therapy*, 9: 13–22.

Jacobson, N.S. and Margolin, G. (1979) *Marital Therapy: Strategies Based on Social Learning and Behaviour Exchange Principles*, New York: Brunner/Mazel.

Spanier, G.B. (1976) 'Measuring dyadic adjustment: new scales for assessing the quality of marriage and similar dyads', *Journal of Marriage and the Family*, 38: 15–28.

Weiss, R.L. and Margolin, G. (1977) 'Marital conflict and accord', in A.R. Ciminero, K.S. Chalhoan, and H.E. Adams (eds) *Handbook for Behavioural Assessment*, New York: Wiley.

CHAPTER 10

Billings, A.G. and Moos, R.H. (1982) 'Social support and functioning among community and clinical groups: a panel model', *Journal of Behavioural Medicine*, 4: 139–57.

Curran, J. (1979) 'Social skills: methodological issues and future directions', in A.S. Bellack and M. Herzen (eds) *Research and Practice in Social Skills Training*, New York: Plenum Press.

Goldstein, A.P. and Keller, H. (1987) *Aggressive Behaviour: Assessment and Intervention*, Oxford: Pergamon Press.

Kazdin, A.E. and Mascitelli, S. (1982) 'Covert and overt rehearsal and homework practice in developing assertiveness', *Journal of Consulting and Clinical Psychology*, 50: 250–8.

Linehan, M.M., Walker, R.O., Bronheim, S., Haynesk, F., and Yevyeroffey (1979) 'Group versus individual assertion training', *Journal of Consulting and Clinical Psychology*, 47: 1000–2.

McFall, M.E., Winnett, R.L., Bordewick, M.C., and Bornstein, P.H. (1982) 'Non-verbal components in the communication of assertiveness', *Behaviour Modification*, 6: 121–40.

Spence, S.H. (1981) 'Differences in social skills performance between institutionalised juvenile male offenders and a comparable group of boys without offence records', *British Journal of Clinical Psychology*, 20: 163–71.

Trower, P., Bryant, B., and Argyle, M. (1978) *Social Skills and Mental Health*, London: Methuen.

Watson, D. and Friend, R. (1969) 'Measurement of social-evaluative anxiety', *Journal of Consulting and Clinical Psychology*, 33: 448–57.

Winefield, H.R. (1984) 'The nature and elicitation of social support: some implications for the helping professions', *Behavioural Psychotherapy*, 12: 318–30.

CHAPTER 11

Cooper, P.J. and Fairburn, C.G. (1984) 'Cognitive behaviour therapy for anorexia nervosa: some preliminary findings', *Journal of Psychosomatic Research*, 28: 493–9.

Corney, R.H. and Clare, A.W. (1985) 'The construction, development and testing of a self-report questionnaire to identify social problems', *Psychological Medicine*, 15, 637–49.

Cummings, C., Gordon, J.R., and Marlatt, G.A. (1980) 'Relapse: prevention and prediction', in W.R. Miller (ed.) *The Addictive Behaviours*, Oxford: Pergamon Press.

Davidson, R.J. and Raistrick (1986) 'The validity of the short alcohol dependence data (SADD) questionnaire', *British Journal of Addiction*, 81: 217–22.

Erdlen, F.A., McLellan, A.T., La Porte, D., *et al.* (1978) *Instruction Manual for the Addiction Severity Index*, Philadelphia.

Fairburn, C.G. (1984) 'A cognitive behavioural treatment for bulimia', in D.M. Garner and P.E. Garfinkel (eds) *Handbook on Psychotherapy for Anorexia Nervosa and Bulimia*, New York: Guilford Press.

Fairburn, C.G. (1987) 'Cognitive behaviour therapy for bulimia nervosa', paper delivered at symposium, Cognitive Therapy With Adult Psychological Disorders: A Clinical Update, University of Oxford.

Hunt, W.A., Barnett, L.W., and Branch, L.G. (1971) 'Relapse rates in addiction programs', *Journal of Clinical Psychology*, 27: 455–6.

Hunt, G.G. and Azrin, N. (1973) 'A community reinforcement approach to alcoholism', *Behavior Research and Therapy*, 11: 91–104.

Kirkley, B.G., Schneider, J.A., Agras, W.S., and Bachman, J.A. (1985) 'Comparison of two group treatments for bulimia', *Journal of Consulting and Clinical Psychology*, 53: 43–8.

Lewin, K. (1951) *Field Theory in Social Science*, New York: Harper & Row.

Litman, G.K., Stapleton, J., Oppenheim, A.N., Peleg, M., and Jackson, P. (1983) 'Situations related to alcoholism relapse', *British Journal of Addiction*, 78: 381–9.

Phillips, G. (1989) 'Relapse after treatment', in G. Bennett (ed.) *New Directions in the Treatment of Drug Abuse*, London: Routledge.

Prochaska, J.O. and DiClimente, C.C. (1983) 'Stages and processing of self change of smoking: toward an integrative model of change', *Journal of Consulting and Clinical Psychology*, 51: 390–5.

Schachter, S. (1982) 'Recidivism and self cure of smoking and obesity', *American Psychologist*, 37: 436–44.

Scott, M.J. (1986) 'The development of a drug related attitudes questionnaire for treatment of addiction', paper delivered at Cognitive Behavioural Special Interest Group on Hard Drugs Seminar at the University of Salford.

Stallard, A., Heather, N., and Johnston, B. (1987) 'AIDS and intravenous drug use: what clinical psychology can offer', *British Psychological Society Bulletin*, 40: 365–9.

Taintor, L. and D'Amanda, C. (1973) 'Multiple drug abuse in heroin addicts receiving out-patient detoxification', *Proceedings of the 5th National Conference on Methadone Treatment*, New York: National Association for the Prevention of Addiction to Narcotics, 1002–9.

Tuchfeld, B.S. (1981) 'Spontaneous remission in alcoholics: empirical observations and theoretical implications', *Journal of Studies of Alcohol*, 42: 626–41.

World Health Organisation (1979) *Mental Disorders: Glossary and Guide to their Classification in Accordance with the Ninth Revision of the International Classification of Disease*, London: HMSO.

CHAPTER 12

Bandura, A. (1977) 'Self-efficacy: toward a unifying theory of behaviour change', *Psychological Review*, 84: 191–215.

Horan, J.J. (1971) 'Coverant conditioning through a self-management application of the Premack Principle: its effects on weight reduction', *Journal of Behaviour Therapy and Experimental Psychiatry*, 2: 243–9.

Janis, J.L. and Mann, L. (1977) *Decision-making*, New York: Free Press.

Janis, J.L. (1983) 'The role of social support in adherence to stressful decisions', *American Psychologist*, 143–60.

Kelly, G.A. (1955) *The Psychology of Personal Constructs*, vols. 1 and 2, New York: Norton.

Larsen, D., Attkisson, C., Hargreaves, W., and Nguyen, T. (1979) in *Evaluation and Program Planning*, 2, 197–207.

Marlatt, G.A. and Gordon, J.R. (1985) *Relapse Prevention*, New York: Guilford Press.

Miller, W.R. (1983) 'Motivational interviewing with problem drinkers', *Behavioural Psychotherapy*, 11: 147–72.

Prochaska, J.O. and DiClimente, C.C. (1982) 'Transtheoretical therapy: toward a more integrative model of change', *Psychotherapy: Theory, Research and Practice*, 19: 276–88.

Tuchfeld, B. (1976) *Changes in patterns of alcohol use without aid of formal treatment*. N. Carolina: Centre for Health Studies. Paper for Research Triangle Institute.

van Bilsen, H.P.J.G. (1987) 'Motivational Milieu Therapy', paper presented at British Association for Behavioural Psychotherapy summer conference, University of Exeter.

CHAPTER 13

Corney, R.H. and Clare, A.W. (1985) 'The construction, development and testing of a self-report questionnaire to identify social problems', *Psychological Medicine*, 15, 637–49.

Litman, G.H., Stapleton, J., Oppenheim, A.N., Peleg, M., and

Jackson, P. (1983) 'Situations related to alcoholism relapse', *British Journal of Addiction*, 78: 381-9.

Marlatt, G.A. and Gordon, J.R. 'Determinants of relapse: implications for the maintenance of behaviour change', in P.O. Davidson and S.M. Davidson (eds) *Behavioural Medicine: Changing Health Lifestyles*, New York: Brunner/Mazel.

Prochaska, J.O. and DiClimente, C.C. (1982) 'Transtheoretical therapy: toward a more integrative model of change', *Psychotherapy: Theory, Research and Practice*, 19: 276-88.

CHAPTER 14

Barna, S., Biddler, R.T., Gray, O.P., Clements, J., and Garner, S. (1980) 'The progress of developmentally delayed pre-school children in a home training scheme', *Child Care, Health and Development*, 6: 157-64.

Beutler, L.E., Scogin, F., Kirkish, P., Schretten, D., Corbishley, A., Hamblin, D., Meredith, K., Potter, R., Bamford, C.R., and Levenson, A.I. (1987) 'Group cognitive therapy and Alprazolam in the treatment of depression in older adults', *Journal of Consulting and Clinical Psychology*, 55: 550-6.

Birchwood, M., Cochrane, R., and Moore, B. (1987) 'Family coping behaviour and the course of schizophrenia: a follow-up study', *Psychological Medicine* (in press).

Falloon, I.R.H., Boyd, J.L., McGill, C.W., Williamson, M., Razini, J., Moss, H.B., Gilderman, A.M., and Simpson, G.M. (1985) 'Family management in the prevention of morbidity of schizophrenia', *Archives of General Psychiatry*, 42: 887-96.

Fry, P.S. (1984) 'Cognitive training and cognitive-behavioural variables in the treatment of depression in the elderly', *Clinical Gerontologist*, 3: 25-45.

Goldstein, M.J. (1984) 'Family intervention programs', in A.S. Bellack (ed.) *Schizophrenia: Treatment, Management and Rehabilitation*, New York: Grune and Stratton.

Gurland, B., Dean, L., Cross, P., and Golden, R. (1980) 'The epidemiology of depression and dementia in the elderly: the use of multiple indicators of these conditions', in J.O. Cole and J.E. Barret (eds) *Psychotherapy in the Aged*, (37-62), New York: Raven Press.

Hogarty, G.E., Anderson, C.M., Reiss, D.J., Kornblith, S., Greenwald, D.P., Javna, C.D., and Modonia, M.J. (1986) 'Family psycho-education, social skills training and maintenance chemotherapy in the after-care treatment of schizophrenia. One year effects of a controlled study on relapse and expressed emotion', *Archives of General Psychiatry*, 43: 633-42.

Intagliata, J. and Willer, B. (1982) 'Reinstitutionalization of mentally retarded persons successfully placed into family care and group homes,' *American Journal of Mental Deficiency*, 87: 34-9.

REFERENCES

Kelly, G.A. (1955) *The Psychology of Personal Constructs*, vols 1 and 2, New York: Norton.

Kuipers, L. (1979) 'Expressed emotion: a review', *British Journal of Social and Clinical Psychology*, 18: 237–43.

Leff, J.P., Kuipers, L., Berkowitz, R., Eberlein-Fries, R., and Sturgeon, D. (1982) 'A controlled trial of social intervention in schizophrenic families', *British Journal of Psychiatry*, 141: 121–34.

Lindsay, W. and Kasprowicz, M. (1987) 'Challenging negative cognitions', *Mental Health Handicap*, 15: 159–62.

Mathews, A. and MacCleod, C. (1987) 'An information processing approach to anxiety', *Journal of Cognitive Psychotherapy*, 1: 105–15.

Meichenbaum, D. (1977) *Cognitive-Behaviour Modification: An Intergrative Approach*, New York: Plenum Press.

Myatt, R. (1983) 'Evaluating parental intervention projects', paper at the London Conference of British Psychological Society.

Nisbett, R.E. and Ross, L.D. (1980) *Human Inference: Strategies and Shortcomings of Informal Judgements*, Eaglewood Cliffs, N.J.: Prentice Hall.

Nooe, R. (1977) 'Measuring self-concepts of mentally retarded adults', *Social Work*, 22: 320–2.

Pahl, J. and Quine, L. (1984) *Families with Mentally Handicapped Children. A Study of Stress and Service Response*, Canterbury: University of Kent Health Services Research Unit.

Paul, G.L. (1967) 'Strategy of outcome research in psychotherapy', *Journal of Consulting Psychology*, 31: 109–18.

Vaughn, C. and Leff, J. (1976) 'The measurement of expressed emotion in the families of psychiatric patients', *British Journal of Social and Clinical Psychology*, 15: 423–9.

Yost, E.B., Beutler, L.E., Corbishley, M.A., and Albinder, J.R. (1986) *Group Cognitive Therapy: A Treatment Approach for Depressed Older Adults*, New York: Pergamon.

NAME INDEX

NAME INDEX

SUBJECT INDEX

For Product Safety Concerns and Information please contact our EU
representative GPSR@taylorandfrancis.com
Taylor & Francis Verlag GmbH, Kaufingerstraße 24, 80331 München, Germany

www.ingramcontent.com/pod-product-compliance
Lightning Source LLC
Chambersburg PA
CBHW061720270326
41928CB00011B/2046